DATE DUE

MAY 26 '92		1998	
JUL 9 '92			
ILL 9/14/92			
DEC 1 8 '92			
JUL 05 '93			
NOV 0 9 '9			
MAR 0 7 '9			
MAR 2 8 '9			
MAY 06 '94			

DEMCO 25-380

SYLVIA PORTER'S

YOUR FINANCES

IN THE

1990s

PRENTICE
HALL
PRESS

New York   London   Toronto   Sydney   Tokyo   Singapore

PRENTICE HALL PRESS

Simon & Schuster, Inc.
15 Columbus Circle
New York, NY 10023

A J.K. Lasser Book
Published by Prentice Hall Press

Prentice Hall Press and colophons are
registered trademarks of Simon & Schuster, Inc.

Manufactured in the United States of America

1   2   3   4   5   6   7   8   9   10

Cataloging-in-Publication Data

Porter, Sylvia Field, 1913–
    Sylvia Porter's your finances in the 1990s / Sylvia Porter.
        p.   cm.
    Includes index.
    ISBN 0-13-879776-5 : $22.95
    1. Finance, Personal.   I. Title.   II. Title: Your finances in the
1990s.
HG179.P572   1990
332.024—dc20   90-42572
                                                                    CIP

This book is intended to provide general information. The publisher, authors and copyright owner are not engaged in rendering personal finance, investment, tax, accounting, legal, or other professional advice and services and cannot assume responsibility for individual decisions made by readers.

Should assistance for these types of advice and services be required, professionals should be consulted.

References to tax provisions in this book are based on current tax laws and regulations. Revisions in tax law, if adopted, might affect the tax consequences.

CONTENTS

—ACKNOWLEDGEMENTS—

Hundreds of sources have contributed to the body of knowledge reported in this book. They include trade and professional association executives, academics, executives in industry and finance, and independent experts. They are too numerous to list. I am grateful for their willingness to share their knowledge of the world of personal finance, knowledge that is both current and visionary.

My associate, Dennis E. Powell, has spent months at his computer digging out and organizing information and doing it cheerfully. Arthur Rogoff, with singular diligence, has compiled many tables and charts so you can master it all at a glance. Some of the charts have been reprinted from issues of "Sylvia Porter's Active Retirement Newsletter."

Carole Sinclair, president of the Sylvia Porter Organization, has shepherded this project with insight and skill since its inception. I am grateful to my first critic and husband, James F. Fox, and to Caroline Urbas, Eleanor DeLynn Bookin, Robert McBride, JoAnna Zulli, and a host of business and personal friends, all of whom contributed in their own ways to the creation of this book.

Finally, my thanks to the editors and staff of Simon & Schuster, who welcomed me home.

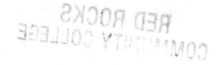

── INTRODUCTION ──

Look around you.

That may seem an odd way to begin a book on personal finance, but it is the underlying theme of all you read here.

The training director of one of the world's largest banks once told me, "I can't teach, but people can learn. It has to be self-development."

So it is with us. I can provide a map, but it is you who must learn to use it. It is your alertness and inquisitiveness that will enable you to secure your own financial future. I urge you:

Be aware of change. See the scores of objects that were unknown to your grandparents—television, computers, jet planes, plastic materials, new medicines and more.

Note the intangibles in our lives that have changed the way we live and eat and learn, the laws that govern us.

Check the speed of change that has become so rapid that change itself frequently surprises us. What we knew a decade ago may no longer be true.

Nowhere is this more apparent than in the world of economics. A decade ago we were concerned with "voodoo economics," but to our surprise, in a watered-down version, it did not lead to a general collapse. Late in the last decade there was an unprecedented stock crash, but nothing much happened as a result.

The rules that govern the accumulation and growth of personal wealth are also changing. The typical person a decade ago could not have predicted the extent of the global communications evolution, or the growth of foreign investment.

Purchasing your own home, the one investment sure to pay off, isn't nearly so sure a bet today. If you followed traditional wisdom and abandoned the stock market in 1987, you might as well have burned your money. If you waited it out or increased your stock purchases at the time, you made money.

Nothing is certain, but there are some trends you can identify to help your own planning. One is the aging of the baby boomers—70 million of them—who are becoming the leading players. They will enrich and deplete the nation's retirement system. They will require homes that, later, will have no eager buyers. Ultimately, they will require medical care which, if they fail to provide for it, may be denied them.

Another is the growing role of the rest of the world in the U.S. economy. Our geographic isolation matters little now.

A third is the influence of electronic communications. There will be new automated ways of doing your job, planning your leisure and making your purchases and investments from a home computer. Only a few years ago you could not have imagined the uses to which you would be putting your telephone.

Medicine, before many years have passed, will have the capacity to keep almost anyone alive almost forever. But the price? Almost no one could afford it.

Our concept of "retirement" is changing and has become a major issue facing the nation. Most of you will work, at least part-time, long past the now-traditional age of retirement.

What you read here will be sensible, informed advice about how to deal with these matters you can anticipate and those you can't. Sometimes, conventional wisdom will suffice; sometimes it won't, because things are changing so rapidly.

This book is divided into three parts:

• The acquisition of wealth, through your job or career, and through your savings and investments.

• The preservation of your wealth as your taxes increase. Insurance issues, legal concerns, and the specter of a retirement crisis threatening your savings.

• The significant areas sure to change in the 1990s and the years to follow. They will affect your life and your pocketbook. These are matters to think about and anticipate in your financial planning.

Knowing how to bait a hook is different from knowing how to catch fish. The successful fisherman learns to read the water.

Today's hard rules may have no meaning tomorrow. But if you learn the ways of thinking for financial success (how to read the water), your stringer—and your portfolio—will be comfortably full.

It is up to you to exercise your wisdom, and to develop more wisdom as you go along. With luck, this book will help you on both counts.

1

YOUR FINANCES IN
——THE 1990s——

It used to be so much easier to look to the future. There were fewer surprises.

But let's look back at the 1980s:

- The decade began with interest rates and inflation at a point where there was some panic. The economy, by all accounts, was in bad shape. But then, as if by a miracle, it recovered, leading to the biggest and longest peacetime expansion in the country's history.

- A president was shot, but he survived. A pope was shot, and he survived. An important leader in bringing some semblance of peace to the Mideast, Anwar Sadat, was shot and killed.

- A drug problem that had pretty much limited itself became an enormous, world-wide industry, with the chief consumer being the United States. Cities became increasingly dangerous and drug-related crimes soared. Millions of dollars were spent in an effort to do something about it, with no apparent results. The cost is measured in billions of dollars and in hundreds of thousands of shattered, unproductive lives.

- Two terrible diseases, completely unknown at the start of the decade, grew to become epidemics. At the beginning of 1990, the acquired immune-deficiency syndrome, AIDS, had claimed more American lives than had the Vietnam War. Its costs defy calculation. Because the disease can be spread through contaminated blood, patients grew wary of receiving transfusions. Blood donors, who (incorrectly) believed they could get the disease by giving blood, stopped doing so. This secondary effect cost an unknown number of additional lives.

1

Lyme disease, named for the Connecticut town where it was first noticed, grew into an epidemic as well. It became apparent, first in a few areas and then nationwide, that an afternoon's stroll in the woods could result in your coming down with a crippling disease. Fortunately, if treated early, Lyme disease can be cured.

Not so with AIDS.

- Social Security was saved from the brink of collapse, but there is reason to believe that it was a reprieve, not a commutation.

- Medical costs soared beyond what anyone would have imagined. Liability issues caused some emergency rooms to close, reducing the amount of health care available. In many cases, inexpensive preventative treatment was foregone, only to be replaced by much more expensive treatment later on.

- A series of scandals rocked government, industry, and the markets. We still do not know, and may never know, what happened in the case involving Iran, Israel, the Nicaraguan contras, and members of the United States government. We do know that many leaders on Wall Street are now enjoying free room and board in federal prisons due to insider trading. Defense contractors, it turned out to no one's surprise, had been overbilling the government—though the degree to which this was taking place surprised everyone.

- Takeovers became a mania. Almost every company either was a takeover target or sought to take over some other company. The result of this was that companies as a whole incurred enormous debt.

- Once a leader in space exploration, the U.S. space program found itself limited to the crippled space shuttle fleet. When a shuttle tragically exploded, the space program ceased to exist at all for two years, during which time it was discovered that the surprise was that more of our space vehicles hadn't blown up, so slipshod had the program become.

- The stock market went into outer space itself. The decade began with people wondering if the Dow Jones Industrial Average would ever break 1,000. It ended with people wondering when it would break 3,000.

- The biggest stock crash in market history took place in October 1987. But nothing much resulted from it, except that small investors, who took the biggest losses, wrote off the market as a place to invest money.

- The computer revolution took hold in ways that could not have been imagined.

- The environment, which had threatened to become an issue a decade earlier, became a big part of the 1988 presidential campaign, and, finally, there is a chance we'll do something to save our planet.

- The Eastern Bloc virtually collapsed. Those countries awakened one morning to discover they were virtually bankrupt. John Reed, one of four Americans buried in the Kremlin Wall, would have been surprised. "I have seen the future," he wrote of the post-revolution Soviet Union, "and it works." As it turned out, it doesn't.

- Marshall McLuhan would have been a little more pleased with the turn of events. The global village of which he wrote came much closer to reality. Certainly the global economy came closer to reality, though divisions between the developed and underdeveloped nations widened.

Some of these things might have been foreseen. Certainly not all of them, and certainly not to the extent that they came to pass.

After the 1980s, one imagines—and almost hopes—that the world will decide to take a breather for a few years. It was an energetic decade, and a brief respite would be in order.

Of course, that won't happen. It is at the same time exciting and terrifying to imagine what our concerns will be as, just a few years from now, we enter a new decade, a new century, and a new millennium.

Certainly, there is no way of identifying all or perhaps even most of those concerns. But we can identify a few, and we can make appropriate allowances for the rest.

FREEDOM IN EASTERN EUROPE

The writer Thomas Mann believed he had found a solution.

The problem was this: He did not want his stories made into motion pictures. They were his inventions, the products of his mind, and he was not about to let someone else interpret them for his audience. If people wanted his stories, they would have to read his books.

His solution, to prevent those in control of his estate from going against his wishes and selling the movie rights, was this: Such pictures could only be made if they were co-produced by East Germany and West Germany. That about sewed it up. There was, of course, no way this could ever happen.

It wasn't very long ago that the idea of thousands of East Germans streaming across the Berlin Wall could be imagined only in terms of NATO retaliation. Those thousands, after all, would have been East German and Soviet soldiers, and the whole business would have been an act of war.

But in what has been a time of unprecedented turmoil in the Eastern bloc, the near-removal of the Berlin Wall is simply the most striking symptom of East embracing West. The events of 1989, following the tragedy in Beijing, were simply beyond the ken of all but those with overly fertile imaginations—indeed, those with a power of invention perhaps beyond even that of Thomas Mann.

There is general agreement that the turmoil in the communist bloc is likely to have profound economic effects far beyond Europe. A lot less clear is what those effects will be.

It will certainly become easier to argue for reduced military spending in the United States. The prospect of reduced military spending injected some enthusiasm into the securities markets, but it reduced the value of shares in defense-related industries. While that was one of the earliest manifestations of change, no one believes it is the most significant one.

Over the next few years, we most likely will be the recipients of some Eastern European products. If it comes to pass that the United States reduces the tariffs to most-favored-nation status, there will be a much greater expansion in trade. A first step came when the U.S. offered that status to the Soviet Union.

The opening of those trade barriers won't at once be a two-way street. There wouldn't really be expanded trade in U.S. exports. The reason is simple: The countries of Eastern Europe have little money with which to buy our goods. Unless they go out and borrow like crazy, they will be handicapped by their low hard-currency reserves. And the environment for lending is just not there. Investors want to see evidence that this is real reform.

The first likely spot for increased two-way trade is Hungary, where reforms have taken hold. Other countries face the problems of building a capital market in a labor economy, a thing not easily done. The problem of displaced workers is an example. To make the means of production more efficient, some workers are likely to be thrown out of their jobs. But in the countries of Eastern Europe, part of one's pay may be one's home—not just the means to pay for it, but the home itself.

The situation is somewhat different in the Germanys, and it is here that the most vivid changes are likely. East Germany has the comparative advantage in terms of labor. West Germany, on the other hand, has the edge in technology and organization. Combining the two, if not through reunification, then through an arrangement to their mutual economic benefit, would produce quite a power. The combined German economy would exceed those of England and France put together.

There is reason to believe this will happen.

They have a common language and cultural background, though not as complete as you might imagine. East Germany has more to gain, because its weakness has been in the production of quality goods. This incentive for the East Germans makes economic cooperation all the more likely, and steps in that direction have been taken.

Such a development could make West Germany a powerful gateway to trade with other Eastern European countries as well. As those economies develop, West Germany's position would grow as well.

These things are of immediate concern to the European community, which is scheduled to meet for economic unification in 1992. But they are of great importance to the U.S. as well. Look for a three-phase development of the economies of Eastern Europe:

- First, the lowering of trade barriers, allowing Eastern European goods into the U.S. at low prices. This would have some impact on our balance of trade.

- Second, as we grow more confident in those economies, our investments there will grow. Those investments would not just be in money, but also in technology and training.

- Third, those economies would reach sufficient strength that they would become competitors with us in the world market.

The move toward market economies in Eastern Europe has been a great step forward for freedom in the world. In our rejoicing, we may fail to notice the equally revolutionary shuffling of the economic deck, which promises to have long-lasting effects.

THE MARKET CRASH

Surprisingly little has changed since 1987's "Black Monday" stock market crash. The markets have installed brakes that won't keep a skid from turning into a crash. They will merely reduce the speed of impact.

The prevailing opinion in the market is that the October 1987 crash was an unusual event that is unlikely to happen again, but that if conditions were right it certainly could.

Preceding the second anniversary of that terrifying day by a couple of weeks was the release of a survey done for the American Stock Exchange.

It optimistically reported that 70 percent of the individual investors questioned did not lose confidence in the market because of the crash. Somewhat less cheerful was the news that 28 percent did lose confidence. Out-and-out tragic was the survey's finding that more than two-thirds of small investors equate stock investment with gambling.

If two-thirds of the country's individual investors think that buying stock is like tossing money around at a casino, why do they do it? A look at the intervening two years might provide a hint. In that time:

- The savings and loan crisis finally came to a head. Those S&Ls that paid the most, in hope of attracting depositors, were hardest hit.

- The one sure investment—homes—actually fell in value in some parts of the country, either because of economic downturns in those areas or because of buying frenzies that had pushed prices too high. As a result, banks in those areas were forced to increase their reserves.

- New scandals surfaced in both the stock and commodities markets.

- Municipal bond default rates were unusually high. The short-term rate on federal paper grew to make it more attractive than long-term issues, in what economists call an "inverted curve."

- There was an almost universal belief that a recession was imminent, the only questions being when it would arrive, how deep it would be, and how long it would last.

This was all very frightening. It's difficult to remain optimistic in the face of such terrible news at every turn. On the other hand, in those same two years:

- While there is no question that the S&L crisis was and is a very serious and expensive matter, individual depositors were able to recover their money, usually within a few business days.

- In most places, homes held their value. Except for those purchased in the hardest-hit areas, or those purchased at the peak of the price curve, they have continued to be a good investment, though they are no longer a sure bet for big appreciation.

- The recession never did arrive or, if it did, it didn't do much damage. Many of those who were preaching recession came to use the phrase "soft landing."

- The traditional panic investments, such as precious metals, plodded along complacently. There was no rush to buy them. Those who had invested in them during the last big panic were now wearing barrels and living in appliance cartons.

- And the stock market had recovered and gone on to set new record highs. Those who bought shares as long-term investments, even before the crash, and who held onto them, have done very nicely. Those who bought stocks the day after the crash and held onto them are now doing quite well indeed.

The moral of the story is that any investment, and investments in general, are apt to move in fits and starts from time to time. But, despite the doomsayers and Pollyannas, a careful investor needn't be unduly worried. If you set your investment goals, make your purchases carefully, avoid the temptation to jump at shiny hopes of quick riches, and stick with it, you are very likely to do well.

The fact that two-thirds of the individual investors surveyed for the American Stock Exchange think of buying stocks as gambling is frightening, because it is a self-fulfilling prophecy. Gambling puts faith in odds that are dependent on sheer blind luck. The investor who counts on luck is, in fact, a gambler.

The investor who researches share purchases carefully, looks at external factors that are likely to affect the company being bought, and who buys shares with plans to keep them for long-term growth is not gambling.

When you invest in several different companies; in a range of industries; and beyond that, in mutual funds, bonds, and other securities—in short, when you diversify—you are not gambling.

It is impossible to make the maximum amount on every single investment. From time to time, you may lose a little on one investment or another. In most cases, these will be temporary losses on paper only. But in any case, diversification will ensure that you will have growth. Some areas, at any given moment, will be doing exceedingly well, while others will slow down a little. Weeks or months later, the situation could easily be reversed. Over the long haul, it all evens out.

Which is precisely the point. You are not a piece of driftwood floating in a sea of investment, subject to its caprices. Instead, you are an investor. You are a smart shopper. You wouldn't go to the grocery store, buy things at random, and then come home and try to figure out what kind of meal you might be able to make with what you've bought. Not at all. You would plan your meal and then purchase the items necessary to put it on the table.

Investing, indeed all of personal finance, is like planning a meal. You must first decide what you want to do. Then tap the markets for the things you need in order to do it.

Of course, just as the grocer might be out of an ingredient essential to your meal, it sometimes happens that circumstances beyond your control force you to change your strategy a little. But, if you're careful, you will have built enough pad into your investment strategy and into your goals so that minor adjustments—or even occasional major ones—can be breezed right through.

THE CHANGING WORKPLACE

As we look to the 1990s, we can see that things are certainly going to change for all of us. The picture is clear in some areas, a little more obscure in others.

During the 1990s, competition for skilled employees among employers, combined with the relentless effect of technology upon the workplace, will result in a drastic change in the way you earn your living. For instance:

- You'll probably work later in life. The traditional retirement at age 65 was formulated when 65 was as long as most people could expect to live. Before long, working to age 70 or even 75 won't be uncommon.
- You will change careers more frequently. Because of changes in the economy and in technology, you'll constantly learn new occupations.
- Job sharing and part-time work will become more common. This more fluid way of scheduling lives and our jobs is expected to maximize productivity by making the most of whatever time you have available.
- You will need to become more technologically literate. Although technology is more important than ever before, many technical fields face a shortage of trained people. This is compounded by the fact that, in many disciplines, what constituted the state of the art two years ago is now outmoded information.

As companies find themselves in hot competition for good employees, they are beginning to offer increasingly attractive benefits plans. Features such as flex-time, child care, parental leave, and elder care will become even more important.

Workers will have to learn the skills necessary to work in increasingly sophisticated settings. It sounds scary, but it isn't: As powerful complicated equipment moves into the mainstream, it also will become easier to use. The more you know, the more your work will be worth, but you won't be shut out of the workplace because you're not, for example, a computer expert.

THE DECLINING SUPPLY OF
SKILLED WORKERS

For the next few years, well into the 21st century, we're going to pay the price for failing to maintain our education system. In the words of Labor

Secretary Elizabeth Dole, we face a "skills gap." We've allowed our children to complete their education without being able to read, write, or perform mathematics at an acceptable level.

The process of retreating from the industrial economy that our parents knew will continue. Secretary Dole says that areas such as government, financial institutions, insurance companies, health care, transportation, and computers will be where an increasing number of future jobs will be. But as we continue to move from an industrial economy to a service economy, we need workers who can have high skill levels. Yet, 25 percent of our young people are dropping out of school, and many of those who graduate are functionally illiterate—unable to read, write, or do math at a high-enough level to get by in today's world.

It's a fact that tomorrow's work force will be increasingly female, immigrant, and minority. (In fact, 60 percent of the new entrants in the work force between now and the year 2000 will be women.) But teen pregnancy will derail the career aspirations of too many young women, and too many minority youth lack access to the quality education that tomorrow's employees will need. In the long run, our nation's shortage of qualified skilled workers will not be remedied until these problems are addressed.

Although government must be expected to take the leading role in solving the problem of a declining supply of skilled workers, businesses must also do their part. According to Dr. Thomas G. Sticht, a San Diego literacy expert, half of all workers read below the 9th grade level—costing businesses $200 million in lost productivity *each day*. This lost productivity will be a powerful incentive for companies to establish new literacy programs. Look for companies to improve their design of technical training programs, and to invest more money in human resources.

Even entry level and unskilled positions suffer from a shortage of workers. That's because today's young adults are having fewer children than their parents. Because of the relatively small number of young people today, there are fewer bodies to supply the country's appetite for entry level and untrained employees. Some service industries have launched campaigns to lure retirees back to work, offering flexible hours and attractive wages. Other companies have recruited employees in metropolitan centers for work in the suburbs. Thus, those companies frequently provide transportation to and from work for these employees.

As a smart employee, you know it is to your benefit to make yourself as valuable as possible to your employer. If you work for yourself, you know that remaining up-to-date is a continuing process that is essential if you are to gain and keep a competitive advantage.

Over the years I've often said that the best investment you can make is in your education. That's never been more true than it is now, though some of the subjects have changed a little.

We are rapidly moving toward a global business community. Because the development of a global economy brings diverse cultures together through the common language of business, it is important to learn a little about those different cultures. Actions and suggestions that are perfectly acceptable in the United States may be greeted with anger or puzzlement elsewhere.

If your work increasingly exposes you to other cultures, it's worthwhile to devote some study to the traditions and manners of those cultures. Fortunately, there are books, tapes, and courses available to teach you the etiquette of international business. Those who expect to survive and thrive will put those materials to good use. It behooves you to keep your head up and to be aware of these changes as they take place. If they do not directly affect you today, they almost certainly will tomorrow.

Right now, one of the best education investments anyone can make is to learn a second language—or even a third. Fluency in—or at least a good working knowledge of—another language is now a virtual requirement of corporate business recruiters visiting college campuses. It is nearly as important as an MBA. Every year the number of companies doing business overseas increases. For some companies, this is as a supplier. In others, manufacturing facilities and joint ventures are established abroad.

Increasingly, foreign-based companies are establishing facilities here. And companies from all sides of the oceans maintain ever larger sales and representative staffs in other countries.

The world situation has the potential to change rapidly. The events in the Eastern Bloc in 1989 were astonishing in their speed—and their magnitude. Obviously, those who were in a position to make the most of the situation made out like bandits. Education allows you to make your own opportunities by imparting the skills necessary to react instantly to changing situations.

Computer literacy is an increasingly valuable, often necessary business skill. It can determine whether or not you get a job or promotion and how much you are paid.

Just a few years ago, only workers in technical, scientific, and engineering fields were able to make much use of computers. That is no longer the case. The computer has wrapped its electronic grip around virtually every field.

A college degree makes you a more valuable employee. Period. But, for a variety of reasons, many employees didn't start or haven't completed college. If you are among these, today is the day to resume your education.

Perhaps you're considering a career change, one that requires more education. If so, today is the day to get started. (See Chart 1.) Or you may wish to go for that graduate degree that would increase your earning potential and open opportunities for advancement. If so, there's no time like the present!

WORKING AT HOME

An accountant tells me he smiles each morning as he watches his neighbors rush to catch trains for an hour's commute into New York City. Before his neighbors have even boarded their train, he begins his work day. He is one of nearly 25 million Americans—more than 20 percent of the work force—who make at least part of their living from home offices.

There are about 15 million home-based businesses in the U.S. right now. The number is expected to double in the next decade. That means that there's a good chance—growing into a very good chance—that you are or will be involved in some sort of money-making enterprise from your home. In addition, more and more large companies are learning that there can be benefits to allowing some employees to work from their homes. The first question you must ask yourself, however, is if you really want to work at home.

If you are, for instance, in real estate, or if you are self-employed in a business where the work is done in an office with most customer contact by telephone, then you can easily make your home your base of business operations. (The advent of cellular telephones has made it possible for some people—plumbers and the like—to actually have automobile-based businesses!)

That doesn't mean, though, that working from your home is right for you. Before you pack up your office and move it into the guest bedroom, give yourself this simple test:

- Why do you want to work from home? Many people believe their work will magically be easier, that less effort will be required, if their business is home-based. They quickly learn that it's just as hard—and in some ways harder—to work from their homes.

- Is your home an appropriate place to do work? The advantages of working at home are also the disadvantages. There are many distractions. Friends will come to think of your work as not really being work at all, so you can expect them to regularly interrupt you. Acquaintances who would never think of asking you to leave your office downtown for an afternoon out will take great offense if you decline such an invitation when you're working at home and, presumably,

CHART 1

Considering Mid-Life Higher Education

	YES	NO
1. Are you sure the education you're considering would be the best way for you to advance or change your career?	☐	☐
2. Have you carefully weighed other alternatives?	☐	☐
3. Would you be able to stop at any point because you concluded that the education was not a good option for you?	☐	☐
4. Are you emotionally up to going back to school for a long period?	☐	☐
5. Will you be able, at this time in your life, to function in a subordinate position to your instructors?	☐	☐
6. If you plan to work and go to school simultaneously, whether full- or part-time for either, do you have the necessary physical stamina to manage it?	☐	☐
7. Are you confident that you have the ability and discipline to persevere and finish your education?	☐	☐
8. Have you considered carefully what work opportunities you'll have after completing this education?	☐	☐
9. Would your family be understanding and supportive of your decision?	☐	☐
10. Are you and your family prepared to cope with a lower standard of living for the time required to complete your education?	☐	☐
11. Can you and your family adjust to the demands on your time that school will make and cope with the possible adverse effects of this on your personal life?	☐	☐
12. If you're going to school without continuing to work, are you prepared to give up the security of the income and fringe benefits of your present job?	☐	☐
13. Is there a second wage earner in your household to provide the back-up of assured family income and group benefits such as insurance?	☐	☐
14. Are you and your family willing to risk "investing" your savings in this education?	☐	☐
15. Are you and your family willing to commit to repay funds that you may have to borrow to pay for this education?	☐	☐

TOTALS ___ ___

How Do You Rate

Some of the questions above are probably more important to you than others. But on an overall basis, you can rate your capacity to handle mid-life higher education on the following scale:

IF YOUR "YES" ANSWERS TOTALED:	HERE'S HOW YOU RATE
14 or 15	Definitely go for it.
12 or 13	Strong disposition to go for it.
10 or 11	On balance, you're in favor of doing it.
8 or 9	Positive leanings outweigh negative.
6 or 7	Negative leanings outweigh positive.
4 or 5	Little inclination. Rethink your goals.
Under 4	Forget it.

setting your own hours. You must figure out how you'll deal with these interruptions—because they will certainly come.

- Do you have the discipline to work at home? At a business office, there aren't many things to do other than your job. At home, with no clock to punch, it is tempting to start work a little later, to take time off to watch that television show, even to fix that dripping kitchen faucet. You must be prepared to impose workplace discipline at home.

- Are you a workaholic? If so, having your home as your office could be the worst thing that could happen to you. To preserve the other aspects of your life, you must learn when to put down your work and go on to something else. This doesn't mean that you can't make the best of that sudden inspiration at 2 a.m., but it does mean that you shouldn't slave away over a hot computer from dawn 'til dusk.

- What does your family think about your working from home? This is a crucial question because your entire family will be affected by the move.

- How will the move affect your business? If you need to meet with clients, or if your business is one in which social contacts are important, a home office may be more trouble than it's worth because you'll have to go downtown to meet your clients anyway. Meeting with clients at home is prohibited under many local zoning laws, and in any case you may feel uncomfortable about bringing clients through your home. Some clients will feel no compunction about phoning at all hours of the day or night, if you work at home. Still others may think of a home office as being unbusinesslike and will seek to have their work done elsewhere.

- Can you put up with the isolation that comes from working at home? This is especially critical if you are an employee moving your base of operations from the main office to your home. Remember, you won't be aware of the office scuttlebutt anymore, nor will you be in a position to pipe up with suggestions and solutions that could lead to advancement. Working from home, you'll come to feel isolated and may suffer from "cabin fever." While others in your business are planning new projects over lunch, you may be making peanut butter and jelly sandwiches for the kids and trying to work over the din of cartoons on the television.

- Does your home lend itself to business? Is there a place that you can set aside exclusively as your office? Or would it end up becoming half-home, half-office, and not very good at either function?

- Have you made an office plan? This includes the physical aspects of your office, such as its location in your home and its layout, the equipment you'll need, and so on. It also includes policy matters: Will you get an additional telephone line? A business-only telephone line is essential in most cases. It can be very unbusinesslike for clients to phone you, only to have the phone answered by your children or, worse, for the phone to be tied up for hours while a client tries to reach you. If your work requires you to use your phone line to connect computers or fax machines, you will most likely need a second business telephone line for data transmission.

As you can see, the dream of working from home can be an unrealistic one, and without the proper planning and preparation it can quickly turn into a nightmare.

MAKING PLANS

By now it should be clear that in order to figure out where you are going, you need to figure out where you are. One of your first tasks in the early part of this decade is to calculate what you have and what you owe. If you haven't begun a savings plan, stop everything at once and begin one! You will certainly need it, if you are not planning to be that piece of driftwood floating to and fro but never getting anywhere.

Arrive at a family budget or, if you are alone, a personal budget. Stick to it. This will involve a compromise between what is probably the fairly relaxed approach that you would like to take and the stern rules of the budget. Don't make a budget that restricts you to the point where you'll give it up. Budgets are like diets in that truly severe ones are rarely successful.

You cannot give flight to your financial goals until you have decided what they are. "To have a lot of money" isn't enough. Identify goals so that you can work toward them.

Get professional help in working out a plan to reach those goals. But don't let it stop there. The responsibility is yours, not your adviser's. You must take the leading, active role, for it is your future that is at stake.

PAY ATTENTION

It is sometimes difficult to follow what is happening in the world, both economically and otherwise. The world has become in many ways a confusion of technobabble, econobabble, politicobabble, hidden agendas, things that are not to be said, and simple misinformation.

Many knowledgeable people who would seek to impart some of that knowledge to others instead fall short and settle for the less noble goal of jabbering in jargon designed less to enlighten than to impress. Others, who lack knowledge, hope to obscure this fact by throwing around ponderous terms. This makes following events even more difficult.

But follow them you must. One of the main purposes of this book is to defuse some of the terms, to explain how and why things work in the financial world, so that you can plug in the day's events and get some sense of whence they came and where they're headed.

When you invest toward your goals, you mustn't sell short your own judgment by failing to appraise and analyze the world around you against those investments. Read the material. Study the prospectus and the annual report. Follow the economic tides so you can determine when it is best to launch a particular ship toward its and your goal. You are, as I said, your greatest asset. Demand full value for and from that asset.

2
BUILDING A PERSONAL
— FINANCIAL PLAN —

It's unlikely that you'd begin a trip with neither a road map nor a planned destination.

You wouldn't begin to build a new home without blueprints in hand.

Nor would you launch a college career without at least an idea of the course of study you'd like to pursue.

Yet many people have no firm financial plan. Their goals are fuzzy things in the distant future, with no particular path toward them.

It's surprising, because financial planning is both simple and enjoyable. (For instance, go over Chart 2.) Once a financial plan is in place, it becomes possible and even easy to make financial goals become realities.

"Where does all the money go?" The question is not the rhetorical equivalent of a sigh to many people: They really have no idea where the money goes!

Don't you be among them.

SETTING FINANCIAL GOALS

Establishing your financial goals is exactly like planning a long vacation by automobile: Not only do you have a destination in mind and things you plan to do when you get there, but there are waypoints you wish to visit. The reason you plan is so you have a route in mind when you pull out of the driveway, so you have a safe and comfortable place to stay each night, and so you don't arrive at a point of particular interest at 2 a.m.!

Just as no two vacations are identical, no two sets of financial goals are

16

CHART 2

Use this matrix to keep track of financial factors that need adjustment because of your life experiences changing up to about age 45. Check relevant boxes below and then adjust relevant factors. For experiences *after* about age 45, see Chart 31 in Chapter 17, "Preparing Now for Retirement."

Check Experience, then Financial Factors	Life Experiences that trigger financial moves	Planning			Career			Money Management			Insurance					Home	Investments by Objectives					Estate	
		Budgeting	Taxes	Inflation	Development	Earnings	Employment Benefits	Checking and Savings	Credit and Borrowing	Government Programs	Medical	Disability Income	Long-Term Care	Life	Property and Liability	Home	Capital Preservation	Income	Growth	Appreciation	Tax Advantages	Planning	Will
	ON YOUR OWN																						
	LIVING TOGETHER																						
	YOU GET MARRIED																						
	YOU HAVE CHILDREN																						
	YOU BUY YOUR FIRST HOME																						
	YOUR CAREER ADVANCES																						
	YOUR CHILDREN GO TO COLLEGE																						

Financial Factors

the same. Still, they have some things in common. Chief among them is a sense of the best path to get there.

Short-Term Goals: These can generally be thought of as ones you hope to achieve in a year or less. Perhaps it's something as simple as saving for a vacation or trip, or a down payment on a new car. It might be money to take a course or buy a special piece of equipment for your home or hobby. Maybe you will need a new refrigerator before long, or want to finally get around to landscaping the backyard.

The first thing to do is get a sense of the cost of achieving your goal. Then set a date by which you hope to have achieved that goal. External circumstances will sometimes set the date for you—landscaping is not to be undertaken in northern climates in January, for instance.

From this point, it's relatively simple to figure what it will take to achieve your goal. Then you can sit down with your budget and decide whether your hopes are realistic. If they are, you can budget for them. If not, you can determine when your goal will become possible. It's as simple as that.

Mid-Term Goals: These are heftier plans and require more preparation. They include everything from major home improvements to a down payment on a home to your children's college expenses to the costs involved for your dream of going into business for yourself.

They are more flexible than your short-term goals, because it is not easy to anticipate the costs of things years in the future. But because they are bigger projects than are your short-term goals, you must begin saving for them much sooner. Identifying them is important because otherwise you cannot budget and save for them.

Long-Term Goals: These are the payoff for a good life well lived. They might include a style of living you've always dreamed of, independent wealth, money to launch a post-retirement second career, and the peace of mind that comes from knowing your children and grandchildren will never want.

Long-term planning can be, and often should be, quite sophisticated. To make the most of it, you probably should seek professional assistance. In any case, it's something toward which you should contribute each month.

YOUR NET WORTH

If planning your finances is like planning a trip, calculating your net worth is like determining where you're starting from on the map. Your net worth is simply how much you'd have left over after you paid off all of your debts and liabilities. In a way, it measures how far along you are on your financial journey through life.

The first step in calculating your net worth is to add up the value of your possessions: your cash and bank account balances; your stocks, bonds, and certificates of deposit; shares in mutual funds, cash value of life insurance polices; investment-grade collections (art, coins, stamps, and the like); home and business equity; and money owed to you. Take a subtotal. These are your immediate assets. You will notice that the figure will change daily. (For help calculating your net worth, see Chart 3.)

To this subtotal add the value of pension plans; employee stock ownership, profit sharing, and 401(k) plans; individual retirement and/or Keogh accounts; and other assets that will be paid to you sometime in the future. These are your deferred assets.

Then you should add the value of your automobile, furniture, and other personal possessions. These are part of your net worth, even though it's unlikely you would liquidate them. Be sure to be realistic in placing a value on these items.

The total of all of the above constitutes your total assets.

Now it's time to begin subtracting.

Add the money you owe: your total outstanding mortgage and other real estate mortgages; the outstanding balances of any home equity loans you may have taken; the amount you owe on your automobile; the balance of college loans, and any other installment debts, including money owed to individuals; and, finally, the amount you owe on credit cards. Subtract this total—your liabilities—from your total assets. This figure is your net worth.

Don't be unduly alarmed if you owe more than you have, especially if you are a homeowner. While you should be concerned if you are in hock to the eyebrows with high-interest debt such as credit cards, long-term, relatively low-interest debt such as student loans that you're continuing to pay or a mortgage on your home (especially if you've bought it recently) could make your picture look much bleaker and less controlled than it really is.

With a sense of where you are, you can begin to plan a way to get where you want to be.

A WORKING BUDGET

Your net worth is a snapshot. By the time you've figured it out, it will have changed—especially if you've invested heavily in volatile stock issues, whose value can change daily (or even faster), sometimes giving a misleading value on paper that doesn't really exist unless you sell.

CHART 3

Your Current Financial Statement and Inventory

Date: _____

ASSETS

Liquid Assets (Readily Convertible to Cash)

Cash and checking; savings; money market accounts; CDs .... $ _____

Money market mutual funds .... _____

Cash in stockbrokerage accounts .... _____

U.S. savings bonds .... _____

Cash value of life insurance, annuities, employee benefit plans .....

Other .... _____

TOTAL LIQUID ASSETS .... ══════

Marketable Investments

Stocks .... _____

Corporate bonds, government securities .... _____

Stock/bond mutual funds .... _____

Options, futures, commodities, precious metals .... _____

Other .... _____

TOTAL MARKETABLE INVESTMENTS .... ══════

"Nonmarketable" Investments

IRAs, 401(k)s, Keoghs, SEPs .... _____

Real estate .... _____

Limited partnerships .... _____

Deferred employment income .... _____

Vested interests in employee benefits .... _____

Business interests/partnerships .... _____

Loans to others .... _____

Collectibles for investment .... _____

Trust funds .... _____

Other .... _____

TOTAL "NONMARKETABLE" INVESTMENTS ══════

Personal Assets

Residential real estate .... _____

Autos, other vehicles .... _____

Jewelry, furs, furnishings, personal collectibles .... _____

Other .... _____

TOTAL PERSONAL ASSETS .... _____

TOTAL ASSETS .... $ ══════

LIABILITIES

Charge account, credit card balances .... $ _____

Other bills to be paid .... _____

Mortgages on residential and investment real estate .... _____

Loans, notes, margin accounts .... _____

Balance due on installment payments .... _____

Borrowed from your employer or against employee benefit plans _____

Estimated liability for income taxes .... _____

Other .... _____

TOTAL LIABILITIES .... $ ══════

NET WORTH   TOTAL ASSETS LESS
TOTAL LIABILITIES .... $ ══════

To make sure that the bottom-line figure grows, you must establish a budget. This is a business plan for your household. The goal is to have the household operate at as much of a profit as is possible without incurring undue hardship.

A word of caution: Many budgets are put together by zealous people eager to turn over a new leaf and put their financial house in order. Nothing could be more worthy of praise—but sometimes that zeal leads to an unrealistically austere budget, one that cannot be realized. The results are that it is abandoned, zeal gives way to despair, and the same old bad habits are embraced again. It is essential that you be realistic in establishing a household budget. Don't budget for things you can't live with. If, despite your best efforts, you end up spending more than you bring in, it's time to get help.

In addition to your working budget, you should formulate a yearly projection, which is a summary of your combined monthly budgets, put together on a single sheet to make something like a yearly "super-budget."

Look at the accompanying Chart 4—"Guide Toward Preparing Periodic Statements of Your Family's Personal Finances." Your working budget can be derived from this.

Your working budget can be for the year, for a quarter, for a month, for a week, or combinations of these. Monthly is best for most people. The "Income" and "Expenses" in the accompanying "Guide" will fluctuate, of course. Calculate annual totals for each item and then refigure them for the period you're working with. For example, say you've a monthly budget and expect to receive dividends from a mutual fund totaling $1,200 for the year. Divide by 12 and enter $100 from that source in your monthly budget's income.

Here's the basic structure for your budget:

YOUR BUDGET. PERIOD: _____

	Expected This Period	Actual	Actual vs. Expected (plus or minus)
Income items	$ _____	$ _____	$ _____
Expense items:			
Fixed expense items	$ _____	$ _____	$ _____
Variable expense items	$ _____	$ _____	$ _____
Net (income less expenses)	$ _____	$ _____	$ _____
Net application (into savings, investments, specific goals)	$ _____	$ _____	$ _____

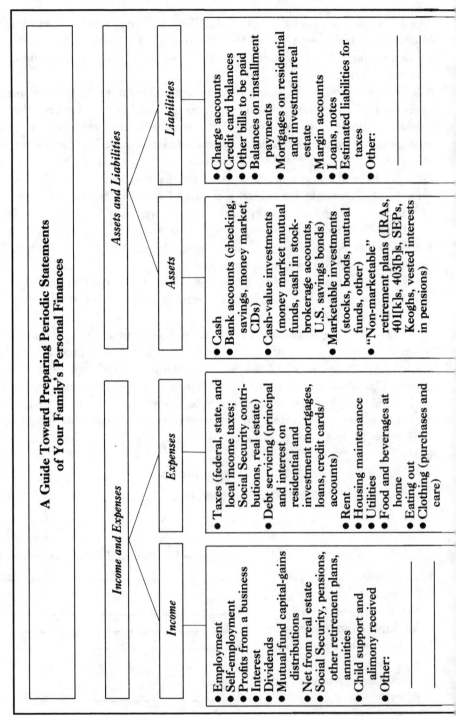

CHART 4

**A Guide Toward Preparing Periodic Statements
of Your Family's Personal Finances**

Income and Expenses

Income

- Employment
- Self-employment
- Profits from a business
- Interest
- Dividends
- Mutual-fund capital-gains distributions
- Net from real estate
- Social Security, pensions, other retirement plans, annuities
- Child support and alimony received
- Other: _____

Expenses

- Taxes (federal, state, and local income taxes; Social Security contributions, real estate)
- Debt servicing (principal and interest on residential and investment mortgages, loans, credit cards/accounts)
- Rent
- Housing maintenance
- Utilities
- Food and beverages at home
- Eating out
- Clothing (purchases and care)

Assets and Liabilities

Assets

- Cash
- Bank accounts (checking, savings, money market, CDs)
- Cash-value investments (money market mutual funds, cash in stock-brokerage accounts, U.S. savings bonds)
- Marketable investments (stocks, bonds, mutual funds, other)
- "Non-marketable" retirement plans (IRAs, 401[k]s, 403[b]s, SEPs, Keoghs, vested interests in pensions)

Liabilities

- Charge accounts
- Credit card balances
- Other bills to be paid
- Balances on installment payments
- Mortgages on residential and investment real estate
- Margin accounts
- Loans, notes
- Estimated liabilities for taxes
- Other: _____

- Other "non-marketable investments (real estate, limited partnerships, business interests, loans to others, collectibles for investment, trust funds)
- Personal assets (cars, other vehicles, jewelry, furs, furnishings, personal collectibles)
- Other:

- Transportation (public, car)
- Insurance premiums
- Medical and other health costs (unreimbursed)
- Entertainment, recreation, vacations
- Grooming and other personal care
- Education, day care
- Child support and alimony paid
- Pets
- Contributions, gifts
- Other:

Net Worth
(Assets less Liabilities)

Net Cash Flow
(Income less Expenses)

Fixed expenses include rent or mortgage payments, payments on other debts, insurance premiums, and the like which you can't do much about changing. Your variable expenses might change; these include food, clothing, entertainment, and recreation. "Specific goals" into which you may apply your net income (additional to net income into savings and investments) are objectives such as the down payment to buy a home, for a vacation trip, for college educations, for a new car, and the like.

Two cardinal rules: One, make sure your budget is realistic—don't anticipate income or greatly understate likely expenses. Two, every once in a while you'll go off your budget, just like with a diet; and like with a diet, get right back on it.

A simple budget that provides instant updates on how closely it's being followed consists of two columns, one filled in, the other blank.

The column that's filled in lists all the projected amounts you planned to spend for a particular item or category. The blank space that follows is for the amount you actually spend.

While it is possible to produce weekly or even daily budgets, the most practical one for most people deals with income and expenses a month at a time.

Your worksheet should begin with your monthly income. This includes your take-home pay plus income from investments, outside work, and any other money that comes your way. That's it for the good news.

From now on, you're subtracting.

The first thing you should subtract is the amount you save and invest. This is your stake in the future and must be paid each month. This can be broken down further on a separate sheet to include retirement planning, as well as other long-, medium-, and short-term goals.

The second item on your list should be your emergency fund. This is exactly what its name implies: money set aside to enable you to deal with unforeseen circumstances without having to dip into savings or liquidate assets. (Remember, if you're disabled, disability insurance will kick in after a few weeks; if you're laid off or fired, you'll be eligible for unemployment insurance.) It should be at least three months' living expenses; six months or more is better still.

While its accessibility is of primary importance, that doesn't mean it should sit idle. It could, for example, be put in an interest-bearing negotiable order of withdrawal (NOW) checking account, or in a conservatively managed fund that offers checking privileges. Though tempting by virtue of its availability, this money is not an entertainment or luxury fund. It's for emergencies. Once you've built your fund to the level you have settled upon, you need only to add to it to rebuild it when it is tapped, and to keep pace with increases in your own cost of living.

Housing payments—either mortgage, mortgage/maintenance, or rent—come next. These are fixed and predictable.

Payments on home equity and home improvement loans are next, followed by other debt payments—car loan, credit cards, college loans, etc. It can be a big money-saver to pay more than you are required to each month. This reduces the principal, and as a result, can reduce the amount on which you'll pay interest in the future, depending on the kind of debt involved.

Automobile and transportation expenses are next on the list. You may find in the first few months that your budgeted estimates are only noddingly close to your actual expenses. This might draw your attention to ways you can save money, once you realize how much it costs to operate your car. Don't forget to include the prorated amount you spend for car insurance, too.

You and your family eat. Budget for it. Again, your actual costs may be widely different from what you imagine them to be, and the importance of finding ways to save in this area may become apparent.

Your utility bills are next. Unless your plan averages your bills so that a fixed amount is paid each month, this may vary a great deal from month to month, with the biggest bills coming in the summer air-conditioning and winter heating seasons.

If you have children, you must budget for child-related expenses. These include child care, school lunches, and things like clothing, birthdays, allowances, and activities.

If you expect to owe income taxes, set aside a prorated amount each month to cover your tax liability. Don't forget state and local taxes and property taxes.

You'll find that many of the categories are remarkably consistent from month to month. But there are a few that are likely to be quite large one month and nonexistent the next. One good way to budget for them is to estimate them on a yearly basis and put money aside for them each month. Then, when the expenses are incurred, you won't have to take on new debt or dip into the emergency fund.

These unexpected expenses include home repairs and maintenance costs, insurance payments, major car repairs, clothing, medical expenses, and the like. Items such as braces for the children's teeth would fall into such a category. The point is to anticipate these expenses as much as you can.

There is another, very important category: fun. Don't forget to earmark a little each month for the occasional dinner out, or a movie or ballgame.

This category includes longer-term recreational activities, such as vacation savings and major family purchases (a boat, perhaps, or membership in a club or swimming pool association), too.

If you have difficulty making ends meet, putting together a budget will help you find the problem, and a solution might prove to be as simple as economizing in one or two areas, such as being careful not to leave appliances and lights turned on, eating out a little less, and so on. You may find that you're seriously overextended with credit card debt. Perhaps your income does not meet your projections.

No one can live outside his or her means for long without disaster taking place (you are not, after all, the U.S. Government). But even if you find that you spend more than you take in, a budget that illustrates this unhappy fact is of use to you. With it, instead of giving way to panic and despair you can take a rational look at your situation and make the choices and decisions necessary to solve the problem. This can range from belt tightening to seeking credit counseling, to refinancing high-interest debt, even to considering bankruptcy if things have gotten far out of hand (a thing that is far less likely to occur if you put together, and follow, a sensible budget).

Taking Stock: You'll be able to fill out much of your actual expense column when you sit down to pay your monthly bills. The rest may not be apparent until the end of the month.

When the numbers are filled in in both columns, you can do your subtraction and find out how well you did. Here's where it gets tricky. The first column you complete, your budgeted column, will specify a certain amount left over. The second column will too, unless you spent more than you took in. But it's not at all likely that the amount you have left over and the amount you think you have left over will correspond.

There are a multitude of little expenses, everything from chewing gum to magazines purchased at newsstands, that don't seem like much at the time but that can really add up. While it would require incredible discipline to get a handle on this category of expenses, you can at least arrive at an estimate, budget for it, and do what you can to economize.

Semi-Annual Inventory: It's a good idea to go over your budget every six months or so—halfway through your budget year. This enables you to see how you're doing and how close you are to your year's projection. It also lets you make adjustments where needed and where possible, and makes trends that require your attention more visible.

All that's really necessary is to add up all your monthly budgets so far, and see how big the discrepancies turn out to be. You might even average your actual expenses and adjust your budget for the second half of the year in order to reflect them.

The Year-End Scorecard: At year's end, it's time to compare what you thought would happen to what actually happened. It can be a happy, sad, or bittersweet experience. If you've budgeted carefully and followed your budget closely, you'll be pleased to see that you're better off than you were a year ago. What's more, you'll have the peace of mind that comes from having taken control of your financial situation.

Then, armed with the knowledge that comes of experience, you can begin making out your financial projection and monthly budgets for a new year.

SAVINGS: THE BUILDING BLOCKS

One of the most important things you can do is come to think of savings as you think of paying your bills—something you do every month, without fail. In fact, you should think of savings as a bill you pay to yourself.

You may be one of the many who are always planning to save, but are constantly confronted with other ways of spending money earmarked for savings. Certainly, saving requires discipline in an age when self-discipline is often overlooked.

If you are one of the disciplined few who make those deposits from each paycheck without fail, good for you. Keep it up! But if you're not, there are a lot of ways to make savings seem a little more like one of the monthly bills. There's a good chance that one or more of these is for you.

Here are some of them:

U.S. Savings Bonds remain one of the soundest investments you can make. Unsurpassed in their security, savings bonds now offer competitive interest rates when held to maturity. (See Chapter 8 for more.)

One of their most attractive features is that most people can purchase them through the payroll savings plan where they work. (If you can't, you can easily buy them at your bank.) This means that part of your paycheck comes in the form of a savings bond. You never see the cash, so you have no chance to spend it.

No-load mutual funds offer unusual flexibility in both investment options and ways of making regular payments. Some offer plans in which you send a check. Others make payroll deductions or automatic deductions from checking accounts in fixed amounts. (Chapter 10 discusses mutual funds in detail.)

You can key your monthly contribution either to a fixed amount you want to spend or to a fixed account value. If you want your account's value to grow by $50 each month and market values have dropped, then you'll have to put in your monthly $50 plus whatever amount you lost in the tick downward. In the long run, you'll end up saving more this way.

Many funds allow you to switch all or part of your account to more stable investments when the market in shares grows stormy.

Employee stock investments offer shares in your company, in a range of companies, or both. Employee contributions may be matched by the company, usually in shares of its own stock.

You can invest a portion of your income before taxes, with dividends and interest untaxed until you begin withdrawing the money. The before-tax investment, though, cannot be withdrawn until you reach age 59½, unless you prove financial hardship.

You may also invest part of your after-tax income. This is nearly as liquid as are investments in a brokerage account, without the expenses—although, of course, your investment choices are limited.

Employee stock plans are especially attractive because your contributions are usually deducted regularly from your pay. You have no opportunity to spend the money. When the company matches part of your contributions, the investment becomes even better.

Credit unions offer savings accounts, often at attractive rates. Usually not as liquid as a bank savings account, credit unions do give you access to your money. Your account can be increased through payroll deductions.

Checking account deductions can be made through your bank or your broker. A specified amount can be placed into a savings account or one of the many funds now available. If you choose the savings account, make sure that you move the money regularly into CDs or other safe, higher yield investments. Savings accounts offer liquidity, but they are not the best place to earn money on your investment. Remember that higher yields come at the cost of security, liquidity, or both. You should keep enough in savings to cover emergencies. The rest should be somewhere else, such as CDs.

Personal saving is more important now than ever before. With uncertainty over the adequacy of pension systems, growing medical and education costs, and the ever-present possibility of unpleasant financial surprises, it is crucial that you save as much as you can every single month. Plans like these make it easy.

A lack of discipline is no longer an excuse.

3

═══ BANKS ═══

Banking in the '80s was characterized by four notable events: deregulation, the S&L crisis, enactment of the Bank Secrecy Act, and the growth of the automatic teller machine. These three events have combined to make banking a totally different proposition in the '90s.

Banking used to be pretty straightforward. Today it's anything but.

DEREGULATION

The Depository Institutions Deregulation and Monetary Control Act of 1980, designed to allow banks and thrifts to pay competitive interest rates, completely revamped the banking system. For example, it allowed creation of negotiable order of withdrawal (NOW) accounts, which are in effect interest-bearing checking accounts. It permitted open-rate money-market accounts at banks and S&Ls. It allowed S&Ls to issue credit cards.

Today, it's becoming less certain exactly what a "bank" is. Credit unions and brokerage houses now offer many services once handled by banks. Many banks are no longer eager to offer those services to small depositors, choosing to cultivate their business clientele instead.

Savings and loans—many of which are quite healthy, despite the hundreds closed by regulators in recent years—are rushing to change their names and charters to those of savings banks. That way, they believe, they can escape the public perception of an industry on the verge of collapse. This is good public relations for them, but it again clouds the issue of what is and what is not a bank.

Because of the deregulation that took place in 1980, there is now a much broader range of services offered at a much broader range of rates and fees. Where before you might have chosen a bank solely on the basis of, for instance, its physical location and convenience, today that would be only one small figure in the total equation. It has become more than sensible to shop for a bank, just as you would shop for other goods and services.

The fact that banks currently provide services that were formerly the exclusive domain of brokerage houses, and that brokerage houses provide services that were once in the bank's bailiwick, has widened your shopping choices while also increasing the confusion. (As a result, the areas of investment that banks now share with investment houses are dealt with in the chapters on those kinds of investments.)

For a rundown of banking services, see Chart 5.

THE BANKING CRISIS

Despite the scandalous collapse of the savings and loan industry—with the bankruptcy of the Federal Savings and Loan Insurance Corporation, the seizure of hundreds of S&Ls by federal regulators, and a federal bailout that is estimated to carry a price tag of $800 for every family in America—except in a very few isolated instances depositors didn't lose a penny, nor did they lose access to their money for very long.

The underpinnings of this American tragedy were innocent enough. Deregulation put banks and S&Ls into competition for new deposits by removing interest rate limits. Sparked by double-digit inflation, interest rates rose in the late 1970s to 20 percent and above. But S&L assets were chiefly in home mortgages granted years earlier. New deposits had to be paid higher interest rates than the S&Ls earned on the old mortgages that had been issued when deposit rates were capped at 5.5 percent.

The S&L's, faced with this combination of low-income assets and high-cost liabilities, suffered a wave of losses. In response, Congress passed the Garn-St. Germain deregulation bill, which allowed S&Ls to enter new lending areas.

Unfortunately, the lending luck of the S&Ls was often bad. The following are some examples.

When oil prices fell, the oil companies, seeking to cut their losses, laid off newly hired employees. Unemployed, these employees could not pay their mortgages. Small businesses that had borrowed to start the support companies for these newly thriving oil communities saw business fall off.

There were wholesale foreclosures. But because these homes and commercial buildings were in now-depressed areas, they could be sold for only a fraction of their earlier value. Billions of dollars simply disappeared.

A similar situation occurred with midwestern farmland, as farmers went

CHART 5

Types of Checking, Savings and Investment Accounts Offered by Banking Institutions*
*Institutions include commercial banks, savings banks, savings and loan, and credit unions. Account names may vary at some institutions from those below. All types of accounts are not available at all individual institutions.
• Regular checking. • Special or economy checking. • NOW (checking with interest). • Super NOW (checking with interest). • Money market deposit. • Money market mutual funds (offered by bank subsidiaries and affiliates as well as by mutual funds themselves). • Sweep (combines both NOW and money market rates). • Multiple asset management (includes money market deposit account and/or mutual fund). • Passbook savings. • Statement savings. • Super savings. • Certificates of deposit. • U. S. Savings Bonds. • U. S. Treasury securities. • Christmas, Chanukah and other types of savings clubs. • Brokerage services: stocks; corporate, U. S. government and municipal bonds; mutual funds; other securities.

far out on a limb to buy as much land as possible. Droughts and so-so harvests caused many farms to go bust. Again, foreclosure followed but failed to recover the money the S&Ls had lent.

By the mid-1980s, the value of S&Ls had declined. But this just made them affordable by unscrupulous takeover operators. These crooks recognized that the appeal of federal insurance on deposits could be exploited to attract billions of dollars of deposits at high rates.

With the deposits in hand, the S&L operators looted the vaults. They spent the money people deposited; lent it to friends, relatives, and shady associates without requiring much security, or simply pocketed it. Some were caught and prosecuted, but many appear to have gotten away with it.

The S&L crisis has been so grave that the FSLIC ran out of money to repay depositors. It has been replaced by a new government organization, called the Resolution Trust Corporation.

The RTC's job is to sort things out and salvage what it can. First, it tries to get a healthy bank or savings and loan to take over and merge with one that has collapsed. If that fails, it "sells" the assets of the bad S&L—by getting other lending institutions to take over the good mortgages, for instance. The loans that have gone bad, to companies and individuals who are no longer repaying, are foreclosed, and the security is sold.

In many cases, there is more owed on the property than the property is worth, so the RTC has to make up the difference. This is why the bailout will cost at least $166 billion. The individual depositors are insured—up to $100,000 per person; twice that if one account is an IRA. The depositors didn't lose money.

The actual closure and liquidation of insolvent S&Ls is handled by the FDIC, which has beefed up its battalion of examiners. The agency is determined never to allow things to get this bad again.

But more trouble may be looming ahead. Just as the smoke was beginning to clear from the S&L bailout, word came that many banks in the Northeast were increasing their reserves due to an increase in bad loans, brought about in part by a decline in real estate values. They did not seem in danger of closing, but their profit picture was not rosy.

Similar unhappy events can be expected as prices drop in other regions where real estate buying panics led to unrealistically high prices. Foreign debt, simply because of its size, is always a wild card, too.

The fortunes of banks rise and fall, of course, with the economic conditions in the areas where they're located. The bigger ones have had embarrassing Third World debt exposures arise, which have cut into their profits. But this has more to do with the wisdom of buying shares in the bank than it does with whether it's safe to put your money—or borrow some—there.

If you're contemplating dealings with a thrift, you can reassure yourself, if you want, by looking at the S&L's financial statement, which is available to you. This will tell you instantly whether or not the institution is making or losing money. You might also want to find out its safety rating as measured by one of the bank and S&L rating companies.

THE BANK "SECRECY" ACT

As we enter the '90s, the confidentiality that most of us came to expect from our banking transactions has been compromised, at least to some extent. If your business handles large sums of cash, or if you are personally involved in large cash transactions, Uncle Sam is likely to pop in to see what's going on.

You can thank drug dealers, because the war on drugs is a big part of the reason. In an effort to track pushers' ill-gotten gains, a smorgasbord of federal enforcement agencies now have access to details of your cash transactions.

Beginning in 1970, a thing misleadingly called the Bank Secrecy Act required all banks and savings and loans to report to the IRS all deposits and withdrawals involving $10,000 or more in cash. In 1985, the requirement was extended to dealers of big-ticket items as well as, for instance, companies that sell money orders or transfer cash.

So far, though, the information was available only to the Internal Revenue Service. That all changed with the passage of the Anti-Drug Act of 1988. Now, those transaction reports are available to the FBI, the Drug Enforcement Administration, and U.S. Customs.

Additionally, the IRS has beefed up its enforcement of the Bank Secrecy Act, and its scrutiny of those reports. The IRS has more than quadrupled the number of investigators in some areas where there seem to be a disproportionate number of large cash transactions.

The information about cash transactions can then be compared to an individual's income tax return. Someone who pays cash for a $25,000 car on a reported income of $10,000 is likely to pique the interest of the IRS and, perhaps, the other agencies as well.

"The money is the key, always the key," says a New York-based Treasury Department investigator. "It has led us to everything from people dealing large quantities of drugs to large caches of illegal weapons to people who simply think they can avoid paying their taxes." The reporting requirements frequently lead to money-laundering operations, he said. "Follow the money and you'll find the bad guys."

This new, intense scrutiny of cash transactions means that legitimate businesses must make extra efforts to be able to explain the nature of those transactions. The law requires that businesses report the name, address, Social Security number, and other information about anyone involved in such a transaction. Information about the transaction itself must be reported as well.

As is true with most information received by the IRS, only a small portion will be subjected to closer scrutiny. But individuals who have been participants in such transactions should be prepared to answer the government's questions. Among them:

- Where did you get the money?
- Was it from a source that requires reporting on your tax return?

- If not, do you have documents to support your explanation of the money's source?

The IRS says that a typical person who, for example, buys a car that appears to be within his or her income is not likely to raise many eyebrows. Indeed, now that the tax law makes borrowing to finance such purchases less attractive, an increase in such transactions is expected.

What will draw the government's attention is a pattern of such transactions by an individual or business that seems to have no reason to be involved with large amounts of money. To identify these, though, all transactions can be subject to some scrutiny.

Failure by a business to report large cash transactions can result in a fine of $10,000 for each violation. If a business continues to ignore the law, a fine of as much as $500,000 and a prison term may be imposed. There are also penalties that may be levied against those who attempt to persuade a business to forego reporting a transaction.

To the IRS and other enforcement agencies, the tough new reporting laws and increased enforcement are powerful tools in their effort to slow the flow of contraband into the U.S. But they have an additional enforcement side effect, making more and more financial records available to the government.

What that means to you is that you must make an additional effort to keep your financial records pristine, so that in the event a question should arise, you can prove that your transactions are legitimate ones, well within the law.

It can spell the difference between a simple "sorry for the inconvenience" and a lengthy and expensive hassle with the government.

AUTOMATIC TELLER MACHINES

ATMs have been around since the mid-1970s, but they have proliferated over the past few years. Now networks allow card holders to withdraw cash across the country, and make gasoline and other purchases.

In the '90s, look for ATM cards to become even more versatile, making inroads into markets once reserved for credit cards. Currently, you can use them to move funds from savings into checking and vice versa, and make credit card and loan payments. Soon the use of ATMs to pay utility and telephone bills will become widespread as well. When you use these machines, you reduce the number of checks you need to write.

As ATMs have become more and more useful, service charges for their use have become commonplace but not universal. If you use your cash card a lot, it's worthwhile to shop around for a bank that doesn't charge for ATM use, or at least for one that offers enough services that the service charge saves you enough time to be a bargain.

The biggest problem with ATMs is that there's no human teller you can correct immediately when a mistake is made concerning your account. You have to use extra care when using ATMs:

- Never deposit cash in an ATM. Receipts from an ATM are not legal evidence of a transaction, and if there's a dispute, it's just your word against the bank's. Guess who wins? Check deposits are different, because the check itself can be traced.

- Never write your personal identification number (PIN) on your card, or keep it in your wallet. If thieves steal your card and use your PIN, it's difficult to prove that your losses are the result of theft.

- Don't use your name, address, or birth date as part of your PIN. A PIN that's easy to guess is as bad as writing your PIN on your card.

- Keep all your ATM receipts and compare them with your monthly statement. Errors sometimes occur.

- If a malfunction occurs, report it immediately to the institution that houses the machine, *and* to the institution that issued the card.

- Be careful when using ATMs that you're not familiar with. An editor from New York used an ATM in Maryland for a large cash withdrawal. The Maryland machine operated differently from the machines in New York, and he inadvertently cancelled the withdrawal after his New York account had been reduced, but before he received the cash in Maryland. It took weeks for the New York bank to clear up the mistake.

What's the biggest cause of ATM fraud? Bank customers. They account for 60 percent of the dollar losses from fraud and 23 percent of the total number of cases. More money is lost due to direct customer fraud than to unauthorized use of lost or stolen cards. Customers commit fraud by depositing empty envelopes and then claiming that they deposited cash, depositing worthless checks, and overdrawing their accounts.

If your ATM card is lost or stolen, notify the bank immediately. You're liable for unauthorized withdrawals up to $500, but if the bank is notified within two business days after you discover the loss, you're only liable for $50 of unauthorized withdrawals. Keep any evidence concerning the circumstances of your loss; banks won't always take your word for it when you claim withdrawals are unauthorized.

Consumer disputes about ATMs are regulated through Regulation E of the Electronic Funds Transfer Act of 1978. Under the regulation, banks must respond within 10 business days to customer complaints. They have to investigate and come up with a final disposition within 45 days. During this period, they must provisionally credit the customer's account.

Some seers have predicted that within just a few decades, cash transactions will be a thing of the past. Some companies already refuse to accept cash. This makes a bank affiliation necessary instead of just highly desirable.

The reshuffling of the financial deck is done constantly by high-speed computers, with no actual money physically exchanged. This has caused headaches among economists, who have to update their definition of money almost daily. When indicators such as the money supply are important to economic planners, it becomes crucial to know what money is.

This technological-economic revolution has trickled down to small companies and individuals. It is now possible, through banks, other financial institutions, or stand-alone service companies, to have some or all of your bills paid automatically each month. You deposit money in your account, and it is paid out as needed. Fixed payments are entered once, while those that vary from month to month must be reported to the institution or company as they are received. Electronic transactions are then made where possible. Otherwise, checks are issued. You can expect more of the former and less of the latter as time goes on.

An increasing number of banks actually provide a special telephone that you take home and use. It works like an ordinary telephone, but it also works like an on-site ATM, allowing you to push a few buttons to conduct transactions. These will become more commonplace, even as did the ATM in the 1970s.

CHECKING ACCOUNTS

Chances are that your chief association with your bank is through a checking account. There are more checking options than ever before. This means that it takes a little careful thought to decide on the kind of account that's best for you.

If you keep more money in your checking account than you need to cover checks, for instance, you might be losing money. That's because any funds beyond those necessary to cover bills could be earning interest or dividends virtually anywhere else.

Moving money from account to account, to make sure that you aren't keeping more money than is needed in checking, has become easier, too. The simplest and most common method is through the use of automated teller machines (ATMs).

According to the Federal Reserve, if you keep a $1,500 average balance in your checking account, your bank will have about $200 per year in revenue from that money—nearly a third of which is profit.

There are ways to make that profit your own. First, make sure you have an interest-bearing checking account. Shopping around will determine which banks offer interest for the lowest minimum balance.

Frequently, if you have a savings account or CDs issued by the same bank, checking is free of service charges. This can be a good deal, but it isn't always. It is a false economy to accept a lower interest rate on cash investments in order to save a few dollars on checking. So add up the entire equation before taking out a CD, or opening a savings account, if you can get interest rates elsewhere that will more than cover charges for checking.

Second, choose the checking account that best suits your needs. Some will allow you to write a few checks each month for no additional service charge—but the charge is high for checks written after the limit is reached. Others offer a flat rate per check which is more economical for people who pay a number of bills by check each month.

Third, consider alternative forms of checking account. There's a whole new crop of full-service financial institutions that offer the things you would normally get from a bank, plus a broader range of investment options. Check-writing privileges from these companies can include heavy service charges, but not always.

There is yet another kind of checking account: the one state law may require a bank to make available to you. Because of high costs, many banks have come to eschew small checking accounts. But many people, especially the elderly, need these accounts in order to pay their bills. As a result, a growing number of states are requiring banks to issue accounts to people who meet certain requirements.

The point is that in the last few years, your checking options have become almost limitless. One size no longer fits all.

Again, when considering these services, check to find out if there are any service charges or other "hidden" costs. These may vary depending on the amount of business you do with the bank, and may differ from bank to bank. For a detailed listing, see accompanying "Bank Fees" chart.

Take a good look at your checking account. You should consider the costs involved and the multitude of options available. But you would be wise to add another factor: convenience. Never forget that your time has value, too. Saving a few dollars at the expense of many hours is a false economy. An institution that is conveniently located may prove to be a bargain over one clear across town, even though the nearby bank has slightly higher service charges or offers fewer services.

BANK FEES

All of the services below are not available at all banks. All of the banks affording these services do not charge fees for all of them. Fees charged vary by individual banks.

Services	*Fees*
CHECKING	Charges for regular checking accounts and special checking accounts with no minimum balance or when balances fall below the minimum. Fees may be flat service charges and/or charges for items processed (which items may be both checks and deposits). Some banks permit balances in other types of accounts to be added toward required checking minimums.
	Most checking accounts (including checking-with-interest, money-market, savings, sweep, and multiple-asset) charge for ordering checks (some charge extra for specialized designs and for name/address imprints) and for bounced checks.
SPECIAL CHECKS	Fees per check for cashier's checks, certified checks, traveler's checks, and gift checks.
CDs	Charges for withdrawal (cashing in) of a certificate of deposit prior to its maturity date.
SECURITIES	Commissions for purchases and sales of U.S. government, municipal, and corporate bonds, of common and preferred stocks, of mutual funds, and of other securities provided by brokerage entities (usually "discount brokerage") of some banks.
RETIREMENT	Fees charged on IRA, 401(k), 403(b), IRA-Rollover, SEP-IRA, Keogh, and other retirement accounts with the banks.
INVESTMENT ADVICE	Generally for clients with higher incomes (often $100,000 minimum). Usually through a bank's trust department (below).
TRUST DEPARTMENTS	In addition to investment (and other financial) advice (above), bank trust departments manage accounts for estates, minors, incompetents, and others who cannot or do not want to manage their own financial affairs.
FINANCIAL PLANNING	Some banks have financial planning departments offering consumers a range of services. Sometimes these departments work with trust, investment advice, real estate, estate planning, and/or other bank departments. Fees usually depend upon various factors, such as planning-time involved, assets involved, and complexity.
SAFE DEPOSIT BOX	Annual fee based upon size of the box.

BANK FEES *(continued)*

Services	*Fees*
LOANS	Interest, and sometimes setting-up, charges for first-mortgage, second mortgage, home-equity, home-improvement, automobile, education, personal, credit-card, and other borrowings. Charges on secured loans (such as secured by publicly-traded securities) generally are less than for unsecured loans (such as on-your-signature).
INSURANCE	Most banks sell life, health, disability, property, and other insurance policies whose premium rates are competitive with other sources.
TAX PREPARATION	Some banks offer a tax preparation service for a fee which depends upon such factors as complexity and time involved.
CREDIT CARDS	Yearly charge plus interest on balance outstanding after prescribed grace period after each month's billing. Some banks may assess a small fee in months when no purchases are made with a card. See "Loans" above, which includes credit-card loans.
ATMs	A "transaction" card has your personal identification number (PIN) which serves as a code identifying you to automatic teller machines (ATMs). You can get cash, make deposits, check your balance, and transfer funds from one account to another. Some banks charge fees for ATM usage additional to any charges for regular accounts.
DEBIT CARDS	You have a debit card and a bank account. A store has an automatic teller machine (ATM) in the store and a bank account. You make your purchase and pay for it by your debit card being put in the store's ATM. Funds are immediately transferred from your account to the store's. As with their own ATMs (above), some banks charge fees for debit-card usage additional to any charges for regular accounts.
AT-HOME BANKING	Some banks by themselves and some service networks in association with banks provide at-home banking. Some services use a home computer, others use a television set hooked into a cable system, still others use a special terminal which gets information via telephone lines. At-home banking services may include your balances, which of your checks have been cashed, shopping, paying bills, and buying and selling securities. Fees will vary depending upon the system being used, services provided, and extent of services used.

Checking accounts, like much of banking, are constantly changing. It behooves you to appraise your needs and then go shopping for the account that most efficiently and economically does the job for you.

SAVINGS ACCOUNTS

It's a good bet that the first investment you ever made was a deposit in a savings account. There is something very wholesome and heartwarming about a young person proudly showing off his or her first passbook.

For many, this rite of growth followed a lecture from a parent about the importance of thrift and savings. Then, the contents of the piggy bank of childhood were taken after school—or on Saturday morning when, until just a few years ago, banks were open—and placed in the bank account of adulthood.

Those accounts didn't pay much in the way of interest.

They still don't. Today, the ritual of a first passbook account is just one step toward thriftiness and investment discipline for young people. For the rest of us, a passbook account, because of its low yield, has limited appeal.

Passbook accounts are easy to open and have little or no minimum deposit. You can add to them in any amount at almost any time—even with automatic teller machines—and you can make withdrawals of any size any time as well. Their advantage is liquidity.

They also provide an opportunity for those who are just starting out, and who therefore can only save a little each week, to build a nest egg that can later be placed in higher-paying investments that have higher minimums. (Of course, in such a situation you shouldn't make the switch the minute you can, because you can be left in a pinch in the event of an emergency requiring you to dip into savings.)

Similar to passbook accounts are statement accounts, which have a monthly or quarterly statement instead of a passbook.

CERTIFICATES OF DEPOSIT

CDs are the leading investment instrument at banks. They offer high safety and a high yield.

The reason certificates of deposit pay more than other kinds of accounts is that the bank knows from the outset how long your money will remain on deposit. This, in turn, aids it in making long-term lending commitments.

CDs are available in a wide selection of denominations, with a typical minimum of $500. They are also available with a range of maturities, from as little as a week to years. The rates are higher for longer-term issues, for two reasons. One is that your money is worth more to the bank over a longer term (unless interest rates collapse, which is highly unlikely). The other is that you are likely to be concerned that interest rates might head upward, leaving you locked into a lower rate for a long-term issue. There would then be every reason for you to choose shorter-term CDs, giving you more frequent opportunities to reinvest.

The disadvantage of a CD is its illiquidity. Once you've purchased a certificate of deposit, your money is tied up for the term of the CD. It is possible to "break" the CD, but it will cost you, in most cases, far more than the difference had you put the money in some other kind of account, albeit one that yielded less. The key, then, is to invest only those funds you are certain you will not need, and to invest only for the term that you feel confident in that certainty.

When investing in CDs, by all means shop around. Read the fine print, because things like frequency of compounding (the frequency with which interest is added to principal, increasing the amount on which interest is paid) can make a seemingly high rate effectively much lower. The figure that should interest you most is the effective annual yield.

It is important, though not crucial, to investigate a bank's quality. The safety of deposits in specific banks is measured by several companies; your broker should be able to provide you with the information you need. The safety issue is not a big one because your deposits in a given bank—up to $100,000 total—are protected by the FDIC. If you have more money than this to put into CDs, put the money in different banks, with no more than $100,000 in any one of them. That way, safety is nearly absolute, even though yields are high.

CREDIT UNIONS—A GOOD PLACE TO SHOP FOR CREDIT

If you are shopping for a car loan, looking for good rates and terms for a credit card, or want to open a home equity line of credit, then you may be surprised by the deals you can get at a credit union.

At the end of 1989, there were more than 60 million Americans who were members of credit unions. You probably should join them.

Because credit unions are nonprofit organizations, credit unions can afford to offer a broad range of financial services at low costs. They pay more interest on deposits, and they charge less interest on loans. You can't beat that. It means you'll have lower monthly payments than you would have if you were dealing with a commercial bank, savings and loan, or mortgage company.

Take credit cards, for instance. One recent survey found that interest on credit union credit cards was more than 2.5 percent less than the average on all such cards. The annual fee was one-third that of credit cards overall. These are savings worth noticing.

The financial services offered by credit unions vary widely. Only about one-third, for instance, offer personal checking accounts. (In credit unions, these are known as share drafts.) Only one credit union in five offers credit cards. Fewer than one-third offer first mortgages, and only one-fourth offer home equity loans. These numbers can be misleading, though. That's because, as stands to reason, the widest variety of services is offered by the largest credit unions, which, of course, have the most members. This means that all of the services above are available to the majority of credit union members. (For a broad view of loan services, see Chart 6.)

Those members are extremely happy with their credit unions. Survey after survey has shown that credit union members are far happier with the quality and kind of financial services they receive than are customers of banks and savings and loan institutions. And compared with bank and thrift customers, more than twice as many credit union members say the quality of services is actually improving.

How do you join a credit union? First check with your employer's benefits office. Half of all Fortune 500 companies sponsor credit unions for their employees. If your company is part of a larger company, there's a good chance that the parent company's credit union is open to you. You may belong to an organization or other group that enables you to join. Ask around.

To learn more, if you have not been provided with the answers you seek, drop a note to the Credit Union National Association, Dept. SP, Box 431, Madison, Wisconsin 53701.

SAFETY DEPOSIT BOXES—A VERY IMPORTANT BANK SERVICE

Like drawing up a will, renting a safe deposit box is something that many people intend to do, but never get around to.

Like failing to have a will, overlooking a safe deposit box can be disastrous. (Having both can be disastrous, too, if you don't inform your spouse, lawyer, or a trusted friend of their locations.)

With FBI statistics showing crime at record levels, plus news reports of drug abusers who support themselves and their addictions through burglary, a safe deposit box is more important than ever.

Think of the important papers, valuables, and small heirlooms you have stuffed into drawers around your home. Not being able to find an important paper when you need it is at least annoying. Some items are irreplaceable, and some can be replaced only after spending a lot of time and money. Their loss, through fire or other disaster, could make an already tragic situation much, much worse.

A safe deposit box is a simple, cheap solution. A small box can be rented at most banks for very little—and under some circumstances, the cost is tax deductible. A few banks may waive the rental fees if your balance in other accounts is high enough.

The safe deposit box is where you should store your passport, birth certificate, insurance policies, stock certificates, and bonds, plus the title of your car and the deed to your home. If you have a few gold coins you bought on a whim a few years ago, they should go into the box, too. If you invest in rare coins, this is the place to keep them. The percentage of the box that is used to store investment-related items can be deducted from your taxes.

A copy of your will, but not the original, should be in the box also. The original should remain with your lawyer or other designated representative. This is because the law in some states requires that safe deposit boxes be sealed following the box holder's death. In those states, the box may be opened only after the will is read and the estate distributed.

While safe deposit boxes enjoy the same high physical security as do other bank deposits, there are important differences. For instance, should the contents of your box be stolen—a highly unlikely event, but it's been known to happen—the bank is not automatically liable for the contents, nor are the contents insured by the FDIC. On the other hand, you do not lose any part of the contents of your box if the bank becomes insolvent.

Over the course of time you may discover that you frequently need information from papers kept in your safe deposit box. This necessitates frequent trips to the bank and inevitably results in your ending up with these papers at home again. Better to photocopy the documents so that you have a set, though not the originals, at home. Then you can use them and protect them, too.

(If you store Certificates of Deposit, for instance, in your safe deposit box, make sure to keep a list of the dates they mature, because you'll want to re-invest the money at once and you may not want to roll it over into another CD at the same bank.)

Make certain, too, to list the tangible contents of your safe deposit box

CHART 6

Your Guide To Personal Loan Sources	
Lending Sources and Principal Types or Purposes of Personal Loans	*Significant Advantages and/or Disadvantages*
Commercial Banks: Home mortgage Home second mortgage Home equity credit line Home improvement New auto, mobile home Education Personal secured Personal unsecured	**Advantages:** No trouble obtaining loans if credit is good. Can borrow large amounts through home second mortgage or home equity credit line. Generally have convenience of numerous branches in urban and suburban neighborhoods. Also can make business and investment loans. **Disadvantages:** Costs of home second mortgage or home equity credit line may be steep. Personal secured loan can tie up assets collateralizing the borrowing (such as checking or passbook savings accounts, or securities) that may be needed on short notice. Unsecured personal loan costs higher because bank's risk is greater.
Savings and Loans*: Home mortgage Home second mortgage Home equity credit line Home improvement New auto, mobile home Education Personal secured Personal unsecured	**Advantages:** No trouble obtaining loans if credit is good. Can borrow large amounts through home second mortgage or home equity credit line. Costs, particularly with various types of home loans, usually are less than commercial banks'. Service, particularly with various types of home loans, often is superior to commercial banks'. **Disadvantages:** *In some states S&Ls are only permitted to grant loans for home mortgages and home improvements. Costs of home second mortgage or home equity credit line may be steep. Personal secured loans can tie up assets that may be needed on short notice. Unsecured personal loan costs higher because S&L's risk is greater.
Savings Banks: Home mortgage Home second mortgage Home equity credit line	**Advantages:** No trouble obtaining loans if credit is good. Can borrow large amounts through home second mortgage or home equity credit line.

CHART 6 (continued)

Lending Sources and Principal Types or Purposes of Personal Loans	Significant Advantages and/or Disadvantages
Savings Banks (*continued*) Home improvement Personal secured Personal unsecured	Costs of various types of home loans and personal loans secured by passbook savings accounts usually are less than commercial banks'. Service, particularly with various types of home loans, often is superior to commercial banks'. **Disadvantages:** Exist in only about one-third of the states, mostly in the northeastern U.S. Costs of home second mortgage or home equity credit line may be steep. Personal secured loans can tie up assets that may be needed on short notice. Unsecured personal loan costs higher because lender's risk is greater.
Credit Unions: Home mortgage Home second mortgage Home equity credit line Home improvement New auto, mobile home Personal secured Personal unsecured	**Advantages:** No trouble obtaining loans if a member in good standing. Lowest rates anywhere. Generally better service than elsewhere. **Disadvantages:** You have to be a member (usually formed by employees of a business or members of a labor union, club or lodge).
Mortgage Firms: Home mortgage Home second mortgage Home equity	**Advantages:** Can borrow large amounts through second mortgage or home equity loan. Competitive rates and terms. **Disadvantages:** Costs of home second mortgage or home equity loan may be steep. Does not add to broader-based customer relationships as with banks and S&Ls.
Sales Finance Companies: Auto Mobil home Boat Major appliances	**Advantages:** Convenience: you're extended credit when you buy a high-priced item; down payment with remainder paid in regular weekly or monthly amounts from several months to several years. It's possible to get a good deal during special promotions when rates are reduced. **Disadvantages:** Rates are high: the retailer adds a finance charge to the cash price. You do not own what you bought until you have completed your payments.

CHART 6 *(continued)*

Lending Sources and Principal Types or Purposes of Personal Loans	Significant Advantages and/or Disadvantages
Small Loan Companies: *(Sometimes known as consumer finance or personal finance companies)* Auto Other high-priced items Personal secured Personal unsecured	**Advantages:** One of the easiest places to get a loan. May be the only place if you have a poor credit rating. Afford both single payment and installment loans. **Disadvantages:** Rates are high. Security might be personal assets such as a chattel mortgage on your furniture. If your credit rating is poor, you may have to have a co-signer to guarantee payment.
Insurance Companies: General purpose use (you may generally borrow up to 95 percent of your life insurance policy's surrender value)	**Advantages:** Simple loan to obtain. Little paperwork. Low rates. **Disadvantages:** No obligation to repay loans and accumulating interest—and payments to your heirs will be reduced commensurately.
Stockbrokerage Firms: General purpose use (you "margin"—borrow against stocks, bonds or mutual funds that you own) ["Advantages" and disadvantages" at right relate only to margin accounts, not other lending services some brokerage firms may provide, directly or indirectly]	**Advantages:** Easy and quick to get once you have set up a margin account. Interest rates are low relative to some other lending sources because a margin account is secured by liquid collateral. **Disadvantages:** Rates can fluctuate widely as margin requirements change. If margin requirements are increased or the value of your pledged holdings declines sharply, you will have to put up additional collateral on short notice or have some of your securities sold out. No obligation to repay so you might let interest accumulate substantially.

OTHER SOURCES

Credit Card Loans: easy to get since you are drawing on your credit line, but this may lure you into impulsive, unwise spending.

Executive Loan Services: arranged mainly by mail and phone to executives with high incomes.

Industrial Loan Companies: arranged mostly with industrial workers for most uses.

Pawn Shops: pawnbroker holds your pledged asset for the life of the loan; you can borrow only a small amount of the auction value of the item, and you pay a very high interest rate.

Forms of credit other than loans: include credit cards, charge accounts and debit cards to purchase goods or services on an "open-end" (revolving) credit basis.

on your homeowner's insurance policy. This is done through the addition of an inexpensive rider to the policy. Then, in the off chance that your bank is burglarized or swept out to sea or falls victim to some other kind of disaster, you'll be at least partly protected.

Conversely, the safe deposit box is the place to keep a list of all valuable items in your home, along with their serial numbers. This can be very valuable if disaster strikes.

Married couples may want to rent the box jointly. This is an additional headache if there is a divorce or dispute, but it is usually advantageous. Do make sure that you know the rights of the surviving spouse in the event of the death of one spouse, because those rights vary from state to state.

Be sure also to read the fine print in your box rental agreement. Some institutions forbid the storage of some kinds of valuables, and if they're on your list, you might have to seek a safe deposit box at another institution.

FOUND MONEY

A friend going through family files once found three savings account passbooks, each more than 20 years old. The accounts each showed balances of several hundred dollars. They had been long forgotten.

She wrote a letter to the bank, which was in a state from which she had moved nearly two decades ago.

The bank had undergone several name changes, had been bought and sold, and wrote back that it had no record of the accounts.

What was she to do? She had certainly deposited the money and had simply left it in the accounts. Now it seemed there was no way of getting her principal, never mind interest that would have greatly increased the balance.

Where did the money go?

After a number of letters back and forth, she found out that the money was turned over to the state as unclaimed property. In due course, she was able to track it down and recover her deposits plus some interest—though not all that she would have earned had the money remained in the account.

Each state has some sort of abandoned or unclaimed property division, usually as part of the state treasurer's office. After a period of time, that varies from state to state, accounts in which there has been no activity and whose owners cannot be found easily are turned over to the state. (This also applies to stock dividends where the stockholder cannot be found, and to other payments and refunds.)

There the money remains, unless it is claimed, forever. Of course, the state can go ahead and use the money—but it must repay it if it is claimed.

Most states pay no interest on these unclaimed funds, though a handful pay some interest.

More than $3 billion currently sits in these state repositories. Surprisingly, the chances are good that you have some money there—especially if you've moved fairly frequently over the years. It might not be much. But it's easy to overlook never having received the refund on a utility deposit, an insurance payment, or a small state tax refund.

If a relative has recently died—and especially if you are executor of the estate—it's a good idea to check with the state to see if there are unclaimed funds in his or her name there.

The process is remarkably simple. In fact, the most difficult part is finding out who to contact to learn if the state coffers hold unclaimed treasures for you. The best thing is to drop a note to the state treasurer's office, requesting the address of the unclaimed or abandoned property division. The majority of states accept telephone inquiries about abandoned funds—be sure to ask if there is a toll-free number.

Once you know who to contact, go for it! Inquire, also, to see if your children or other relatives have money in their names. The accounts are listed on a computer, so it's easy for the state to run a check. If your given name is different from the name you go by, have them run a check on both—this is where mix-ups often take place.

If you own a company—or are a financial officer with a company—it's worthwhile to check once in a while to see if company money might have found its way into the unclaimed property file. It frequently happens.

One thing you should avoid is companies that will conduct the search for you. As you can see, it's very easy to make the search yourself, so you don't need any help. And those companies usually take a large percentage of whatever you recover, as a bounty.

Once you have determined that the state is holding money that belongs to you, find out what you need to do to recover it. In some cases you may have to provide proof that the money is really yours—but not always. In the case of my friend, the bankbooks were proof, so there was no problem. But in any case, you will be asked to fill out a form and provide evidence that you are who you claim to be. You will be asked to provide evidence that you are the proper owner of the money—such as proof that you lived at the address of record connected with the money—and your Social Security number. If you are making the inquiry for a deceased person, you will have to prove your interest in the case, such as being that person's executor.

It's worthwhile also to run a check in other states where you've lived—even if you lived there many years ago. It's easy to forget small accounts that were opened, deposits paid but never refunded, and the like. A few years ago, it was popular for college students to open small cash-value life insurance policies while at school. They graduate and go home, and the company doesn't know where they are. These funds—or the papers connected with them—sometimes end up with the state.

What's more, conducting such a search can be fun. For very little investment you stand a surprisingly good chance of finding money you had forgotten you had.

And in a few cases, really large amounts have come to light and been claimed.

4
CREDIT

You probably owe too much money. I can say that safely because the majority of Americans are in debt to the point that one or two adverse events could bust 'em.

Americans simply carry too much debt. For the last few years, it has amounted nationwide to nearly one dollar in five of disposable income. And that's not including mortgages. It increased 30 percent from 1982 to 1987 alone.

The idea of spending somebody else's money has come to be taken all too casually by everyone from those in the highest levels of government on down. Money borrowed is money that must be repaid with interest. That is an immutable fact. Sometimes economic changes make it a little easier, because the money repaid lacks the value of the money borrowed, but not always.

Credit is a tool. It should be used when it and only it can aid in the performance of a worthwhile task. But just as you would not scramble your eggs with a hammer, you should not look to credit to do more than it should, no matter how much you are urged to do so, and no matter how tempting is the idea. If you don't borrow, you don't owe. Period.

The question really shouldn't be how much debt you can afford to take on, but how much you can afford to save. No matter how much debt you can comfortably incur, if you cannot also save you have little business getting into debt at all.

Credit has its costs, as illustrated in Chart 7.

HOW YOU GET CREDIT

Retailers, financial institutions, leasing companies, insurance companies, credit-card companies, employers, landlords, and others with authorized interest in determining your financial responsibility can get copies of your report from a credit bureau. A credit report includes a history of your loans and credit, payments, delinquencies, and other companies requesting a copy of your report. Some of the parties interested in your credit history will check you out further in addition to your report.

Creditors rate you on what are known as "The Three C's": (1) Character—have you been paying past debts on time, and do you live within your means? (2) Capacity—is your employment stable and will your income and other expenses enable you to pay off new debt? (3) Capital—do you have collateral that may be used to secure your new debt?

Different creditors weigh The Three C's differently; they assess your loan application by giving you points for various attributes that (they think) are indicative of your creditworthiness. This is known as "loan scoring." Different creditors use different formulas in loan scoring, so if you're turned down by one, you may be acceptable to another.

There are various types of loans and credit. "Unsecured" cash loans require no collateral, only your signature. "Secured" loans are collateralized by assets of marketable value, which can be sold to pay off loans on which you may default. Marketable physical assets include your home (for a first or second mortgage, or a home-equity loan), car, and jewelry. Marketable financial assets include stocks and bonds (and mutual funds), savings accounts, certificates of deposit (CDs), and cash-value life insurance.

Some lenders may insist that you have credit insurance, to pay off the balance of the debt if you die or become disabled, or if physical collateral is destroyed or damaged. This insurance is usually a bad buy (typically, it can add 20 percent or more to the cost of financing a car, for instance), and you should avoid it if at all possible.

Be prepared when you apply for a loan. Don't walk in "cold." Have with you documentation to support your application. Try to borrow enough so you won't be caught short. But don't borrow so much that you'll be paying interest for money you don't need. Do try to arrange for a larger line of credit if needed. Try not to put up collateral that's worth substantially more than the amount you're borrowing.

If you're seeking a loan, you usually have a better chance at a financial institution or other source with which you have had prior dealings. Sources from which you may borrow include commercial banks, savings and loans, savings banks, credit unions, sales finance companies, personal finance companies (sometimes known as consumers or small-loan finance companies), insurance companies, stock brokerage firms, mortgage firms, employers, executive loan services, industrial loan companies, and pawn shops.

CHART 7

The Cost of Borrowing What You Will Pay in Interest Charges								
Number of Monthly Payments	ANNUAL PERCENTAGE RATES							
	11%	12%	13%	14%	15%	16%	17%	18%
	FINANCE CHARGE PER $100 OF AMOUNT FINANCED							
1	0.92	1.00	1.08	1.17	1.25	1.33	1.42	1.50
2	1.38	1.50	1.63	1.75	1.88	2.00	2.13	2.26
3	1.84	2.01	2.17	2.34	2.51	2.68	2.85	3.01
4	2.30	2.51	2.72	2.93	3.14	3.36	3.57	3.78
5	2.77	3.02	3.27	3.53	3.78	4.04	4.29	4.54
6	3.23	3.53	3.83	4.12	4.42	4.72	5.02	5.32
7	3.70	4.04	4.38	4.72	5.06	5.40	5.75	6.09
8	4.17	4.55	4.94	5.32	5.71	6.09	6.48	6.87
9	4.64	5.07	5.49	5.92	6.35	6.78	7.22	7.65
10	5.11	5.58	6.05	6.53	7.00	7.48	7.96	8.43
11	5.58	6.10	6.62	7.14	7.66	8.18	8.70	9.22
12	6.06	6.62	7.18	7.74	8.31	8.88	9.45	10.02
18	8.93	9.77	10.61	11.45	12.29	13.14	13.99	14.85
24	11.86	12.98	14.10	15.23	16.37	17.51	18.66	19.82
30	14.83	16.24	17.66	19.10	20.54	21.99	23.45	24.92
36	17.86	19.57	21.30	23.04	24.80	26.57	28.35	30.15
48	24.06	26.40	28.77	31.17	33.59	36.03	38.50	41.00
60	30.45	33.47	36.52	39.61	42.74	45.91	49.12	52.36
72	37.05	40.76	44.53	48.36	52.24	56.18	60.17	64.22
84	43.83	48.28	52.81	57.42	62.09	66.84	71.66	76.55
96	50.80	56.03	61.35	66.77	72.28	77.88	83.57	89.34
108	57.96	63.99	70.14	76.40	82.78	89.27	95.87	102.57
120	65.30	72.17	79.17	86.32	93.60	101.02	108.56	116.22

Comparison-shop to find which lender may offer you the best deal. Be careful to consider all factors that might affect your borrowing costs, including fixed vs. variable rates, non-interest fees, and other charges.

If you're turned down, the Equal Credit Opportunity Act provides that the creditor must let you know in writing. The creditor also must give you the reason or inform you that you have the right to request the reason. You also have the right to know which credit report was used and to obtain a copy from the credit bureau. There may have been a mistake in your report that you can remedy.

With knowledge of the reason for the turndown, you may be able to take steps to improve this defect and reapply and be approved by the creditor. Or you may be able to apply successfully to another creditor whose scoring methods are different.

ESTABLISHING CREDIT

You have just graduated from college. You're on your own. This means that you've taken on financial responsibilities that until now your family has, in all probability, handled for you.

There are some questions that you probably have, but you have no idea of the answers:

- How much debt can you safely assume on your own?

- What burden is assumed by other college graduates in your position?

- Are there any rules?

I've been in this business for quite a while. I've managed to walk without stumbling through an increasingly complex obstacle course of credit options, education loans, automobile loans, and the like. Chart 8 can help you figure out the debt you can afford to carry. Having paid attention to the things I've seen, the people who got into trouble and the people who didn't, I'm prepared to suggest some basics concerning debt:

- Do not take on debt, other than servicing your home mortgage, which adds up to more than 20 percent of your annual after-tax income.

- Do not owe more than one-third of your "discretionary" income for the year. Discretionary income is the amount of money you have left after you pay for necessities such as food, clothing, and shelter.

These guidelines permit a wide range within what you could come to consider an acceptable debt level. They are merely guidelines, though; depending on your income or your needs, they could be a little high or a little low.

They may sound very conservative indeed, but they really aren't. Of course, if you are at the very high income level, and your expenses for necessities are very low, you could afford to incur more debt. But if you can minimize your debt, do so.

Establishing credit is easier than it used to be, and that can become a problem—especially for young people. The easiest way to get credit is

CHART 8

How Much Consumer Installment Debt Can You Carry?**

As a rule of thumb, your consumer installment debt should not exceed 20 percent of your "take-home" income from work. As you reach the retirement planning stages be even more conservative and use *only* net income from work. Don't include interest, dividends and other non-employment income. Hold back this non-work income as a protective cushion that you can put into savings/investments.

If you are retired, assess what you consider to be your "take-home" income—which might include Social Security, annuities, pension plan, IRA, or similar. Do not include the interest or dividends from longer-term investments—say those maturing in five, ten years.

A. Your total annual net income from work .... $ _____

B. The 20 percent installment-payment debt maximum safety level *(20 percent of A.)* $ _____

C. Your present total annual consumer installment-debt payments:
- a. Auto(s) .... $ _____
- b. Other vehicles ....   _____
- c. Furniture ....   _____
- d. Appliances ....   _____
- e. Home entertainment equipment ...   _____
- f. Sports equipment ....   _____
- g. Vacation trip ....   _____
- Other:

_____   _____
_____   _____
_____   _____

- h.   Total ....   _____

D. Amount of total annual consumer installment-debt you can afford—in addition to present amount *(B. minus C.)* $ _____

This amount (D.) is your present margin of safety. If your present amount (C.) exceeds the 20 percent level (B.), you are in trouble already.

E. To figure your current debt ratio, divide your present total debt (C.) by your annual net income (A.) ....   _____ %

**Other than mortgage, education and business loans.

through credit cards. But unfortunately, the credit card route is by far the worst way to do it.

Why? Because easy credit can become an irresistible pit of quicksand to the young and inexperienced. You're offered a credit card and you say, "Why not? After all, I don't have to use it," but it seldom works out that way. Often, people don't recognize the connection between putting a purchase on the card and spending money. Before they know it, they're in more debt than they can handle.

A far better and healthier approach for those who are just starting out is to leave the credit cards at home, or simply refuse them. Here are some guidelines for establishing credit which are based on sounder principles:

- First, open a bank account, preferably a savings account. Establish a relationship with the bank.

- Make regular deposits of a percentage of whatever you earn, even if it's only a few dollars. This builds your account, but more important, it sets a good pattern and helps create self-discipline.

- After you have built up an account, borrow money against it. Don't spend the money. Don't do anything with it. Deposit it in another account. Then, after a month, pay it back. You can do this several times. It establishes a record, and the record looks good. It also familiarizes the borrower with the system. The bank will be willing to make such loans, because they have the money right there. You never lose access to it, so if an emergency—a real emergency—arises, you can get your hands on it.

- While there will be a slight cost in interest, it will be well worth it. You'll end up with a good credit rating, money in the bank, and the discipline and knowledge necessary to make wise choices when credit is really important. You'll be known to the bank, and get better rates, because yours won't be a "high-risk loan."

CREDIT CARDS

Credit card companies have been very successful in marketing their cards as "status symbols." They have spent millions of advertising dollars to convince us that their gold or platinum versions are supposedly somehow more prestigious than the ordinary variety. A friend once remarked to me, "I just received a pre-approved application for a card with a $20,000 limit, which I suppose comes to $35 per month forever!" Similarly, there has come to be a certain cachet attached to having a billfold or purse filled with credit cards and charge cards.

Let me say it: The emperor has no clothes! This business of carrying a huge wad of plastic is silly and dangerous!

The big problem with carrying a lot of credit and charge cards, or carrying ones that have an astronomical limit on the amount you may charge, is that it takes the discipline of a saint to keep from getting deep into debt. Even with a credit limit of $1,200 or so, paying the minimum each month on a card filled to the limit will end up with your paying $35 per month virtually forever.

You can shop around to find credit cards that charge less. But the principal way to save is to cut down on their use, the number you carry, and the resulting credit charges.

If you travel frequently, a credit card from one of the major companies can be useful, sometimes necessary (car rental firms, for example, are extremely hesitant to rent vehicles to people who don't have a credit card). A gasoline credit card can help in record keeping and can make paying the fuel bill an easy, one-shot monthly affair. If you have children, a department store credit card can help in back-to-school and other purchases. Credit cards can be useful in business record-keeping, where you expect to be reimbursed—just make sure there's no slip 'twixt the expense check and the credit card payment!

In some places it is not safe to carry much cash (though you can often get around this by carrying cash in a pocket or someplace other than your billfold or purse, which is a good idea anyway). But it's to your advantage to pay cash whenever possible for non-business dining, entertainment, and purchases. This way, you don't end up running up a huge charge tab that you can't pay off at once, leaving you with very high interest payments.

Carrying a balance on a credit card is one of the most expensive forms of credit you can have. It typically is 1.5 percent per month, or 18 percent per year. That's steep compared to other consumer loans.

For this reason, it's very unwise to take cash advances on your credit card. Interest is usually charged from the day you take the advance, unlike charges, which typically have a 30-day grace period, meaning that if you pay off the entire balance within that time, you will pay no interest.

(Use of a credit card overseas is another matter as well. You will find that, at minimum, you will be billed at the highest possible exchange rates.)

WHAT TO LOOK FOR IN A CREDIT CARD. When you apply for a card, double-check to ensure that your bank doesn't charge you if you pay within the 30-day limit. This is a period during which you may pay for your charges interest-free. Obviously, this means that you have use of the money for a short time at no charge. The credit card company hopes that you decide to let it slide—otherwise, the bank makes no money on your borrowing.

Second, firmly resolve to pay the entire balance each month. Some companies require this anyway. That way, you will usually pay no interest at all.

Third, shop around. Though you plan to pay off the entire balance each month, you still would like to find the lowest fees and interest rates.

It's possible that your dealings with your bank are such that a credit card is offered to you at a reduced rate or entirely free of the annual fee. This sounds like a good idea, and usually is—but don't keep large amounts in low-yielding accounts just so you can receive a free credit card. To do so will make the credit card not free but, over time, very, very expensive. Of even greater concern is an Internal Revenue Service ruling that when free cards are provided for holders of tax-advantaged accounts, such as IRAs, the tax status of the entire account is thrown into question. Be careful and check before you agree to a free card tied to your accounts.

With great care, credit cards can be used to take advantage of truly great bargains, even if you don't pay off the balance all at once. If you purchase an item you really need for $500, and it normally sells for $750, you can pay it off over two or three months and, despite the high interest rate, achieve a substantial saving.

The problem comes when you let a credit card balance ride from month to month to month, merely paying the interest, never reducing the principal. This is simply throwing your money away.

Affinity Cards: Some credit cards are called "affinity" cards. They work like this: Part of the fees and interest you pay are donated to the organization "sponsoring" the card. And the card itself is emblazoned with the logo or name of the group or cause, which is supposed to signify your support every time you make a purchase with it.

They sound like a good idea. But these new and popular accounts usually do not make a lot of financial sense—because with most affinity cards, the interest rates you pay are much higher than the best rate you could receive if you shopped around for a plain old credit card. And the charity the card represents receives very little of the increased costs that you pay.

Here are some things you should consider before you make a decision to open an affinity account:

- How do the rates compare to the best deals you could get for non-affinity accounts? With credit cards, for instance, there can be an interest-rate spread of three to four percent between the higher affinity card rate and the best rate available for an ordinary card.

- What does the organization you support receive as a result of your new affinity account? In most cases, it makes far more sense to get the cheapest rate you can—and remember, credit card interest is no longer tax deductible, even in part—and give the difference to the group you support, as a straight donation. That way, you get the benefit of a tax deduction for your donation, and the organization you support receives far more money.

- Find out before opening an account if you'll be exposed to other fund-raising pitches from the same organization, or get your name placed on mailing lists so that you'll be pummeled with pitches for money from other groups. If so, and you want to be left alone, state explicitly that you don't want to receive other fund-raising pitches and if you do, you'll close the account.

- A question you should always ask yourself: Do you really need another credit card? Credit cards have what amounts to voices of their own. They sit there quietly until your willpower is weakened, then they start begging to be used. The rule with credit cards is that if you can do without one, do so.

Affinity cards and accounts are a very clever marketing idea, but they play on your emotions in an area where cold numbers should be considered. The standard you should apply when you are offered such an account or card is the same standard you should apply in other financial dealings. You should go for the best deal.

Secured Credit Cards: If you watch television, you have probably noticed an increase in the number of advertisements for "guaranteed" credit cards. You would virtually have to be a prisoner—and one serving a long term, at that—to be turned down.

The idea isn't new. The marketing technique is. They're called secured credit cards, and in some cases they aren't a bad thing.

The secured credit card is, says the American Bankers Association, very much like any other kind of secured loan. The security, in this case, is your savings account at the bank. The bank knows it can extend credit to you, because it already has your money in an account and a signed agreement from you that allows the bank to seize the money from your account if you fail to pay.

You should shop around, aided by new regulations mandated by Congress, that require full disclosure of interest rates and terms.

The first place you should check is the bank where you regularly conduct business. There are several things you need to consider:

- The size of the account that you must maintain in order to have a secured card. Most banks, but not all, place a limit on credit card purchases that is equal to the amount on deposit.

- The interest rate charged. Because the card is secured, the rate should be, if anything, lower than the standard card rate, but it doesn't usually work out that way.

- The interest paid on your deposit. Find out if your bank allows you to guarantee your card payments through a deposit that pays higher interest, such as a bond or a CD.

- Additional charges and fees, and the grace period (the time between a charge and the time you can pay it off before interest is charged). Some cards allow you as much as a month; others begin charging interest from the day you make the purchase.

- The potential for an upgrade, over time, to a regular card. One of the strengths of a secured credit card is that it will allow you to begin rebuilding a good credit rating. You should find out how long your record must be perfect before you will be granted an unsecured card.

If your bank doesn't offer a secured card that's to your liking, check with other banks in your town. Finding an arrangement that's flexible enough to meet your needs, at the most favorable rates, is worth the effort.

Find the best deal, make your deposit, and get your card. But think of it as being for emergencies only. You are getting such a card out of need, rather than simply for convenience. It is for use only when you must make a purchase, and then only when cash is not accepted, as when guaranteeing lodging reservations or renting an automobile. Capricious use of it will get you right back into the same kind of fix that the secured card is supposed to help you escape.

PROTECTING AGAINST CREDIT CARD LOSSES. It used to be if you lost a billfold or purse, you'd sit down on the curb and cry.

You can't do that anymore. If you lose your purse, or reach for your billfold only to find an empty pocket, there's a good chance you're in a race with crooks. How quickly you react, and how well you've prepared for such an eventuality, will determine who wins the race.

The prize in this race is your money, your other valuables, and, not inconceivably, your safety. The rules are these: List, report, and replace. First, list everything in your billfold that will require action if you lose it, along with the appropriate telephone numbers and addresses. Keep the list where you can quickly get at it. Second, report the loss at once, and at the same time, arrange for replacement of the lost items.

Stop for a moment and count up the financial instruments you carry: Bank and store credit cards, of course. Probably a card for an automatic teller cash machine.

- You need to report the loss of credit cards. Make note of the time and date of each call, and record the name of the employee to whom you speak, in case it becomes an issue later. You are not liable for any charges made after you have made such a report, and in any case your maximum liability is $50 per card. It is a good idea to follow up with a letter to each store or bank card company. (A tip worth noting: The numbers used to report lost cards are changed frequently, because customers insist on using them for other business. Make sure your list is up-to-date. The correct number is listed with each month's account statement.) This may well be a good time to consider whether you really need all those credit cards.

- Next, report the loss of your automatic teller card. This can be the most expensive card to lose. If someone manages to come up with the access code that, in combination with your card, gets into your account, and you have not notified the bank of the card's loss within two working days, you could lose up to $500. If you fail to report it for 60 days and someone cleans out your account (plus any cash advance privileges you have), you are out the full amount. But if you report the card's disappearance within two working days, your maximum loss is $50. Of course, it's the height of foolishness to write down your access code on the card itself or on anything you carry with it.

You probably carry some items that won't immediately come to mind, but these need your attention, too.

- Many people now carry telephone company credit cards, and it is possible to run up truly heroic phone bills with a stolen card. Report the loss to the phone company at once, again, with a follow-up letter.

- Some brokerage houses provide convenient, card-sized documents listing your account number, the broker's phone number, and other information. Someone finding this card can have a high old time for himself playing the market with your money. The chances of such an individual actually draining your account for himself are very slight, but in a day and age where computer hackers break into giant computer systems just for the fun of it, vandalism is a real possibility. Let your broker know of the loss, and get your account number changed.

- With the new immigration law, there's a hot trade in stolen or phony Social Security cards. This doesn't seem like a big deal, and chances are it won't be. But there's always the possibility that someone else's income will be reported on your Social Security number, which could prove confusing and annoying, to say the least.

- The same holds true with insurance identification cards. People who make their living by stealing other people's possessions aren't above charging their emergency room visits to your policy.

- Don't forget your driver's license. This can be of special concern if you lose your wallet or purse while on a trip. Fortunately, most states will issue a temporary license for travelers caught in just such a bind.

- Then there are the keys. This can end up being quite expensive, because if your keys are in your purse—or if you carry a spare house key in your billfold—you have to change the locks. Don't forget changing the car locks, too, or you might awaken one morning to discover that the family chariot is among the missing.

CREDIT CARDS AT COLLEGE. Parents sending their youngsters off to college may wish to arm them with a credit card of some sort, "for emergencies." This is a good idea, say card companies, but only if strict ground rules are established ahead of time.

The Office of Public Responsibility at the American Express Company offers guidelines.

- The only purchases allowed will be those agreed upon ahead of time.

- The student must save all receipts and send them home.

- There should be a monthly limit set on the amount that may be charged by the student.

- Credit purchases should be paid for with earned income rather than allowances, establishing the relationship between credit purchases, work, and money.

- The parent should co-sign the card, to be able to keep track of purchases and rein in the student if it looks as though things are likely to get out of hand.

CREDIT TROUBLE

It often happens early in a new year, following the holiday spending binge: Many Americans awaken to find fiscal headaches arising from over-indulgence at the cash register. Some will face the new year with charge accounts loaded to the limits.

It's a common story. How can you dig your way out of it?

First thing, take out all those credit cards. Take a pair of scissors and cut all the ones you can possibly do without—and this means most of them—into pieces.

Now add up your total monthly payments. Add in your payments on personal loans. Does this amount to more than 20 percent of your monthly take-home pay? If so, you're flirting with disaster. Don't wait for second and third billing notices or collection notices. Get help now.

Unless you live in a very small town, there is probably a credit counseling agency that can help you get out from under your charge debts. The first thing that will happen is a close inspection of your financial situation in the hope that your payments can be budgeted in.

If your outflow exceeds your income, the agency will help you contact your creditors and arrange a repayment plan. Credit card companies are accustomed to this and are surprisingly flexible. They don't want to go to collection agencies much more than you want them to. They certainly don't want you to file for bankruptcy.

Solving the immediate problem treats only the symptoms—it does nothing to cure the disease. Many people go to credit counselors in a state of high anxiety, eager to get out of their particular jam. But the experience is lost when they fail to pay attention to the important lesson that will be offered, which is how to stay out of trouble to begin with. Especially at the holidays, many people believe that the amount they spend for gifts and entertaining is a measure of themselves as people. The purpose of credit counseling is to eliminate such thinking, which is what gets consumers into trouble to begin with. Remember: It's always safer and easier to prevent a fire than it is to put out a fire.

CREDIT COUNSELING. The best first step is to drop a note to the National Foundation for Consumer Credit, 8701 Georgia Ave., Silver Spring, Maryland 20910. They'll tell you who in your area provides the service.

The last thing you probably want to do is end up spending more money to hire someone to help you figure out how to stop spending so much money. Credit counseling isn't very expensive. Some counseling centers provide their service at no cost, while others expect a small percentage of your monthly payments. Still others urge you to become involved with counseling others a few hours each week. This is an especially good idea, because it helps you remember the anxiety that you felt when you first visited the counseling center—which helps reinforce your resolve to stay out of such trouble in the future.

You may be concerned that if you go to a credit counselor, it will hurt your credit rating. But it probably won't. The first thing a counselor will do is help you to organize your budget, and that may be all that is needed. Even if a special payment plan is arranged, it does not necessarily have to be reflected in your credit report—presuming that you make payments as scheduled and don't get into further credit trouble.

Once you've arranged a payment schedule, there are some other things you can do to dig your way out of the hole. The chief one, as mentioned above, is to get rid of any credit cards that aren't absolutely necessary, and that means almost all of them. Begin or enlarge your savings plan. Formulate a budget and stick to it. It is only after you've developed realistic and responsible approaches to money that you will be able to carry those plastic cards around without giving in to the temptation to use them.

You may consider a debt-consolidation loan, which is a loan that lumps your charge card bills together and pays them off. It's a form of refinancing. Debt-consolidation loans can be a good idea. Shop around to make sure that the interest rate you're paying on the loan is less than that charged by the card companies—otherwise, all you've done is reduce the number of checks you have to write each month. Choose the shortest term you can afford. Remember, too, that if you can arrange a secured loan, with your home or car as collateral, you will get a lower interest rate. And bear in mind that most consolidation loans involve substantial pre-payment penalties. WARNING: This does not now mean that you're free to dive back in with your charge cards and run up new charges. Instead, it means you have been given a second chance. If you take responsible advantage of it, your credit problem will be solved.

Beware Of Credit Doctor "Voodoo": Too many Americans, looking for an easy way out of debt, have sought the help of "credit doctors." In too many cases, though, they've really just wasted money on credit quacks.

Credit doctors are people who, for a fee, offer to "fix" poor credit ratings. In many cases, they do this by "borrowing" other people's good ratings. Here's how the scam works:

You have a poor credit history, but you wish to borrow money. For a fee of $500 or more, the credit doctor presents you with a good rating. You obtain credit. It's possible that nothing more ever comes of it— so long as you make all payments on time.

The credit doctor is either a credit bureau employee or former employee, or someone else who has obtained access to the credit bureau's computer codes. Operating from a home or office computer, the credit doctor enters the credit bureau's machine. During this electronic burglary, he or she looks for someone who resembles you but who has a good credit history. Your files aren't changed. Someone else's are stolen.

You are given new information about yourself. When you apply for new credit, you are in effect claiming to be someone else.

Sometimes this all happens without the "patient" having any idea that anything illegal is happening. Other times, everyone involved knows it's illegal, the purpose being to borrow as much as possible, then skip town. The cleverest of these con artists go ahead and make a payment or two, to confuse things further when time comes to unravel the credit mess the unsuspecting victim comes to be in.

This is in violation of the mail fraud, fair credit, and computer fraud statutes. Both "doctor" and "patient" stand to go to jail if caught. But the Better Business Bureau says this is one of the most popular scams around. The Federal Trade Commission says a prison cell awaits those who offer or receive credit doctoring services.

Other "credit doctors" don't engage in high-tech fraud; they're simply low-class conmen who won't be able to improve your credit rating. Don't be misled by their seeming legitimacy. Advertising in local newspapers or on late-night local television does not guarantee a straight-dealing, legitimate operation. The only way to clean up your credit rating is to reach agreements with the people you owe.

Instead of the credit doctors, seek the services of a reputable credit counselor. Over time, your credit record will be healed.

BANKRUPTCY—THE DEBTOR'S LAST RESORT

You have become heavily in debt. You have explored every possible way to work something out. But nothing has worked. Your creditors will not accept any of various alternatives that you've proposed. You haven't been able to get a loan consolidating your debts into a single manageable package. You even consulted a debt counselor, who wasn't able to come up with anything workable.

Your last resort is bankruptcy. Either you file yourself voluntarily, or creditors can force you with a petition of involuntary bankruptcy.

More than 600,000 individuals filed for Chapter 7 bankruptcy in the U.S. in 1989. That's double the number who filed in 1980. Unlike Chapter 11 and Chapter 13 bankruptcies, which stretch out payments until debts are satisfied, Chapter 7 wipes the debts off the books. More than nine out of 10 of the individuals who file for bankruptcy seek Chapter 7 relief.

That leaves the American credit industry holding an empty $1.6 billion bag, according to a recent study done for a bank credit card company. The costs, of course, are passed along whenever possible in the form of higher prices or rates or more stringent loan-approval criteria. Projected over the country, the cost comes to more than $6 per person per year.

Among the advantages of filing bankruptcy:

- It stops creditors cold. They can't try to collect, can't sue, and generally can't foreclose on assets for at least four months.

- It can prevent the Internal Revenue Service from seizing property for tax debts.

- It allows many debts to be settled for a fraction of their original value. Bankruptcy results in your debts being discharged (that is, settled legally). The debts—particularly unsecured debts, such as credit card debt, or finance company loans—that are discharged may far exceed the value of the property you lose in bankruptcy proceedings.

If you file, you have a choice of what are known as Chapter 7 or Chapter 13 plans, as described below. Chapter 11, for businesses, is similar to Chapter 13, for individuals. However, an individual operating a business as an unincorporated sole proprietorship can file under Chapter 13.

Creditors can file a petition of involuntary bankruptcy against you under Chapters 7 and, if applicable, 11, but not under Chapter 13.

Chapter 7 is the "straight bankruptcy" plan. Your assets (excluding certain regulatory exemptions) are sold and the cash received is distributed among your creditors, eliminating your debts (with certain exceptions).

The assets and their maximum dollar value which can be exempted depend on whether federal or state bankruptcy laws are being applied. These exempted assets may include your home, furnishings, appliances, household goods, books, musical instruments, prescribed health aids, clothing, jewelry, motor vehicles, tools of your trade, and cemetery plot.

Debts not eliminated may include alimony, child support, government student loans, and taxes. But consult an attorney (preferably a specialist recommended by an attorney you trust), because the law is complex and loaded with exceptions to these generalizations. Unless your situation is particularly complicated, an attorney probably will cost you from $200 to $750. You should prepare a detailed list of all your assets and liabilities, and income and expenses, for your meeting with the attorney.

You can file a Chapter 7 only once every six years.

Chapter 13 is the "wage-earner's bankruptcy" plan, for people with regular incomes. The bankruptcy court works out a debt-payment plan for you, which generally may run from three to five years. You, the debtor, make periodic payments to the supervising court-appointed trustee who, in turn, dispenses to creditors.

Income generally exempt from Chapter 13 payments includes disability benefits, pension plans, annuities, Social Security, unemployment compensation, alimony, child support, veterans benefits, and life insurance.

If you go bankrupt again in the future, you can file a new Chapter 13 if your prior Chapter 13 payment plan has been completed.

Chapter 13 is a more complicated plan than Chapter 7, and thus usually costs more.

A bankruptcy will remain on your credit reports for 10 years. Once bankrupt, your credit cards generally are revoked; and new loans and credit, if available at all, will be at the highest interest rate. To re-establish credit, establish an active checking account and apply for a single small loan; make payments promptly, then apply for another larger loan and a credit card with small ceiling, make payments promptly, and so on. Chapter 13 bankrupts generally find it easier to re-establish credit than those in Chapter 7.

Be forewarned that bankruptcy can be a trying and traumatic experience; and although less so than years ago, it's still a stigma. So don't overextend yourself in the first place.

BANKRUPTCY FRAUD. One of the country's leading growth industries is bankruptcy fraud. According to a recent study done for a bank credit card company, more than one-third of individual bankruptcy filings are fraudulent.

The problem, says the credit card company, is that more and more individuals see bankruptcy as a legitimate business strategy, rather than a means of protecting honest unfortunates from total ruin.

The result, beyond increased scrutiny of would-be borrowers, has been a more aggressive attitude in challenging bankruptcy filings. Sadly, some who truly need bankruptcy relief are being forced to face vigorous and expensive challenges due to the frequency of fraudulent filings.

Until recently, with high legal costs and no assurance of victory, chasing abusers of the system hasn't been a good investment. But as the numbers continue to rise, creditors have found that a combined challenge of questionable filings can be cost effective, with the creditors sharing the costs of investigation and legal action.

The most visible of the pooling efforts is a clearing-house system offered to member banks. This system streamlines the process by allowing one investigator and one lawyer to handle several cases in the same court, for example. Several different banks may be involved, but the per-case costs drop dramatically.

There has also been instituted a program of pursuing the worst cases through criminal prosecution, by doing much of the footwork necessary to take the case forward to indictment.

What do investigators look for?

- Sudden, large expenditures shortly before the filing. The purchase of a car is a frequent example.

- Large cash advances against credit cards, or running the cards to their limit, again just before filing for bankruptcy. The pooling of resources among lenders makes this kind of abuse more apparent.

- Evidence that the person filing for bankruptcy has a greater-than-stated income. A lavish lifestyle can torpedo a bankruptcy filing.

- Evidence that assets have recently been transferred, or that there are hidden assets.

The bankruptcy law exists for those who truly need it, and there is much you can do, if you truly need it, to prove you are not engaging in bankruptcy fraud.

Contact creditors when trouble looms. Explain your situation and attempt to restructure your debt. Most creditors realize it is in their best interest to be flexible toward customers who are in over their heads.

If this fails to bring results, find a good credit counselor. Non-profit credit counseling agencies are available in most cities. They can help you where individual action can't, because the creditors know your situation will have been more closely scrutinized by the counselor.

Chances are that you'll be able to avoid both bankruptcy and the kinds of thinking and behavior that can lead you to further credit trouble in the future. But if it turns out that bankruptcy is inevitable, your good-faith efforts to exhaust all other possibilities will make a challenge less likely, and defense against a challenge simpler.

5

THE INSURANCE
── YOU NEED ──

In an increasingly dangerous world, insurance plays a bigger part in our lives than ever before.

Baseball fans will remember the night in 1989 that they tuned into the World Series on television and found not baseball but an earthquake. As events unfolded, two kind of survivors emerged: Those who had insurance and could rebuild, and those did not and therefore could not.

Just weeks before, a devastating hurricane named Hugo struck the southeastern United States, causing immense damage. Those who had insurance against this eventuality are back in business; those who didn't may be, or they may not.

The health care crisis is upon us, and those without insurance are not so much led to bankruptcy but denied treatment entirely. The experience of the 1980s tells us that previously unknown but terrifying epidemics can appear and spread with amazing speed. Just as no company is immune to random disaster, so no person is immune to the capricious twists of fate. Just as no company can presume there will be a government bailout, no person can assume that somehow his or her medical needs will be met.

While life insurance is more of an investment than insurance, it is nevertheless worth noting that none of us know the number of our days. It is satisfying to know that those we love will not suffer unduly for our absence, should that absence come to pass.

The lesson is that a well-thought-out insurance package should be a big part of your financial situation. If it isn't, make it so.

68

INSURING YOUR HOME

As inflation and the booming housing market of the last decade or so have driven the price of homes through the roof, many homeowners have been tragically surprised when, following a fire, windstorm, flood, or earthquake, they learn that their insurance benefits won't even begin to restore their standard of living to what it once was.

It's time now, before you face this kind of tragedy, to review all your insurance coverage so that it reflects the higher amounts and other changes in your income level and property value. There are four major areas that you should consider.

First, and most important, is making sure that you have protection against replacement costs—the amount it would cost you to rebuild your home. In many cases, especially in hot real estate markets, replacement cost will be less than the appraised value.

If your bank requires you to insure your home against fire and other damages up to the amount of the mortgage, however, and that is all the insurance you carry on it, you almost certainly don't have enough coverage to pay to replace your home should something happen to it. Be sure to buy as much insurance as you need if the mortgage amount is less than the projected replacement cost. Your agent can calculate that cost using industry figures.

Upgrade your coverage each year—automatically, if you can—to match inflation. The premiums increase, too, of course, but you don't have to take out a new policy each time.

Don't ignore the huge liability awards so prevalent today. Since the liability side of your homeowners' policy protects you against a lawsuit if someone claims your negligence brought about, or contributed to, his or her injury, review that section of your policy as well.

Many standard homeowners' policies limit liability up to $100,000. That may not be enough for you, and it's relatively inexpensive to buy endorsements that increase your liability protection. Most companies will let you buy up to $1 million liability coverage on your homeowners' policy. If you want or need more, you'll have to look to an umbrella policy.

Some of the verdicts in liability lawsuits in recent years have been so outlandish that it is clear there is little the property owner can do to make certain he or she will never lose such a suit. Insurance protection is your best hope against such a sad eventuality.

Examine your life insurance policy. Many insurance agents recommend a "decreasing term" policy as mortgage protection. These policies have no cash buildup; instead, the premiums remain stable as your mortgage amortizes—and you get older.

An alternative is to buy a straight life insurance policy earmarked to cover your mortgage should something happen to you. If you remain healthy and alive, the policy builds cash value.

If your mortgage is relatively small, you might consider increasing the value of your other life insurance policies by that amount. The reason: Smaller policies are, proportionately, more expensive. As a rule, the bigger the policy, the better the rate.

Don't overlook the availability of discounts or more favorable rates when you purchase both your homeowners' and life insurance policies from the same company.

INSURANCE FOR RENTERS. Now more than ever, insurance for renters is a subject requiring your attention. These days a larger proportion of households are renting. The home ownership rate for households headed by people in their 20s and 30s has declined substantially, as young people are waiting longer to settle down and begin families, with all the responsibilities—including home ownership—that that entails.

Fewer than one out of every four renters have tenants insurance, according to the most recent surveys. But when you consider that 95 percent of all homeowners have homeowners' insurance, if you are a renter who owns furniture, jewelry, specific valuables, clothing, or any other personal property that would cause you significant financial loss if damaged or destroyed, you should consider obtaining tenants' insurance.

Your landlord probably has insurance to cover the house or apartment building where you live if someone is injured in an apartment building hallway or other common area. Beyond that, the landlord's responsibility, and therefore his or her insurance coverage, is extremely limited.

In fact, the landlord would be responsible for damages to your personal property only if the damage is due to the negligence of the landlord, and you are able to prove it.

What, exactly, is tenants' insurance? It is coverage available to renters that may include:

Personal Belongings: You and the direct-writing company or insurance agent agree on a dollar value for the coverage you want. There are limits on how much a company will pay on certain valuable items. (For instance, coin collections, rare gun collections, and the like require special and very expensive policies.) The most you can collect on a standard tenants' policy for certain specific kinds of items is usually about $1,000—unless you purchase a personal articles floater. You may want to buy this extra coverage for an expensive item, say a $5,000 fur or $3,000 diamond bracelet. To help determine how much insurance you need, take a room-by-room inventory.

(This is also a good time to record serial numbers of appliances and other valuable items, to photograph your property, and to assemble other proof that you own it. This material should then be put safely away, perhaps in a safe deposit box, because it will be extremely important if disaster does befall you. This is a good idea for homeowners, too.)

Liability: Similar to homeowners' insurance, tenants' insurance is a "package policy" that includes liability coverage at home or outside for injuries caused by you, someone in your family, or even a pet, although, of course, the coverage does not extend to damage that you may do with your automobile.

The standard minimum liability policy pays up to about $100,000. This may not be enough, especially if you have a large or feisty pet, entertain frequently, or the like. Fortunately, some companies offer coverage up to $200,000 or $300,000. It's worth asking about: The cost of increasing your coverage will probably be lower than you think.

Expenses: If you suffer a catastrophe of some sort and your home is not fit to be lived in due to the damage, you may have to stay in a motel and eat in restaurants while it is being repaired. Tenants' insurance covers the difference between these temporary expenses and your normal living costs up to the predetermined limits on your policy.

Rates vary from state to state, area to area, and by company. You should be able to purchase adequate coverage for well under $200 per year, depending on where you live and the dollar value of what you own.

Just as with homeowners' insurance, it's worth your while to re-evaluate your coverage from time to time, because you will probably find that the replacement costs of your possessions have become higher than you think.

PROFESSIONAL LIABILITY INSURANCE

No matter what your profession, there's a good chance you can get—and may need—some kind of professional liability insurance. While you may often think of professional liability insurance as being the concern only of physicians and lawyers, virtually every profession is at risk.

Increasingly, other businesses and services have decided—or been forced—to get their own kind of "malpractice" insurance. A lot of new legislation has been enacted requiring professions to maintain liability insurance. For instance, following the widely publicized stories of abuses in a handful of day care centers, it became a matter of law in some states—and merely a good idea in others—for operators of those centers to beef up their policies.

Product liability and service liability coverage are now required for almost all of the construction trades. In most states, for example, plumbers must carry that kind of insurance or be able to prove their financial ability to cover damages resulting from a botched job.

Radon inspection, a profession unheard of just a few years ago, has opened a new area of liability. What if the inspector rules that there is a radon danger, thereby reducing the value of a home and sparking costly alterations, only for it to be discovered later that there is none of the radioactive gas after all? Worse, what if the inspector's radon-measuring machine is faulty, and the determination is that there is none when in fact the levels are life-threatening?

In an imperfect, sometimes unfair world, these things can happen in almost any business. But only in recent years have practitioners faced the threat of bankruptcy or worse as a result.

According to a recent article in a major metropolitan newspaper, malpractice insurance is now commonly bought by dog groomers, manicurists, wedding consultants, the clergy, operators of tanning salons, and even masseurs.

An even bigger problem is that of product liability insurance. It is often impossible to determine the ways in which a new product can cause harm to its users. Asbestos building materials, for instance, had been popular for decades before it was learned that exposure to the mineral could lead to lung disease. The companies that produce it nevertheless were held responsible. It is not surprising that product liability insurance is very expensive.

(That is why general aviation aircraft, small two-to-four-seat private planes, are hardly being manufactured at all in this country anymore. It was determined that a company is liable for its planes for as long as they remain in service, irrespective of how many times they have been sold or, to an extent, their maintenance. More than half of the cost of a new small airplane now results from product liability insurance premiums—and a lot of companies decided simply to stop making light aircraft.)

You should be concerned about this because it costs you money, even if you're not paying professional and product liability premiums directly. The cost of everything you buy is increased by those premiums.

Even if you don't think you need such insurance, it is worth checking the extent to which you might under some circumstance be held personally liable from some professional goof.

THE BEST DEAL ON CAR INSURANCE

Many of you are paying too much for your car insurance.

While there has been an enormous hue and cry about the high costs of automobile insurance—including but not limited to the widely publicized referendum in California that sought to cap rates—there's much you can do yourself to lower your premiums. A worksheet, such as the one shown in Chart 9, can help you.

Of the many things you can do to reduce your costs, one of the first is to check with your state insurance commissioner's headquarters to see if they have material to help you. They will probably have information that will help you understand how rates are set and the kind of coverage you really need.

Additionally, a state insurance office can explain options that are available to you, which are not the same from state to state. For example, in some states you can opt for a high deductible in your medical coverage—a wise thing to do if you have other health coverage.

Right off the bat, there are things you can do that can reduce your rates:

- Make sure your insurance carrier's information about your driving record is accurate. If you have no accidents or moving violations, your rate will be lower—but only if your insurance company knows your record is clean. Also, if your record contains violations, they should be wiped from the slate after three years. Check to make sure this has been done.

- Choose a higher collision deductible if you can afford to self-insure your car for the difference. Consider how much more you are paying each year for the greater coverage. How long would it take for you to have paid the entire difference to the insurance company? Is your situation such, and are your driving habits such, that it makes more economic sense simply to save the money?

- Consider whether collision insurance is a good idea for your car. If you drive an old clunker, the amount you pay for collision coverage could, in a couple of years, itself replace your car. That means you'd probably be better off saving the money and insuring yourself in this regard.

- When buying a new car, consider insurance costs when figuring the overall cost of the vehicle. That cute little sports car will likely cost more to insure than a big family sedan—and the difference can run into thousands of dollars, depending on your area of the country and your driving record.

CHART 9

Do You Have Enough Automobile Insurance[1]?		
	Amounts of Coverage	
Type of Coverage[2]	*Present Amounts*	*(After Reviewing:) Amounts You Should have[3]*
Bodily Injury Liability: For death, injury, suffering inflicted on one or more people by your car	$[4]	$
Property Damage Liability: For property accidentally damaged by your car	$	$
Medical Payments[5]: For injury sustained by you and your passengers in your car and on you as a pedestrian by a car	$[6]	$
Uninsured Motorist's[5]: For your medical bills if you are the victim of an uninsured motorist, a hit-and-run driver, and, in some states, the victim of an underinsured motorist	$	$
Collision[7]: For cost of repair of damage to your car or its cash value, whichever is less	$	$
Comprehensive: For theft, glass breakage, fire, flood, and additional adversities other than collision damage, wear-and-tear, and mechanical problems	$	$
Other	$	$

1. Be sure you know how your coverage is affected if your state has no-fault insurance.
2. Type of coverage afforded may vary by individual states. Also, get in touch with your state insurance commission for car insurance minimum legal requirements and for information on car insurance companies.
3. Keep in mind that you might increase the deductible as well as the amount of coverage so that your premium cost may not be higher. Also, be sure your premiums reflect discount possibilities that may be available, such as the safe driving and for multiple car ownership.
4. Is there a maximum amount payable to any one person in any one accident? A maximum amount for all injuries occurring in any one accident?
5. In reviewing the amount of your coverage in your auto insurance, also consider the protection afforded by your regular health-insurance and disability-income insurance policies.
6. Are medical benefits paid promptly without determining who is at fault?
7. Some policies are available which provide replacement cost; benefits are higher, but, of course, so are premium costs.

- If you are in an "assigned risk" group, which is where companies pool the riskiest policies, make sure to find out what is necessary to get yourself removed from that category, which is very expensive.

- Take a defensive driving course. Graduates of approved driver education and defensive driving courses are usually eligible for premium reductions. Enroll your children of driving age in a driver education course rather than teaching them yourself. The small cost of the course will be more than offset by premium reductions.

- Consider an automobile alarm. The kind that are on automatically, called "passive" alarm systems, can produce substantial savings, especially if your car is very expensive or one of the models popular with car thieves.

The one place you cannot afford to reduce your coverage is in liability insurance. In many states, the minimum amount required is unrealistically low—there's a good likelihood that a court would award an amount far higher, with you liable for the difference. Get as much liability coverage as you can afford, consistent with awards in your region.

There are about 1.4 million car thefts in the U.S. each year, according to the National Automobile Theft Bureau. There are 1.6 million thefts of contents of automobiles, and 1.2 million thefts of accessories. In 1978, the last year for which the statistics are available, law enforcement costs in connection with auto thefts were about a billion dollars.

The theft statistics provide some surprises. While the popular sports models are the most likely to be stolen, they are not the likeliest cars to be burgled and have their radios and other accessories stolen.

The seven cars most likely to produce insurance theft claims including theft of accessories are all Volkswagens, according to the Highway Loss Data Institute. This is apparently because Volkswagens come equipped with stereo systems that are prized by thieves. Of the top 10, nine are Volkswagen products.

No wonder removable car radios have become so popular! Ironically, New York City police report that removable radios often cause a thief to break into the trunk, because that is where so many people put the radio after they've unplugged it from the dashboard.

Protecting yourself from car theft is relatively simple, with some precautions paying for themselves through reduced insurance rates. Among the recommendations from the experts:

- Invest in a good passive anti-theft system with alarm.

- Think twice before installing an expensive car stereo system, especially if you live in or near a city.

- If you live in or near a city with a high theft rate, you may even want to choose a model that is unpopular with thieves.
- You may wish to choose a four-door over a two-door model, because the latter are more likely to be stolen.

WHEN THE GUY WHO HIT YOU HAS NO INSURANCE. You've been responsible, but the other driver hasn't. You have insurance. The other driver doesn't.

You could take them to court, but experience suggests that the chances are the default judgement you are likely to receive when they—very likely—don't show up for court won't amount to even enough to pay your expenses in suing them.

Or you could have uninsured or underinsured motorists' coverage. This gives you protection in cases where the other driver had no insurance, or too little insurance to cover the expenses you incurred.

What does this insurance cover? Typically, damages arising from bodily injury and legal liabilities. These may include medical bills, wage losses, pain and suffering, and survivors' benefits.

Only in a handful of states does the coverage extend to damage to your car—but this type of protection is usually included under your collision coverage. Bear in mind, also, that uninsured or underinsured motorist coverage protects you only if you are the victim of a motoring accident. It gives you nothing if you are the driver at fault.

The majority of states require insurance companies to offer you coverage against the uninsured or underinsured motorist. But those states do not require the insurance companies to aggressively market that coverage, meaning that you may not know that you're entitled to buy such coverage. If you're not sure, here's what to do:

- Call your insurance agent and ask how much the additional coverage would cost. (It's a good idea at the same time to find out whether your own liability coverage is sufficient. Remember, prices on everything, including automobiles, have risen considerably in recent years.) You'll be surprised at how little it costs to gain protection from the uninsured or underinsured motorist.
- Make sure you're not duplicating coverage you already have. Your current medical and disability insurance coverage may cover situations likely to arise if you are the victim of an uninsured or underinsured driver. The only additional coverage you would then receive is for pain and suffering, and you must decide whether this justifies the extra premium.

- If you live in a state with compulsory no-fault insurance, your right to sue for pain and suffering is strictly limited, requiring damage to exceed a certain amount or other conditions to be met before you can sue for more. In such cases, uninsured or underinsured coverage would be necessary to meet the bills if your expenses exceeded that amount.

HEALTH INSURANCE—A CRISIS IN THE MAKING

A health-care crisis is underway in the United States. Medical costs have reached the point that they're in danger of bumping into satellites. As a result, a revolution in health care is developing in our country. What will emerge in the 1990s will bear little resemblance to what you know today.

What will force change in the 1990s?

The continued inflation of health-care costs (to perhaps as much as 12 percent of the gross national product) will lead to a revolt. The cost of keeping a patient in the hospital will soar from the present $600–800 per day to an estimated $1,200–1,500. Employers (who pay a large part of the nation's health insurance bill) and their employees will recognize technology can drive up costs, but also that some higher costs are for duplicate medical capacity. As we will see, they are already responding in some ways that employees are certain to find less than desirable.

The outcome is very likely to be something along the lines of what might be called "competitive socialized medicine" as the dominant system of health care in the U.S.

This does not mean the kind of cradle-to-grave, government-controlled socialized medicine found in Great Britain. What's meant basically is a system in which various kinds of managed health-care organizations compete with each other for customers. The most familiar of these is the health maintenance organization, or HMO, in which your cost usually is lower than for the traditional kind of medical insurance. But once you have joined up, you will surrender a certain amount of individual freedom of choice in such areas as selection of doctors and treatment sites. Also ahead are "hybrid" managed programs, appealing to those who want more freedom of choice than that offered by an HMO.

The transition to standardized, controlled, competing health plans will not be smooth. As the various health plans compete with each other for business, the weaker, more poorly managed ones will fall until finally only the strongest and most efficient stand. Hospitals that fail to maintain adequate occupancy rates (likely to become commonplace as systems curtail hospitalization) also will be forced to close.

The result is almost certain to be cheaper and better-quality medical care. During the shake-out, though, things will be rough, and it's up to you to make sure you're not the one getting shortchanged.

Do you have enough medical insurance? Check Chart 10 to find out.

EMPLOYEE HEALTH INSURANCE. The number of companies providing free medical coverage slumped by about one-third during the 1980s. What's more, the number of employers who have raised deductibles in health benefit plans has surged dramatically. Your chances are now nearly one in two that your deductible in a company-sponsored insurance plan has risen.

If that weren't bad enough, the application of deductibles to all types of medical benefits (including hospitalization and surgery) has increased to the point where this now applies to four-fifths of all covered workers in the U.S.—and, again, the trend is continuing.

This trend is likely to continue. Employees will grumble, but in most cases, they'll have to swallow an increased portion of their health insurance costs. (A long, bitter, and sometimes violent 1989 telephone strike had as its core issue whether workers would assume part of the costs of their insurance. The workers ultimately won, but at enormous cost.)

Efforts to hold down the costs of health care have been reported extensively in recent years. But most of the stories you have been reading reflect the corporation's—not the employee's—perspective. Although you, the employee, are directly affected by the cost-containment procedures, you have largely been ignored. You almost surely have not been informed that basic rules have been changed in many areas.

The economic situation in health care today places unprecedented demands on you, the employee, to manage your own medical expenses. Most companies now require higher deductibles and co-payments, as well as extra deductibles for surgery and hospitalization. As a result, the total you, the employee, receive for medical treatment depends on how you go about getting it. If you ignore the the new rules your employers have set up, you can lose part or all of your reimbursement.

The message of all the new provisions? You as an employee must educate yourself on how to become a better health-care consumer. Your financial well-being rests on it.

Here are basic tips that you will probably find useful. If you know them, your neighbor may not, so be sure to pass them along.

CHART 10

Health Protection: Health Insurance, or HMO or other Provider

Compare your coverage with estimated average costs currently in the area where you live, to determine if you need additional protection.

A CHECK LIST OF MEDICAL COSTS

Doctors	Home Services	Hospital	Other Facilities
• General practitioner • Specialist physicians (such as an internist) • Dentist • Opthalmologist • Psychiatrist • Other: _____ _____ _____	• Home-care personnel • Home-care equipment • Visiting nurse • Ambulance • Other medical transport • Other: _____ _____ _____ _____	• Room and board • Laboratory tests • Radiological • Drugs • Medical supplies • Medical equipment • Surgeon • Operating room • Anesthesist • Visiting doctor • Intensive care • Special nurses • Other: _____ _____ _____	• Nursing homes (intensive care, intermediate, custodial) • Adult day care • Diagnostic imaging centers • Emergency care (ambulatory care) • Ambulatory (outpatient) surgery centers • Psychiatric care • Maternity (birthing) centers • Alcohol and drug abuse • Functional rehabilitation • Hospices • Other: _____ _____

The first step, and a very important one, is for you to learn more about your company's benefits plan. Find out about the pitfalls and the incentives. Make notes. If you have questions, ask the company's benefits department for clarification.

Become a discriminating medical shopper. Make sure that any treatment you receive is both necessary and reasonably priced. Get second opinions, which can be the best investment you can possibly make, and in any case, your employer probably will pay for them. If you must undergo minor surgery, try to arrange for it on an outpatient basis. If you require hospitalization, do everything you can to keep hospital stays as short as possible. Your company or its insurance company may limit the number of hospital stays it will pay for.

Coordinate your medical benefits with your spouse's benefits. You can cover the entire cost of certain medical treatments with family plans, as long as the insurance carriers authorize the expense.

If you have flexible benefits, carefully evaluate them using the "low" medical option. Though it requires a higher deductible, you can make it pay like the "high" plan. You merely take advantage of your company's offer to waive the deductible or raise payment when you use Preferred Provider Organizations, outpatient testing, and the like. If you're covered under your spouse's plan, elect the minimum coverage and use your extra credits for other benefits or for cash, which could cover the deductible.

If your company offers a health-care reimbursement account, allowing you to pay for uncovered medical expenses with your pre-tax dollars, take full advantage of it. Don't shy away because of the "use it or lose it" rule. With a little planning, you can calculate your minimum yearly medical costs and earmark this amount of your salary to go into the account. Even if you have to forfeit a few dollars at year's end, you'll probably still come out ahead with the tax savings.

Finally, think prevention. Many employers will subsidize your participation in wellness programs, programs aimed at helping you stop smoking, aerobics workshops, and other programs and activities designed to make you a healthier, more useful employee. For them, healthy employees mean greater productivity as well as lower medical costs.

A major criticism of HMOs is that they tend not to promote the doctor-patient relationship that the traditional fee-for-service system offers. This is one reason employers are looking at ways to maintain fee-for-service medicine while cutting costs. Utilization review (UR) is one way that has been found to reach this goal.

Simply put, UR is based on the idea that checking a doctor's orders—

getting a sort of automatic second opinion—may avoid unnecessary medical treatments and expenses.

It's difficult to say exactly how many employers include UR in their health plans. This is chiefly because there are variations in the way UR is defined. However, one company in four requires that employees get approval before they can be admitted to hospitals for non-emergency care. And almost one-third require that employees get a second opinion for non-emergency surgery and treatments.

This saves money because we generally receive more medicine, medical treatment, hospitalization, and surgery than we need. It forces all involved to look for and consider treatments that are less expensive without being less effective.

To illustrate the problem: One study conducted by the Rand Corporation disclosed that a startling 40 percent of the 1,132 hospitalizations examined were avoidable. The study, published in *The New England Journal of Medicine*, looked at more than 100 hospitals across the country and judged 23 percent of the admissions to be inappropriate. An additional 17 percent could have been avoided by using outpatient surgical facilities.

While utilization review appears to be one way to control unnecessary hospitalization and shorten hospital stays, it is by no means a cure-all. Follow-up and focus on overall quality of care are essential too.

The key question from the employee's perspective is, how do you avoid cookbook medical care? What if you need additional treatment despite the statistics? Would a doctor be intimidated into conforming to the review board's judgment? How can you make sure that out of all this you receive the medical care that you need?

Exactly how effective many of these review boards are in cutting costs is certainly a question that is likely to grow as the reviews become more common. As it stands, much commercial review is done over the telephone. A physician cannot diagnose you by telephone, and there is reason to wonder if a review board can make important decisions about your health by a mere phone conversation.

THE HMO ALTERNATIVE. For more than a decade, the government has been trying to reduce skyrocketing health costs. And prepaid group health alternatives, termed HMOs, are one way being tried. But is an HMO right for you?

There are two types of HMOs. The first is the group model, which usually is in one building. The second is the independent practice association, in which you see the HMO doctor in his own office.

Make sure you understand the difference between a group model HMO and an IPA, or independent practice association. An IPA offers a large number of physicians, and you see them in their own offices, so you'll be doing more traveling and more picking and choosing. Also, IPAs are decentralized and less apt to regulate the quality of treatment provided. If you're happy with your current doctor and he or she belongs to an IPA, then it may be a good bet for you.

Employers may be required by law to offer you a choice between the two types of HMOs if they:

- Are subject to the Fair Labor Standards Act, and pay the minimum wage.
- Have 25 or more full- or part-time employees, which makes them subject to the 1973 HMO Act.
- Have written requests from one or more HMOs asking that they be allowed to offer employees their services.

According to the Group Health Association of America, both private and public employers, including state, county, and city governments, covered above must offer the choice.

But they do not have to offer you more than one of each kind of HMO (group model or IPA) per area. Also, they do not have to sign with the first HMO that asks them.

In theory, HMOs should save employers a great deal of money compared with traditional health insurance. Prepayment of fixed premiums should be an incentive for HMOs to contain costs, and thus charge less. And a 1985 poll the Louis Harris organization did for the Kaiser Family Foundation did find that 85 percent of employers polled thought HMOs kept down health-care costs.

But some companies question whether HMOs really yield savings. This is especially evident in a 1986 study of HMOs that dealt with the insurance practices of 861 corporations and other organizations—believed to be the most detailed survey of this type ever taken. It was determined that a majority of HMOs—61 percent—were thought to cost more than the employer's indemnity plan.

Employers, on average, paid 75 percent of all the employees' family HMO contracts and 86 percent of individual employees' contracts.

Federal law says employers must put the same amount into HMO capitalization fees as they put into premiums for employees who choose the most expensive health insurance coverage. That means that contributions to HMOs for lower-risk segments of the population are being based on the expenses of the older populations in fee-for-service plans.

You should remember that federal regulations must be met, regardless of whether HMOs actually do cut costs for your employer. So if your boss isn't offering an HMO and you think he is supposed to, check with your benefits officer. There may be many reasons: your employer may not be aware of the option or the requirements, he may not have been approached by a federally qualified HMO, or there may not be one in the area.

But millions of people are enrolled in HMOs, with the number expected to rise steadily.

Why HMOs Have Grown: The original reasoning behind HMOs was that prepaid plans would contain costs, since for one fixed price a member is covered for virtually every medical cost. Thus, the more efficient and cost-conscious an HMO is, the more financially successful it is likely to be. This philosophy is very different from traditional fee-for-service health care, which follows the formula that the more care a doctor prescribes, the more money he gets.

Are the lower medical costs of HMOs due to the "maintenance" and preventive treatment for which they were initially conceived? A study cited in *The New England Journal of Medicine* reported that it seemed unlikely that preventive care could account for much of the large difference in hospitalization rates. Instead, the economic incentives to contain costs reduce hospitalization rates.

How can you evaluate whether HMOs are an available and viable alternative to the traditional indemnity insurance your employer currently provides?

Your key question is whether your local HMO is cutting corners—providing reductions in the quality of medical care—to keep its hospital bills low. Or is it successfully avoiding unnecessary hospitalization through preventive, efficient care?

The question takes on a slightly different shading when you are a Medicare patient.

On the one hand, HMOs offer many attractive benefits for Medicare patients: lower premiums and coverage for items not covered by Medicare such as preventive care, health checkups, eye examinations, podiatry, hearing tests, and injectable drugs. Some cover eyeglasses, medicine, and even dental care.

And, of course, you receive the traditional benefits of HMO-style health care: All medical coverage for one fixed rate. If it's a group model HMO—all under one roof—it saves you from traveling to different locations for different doctors.

With HMOs in general, there's no need to worry if a doctor will accept

Medicare for full payment. There are also no deductibles, no co-payments, and no Medicare claim forms to fill out (except for emergencies and certain in-hospital services).

There's no question it sounds terrific, but before you dash off to your local HMO, you must consider what you're getting: If you join an HMO and continue to see your present, non-HMO doctor, you will have to pay for it yourself. Many HMOs don't offer enough orientation and instruction on HMO use, and unpleasant surprises can be the result.

DISABILITY INSURANCE

Too many people overlook their disability insurance. But your chances of being disabled for three months or more are much greater than the chances of your dying before retirement. And when you have to rely on it, you'd be surprised how inadequate most employers' long-term group policy payments—not to mention Social Security and state disability payments—can be.

Adequate disability insurance could be the crucial difference between keeping your house or having to sell it in the event of injury or illness. More than 48 percent of the mortgage foreclosures in the United States in recent years resulted from just such events.

Find out what disability coverage you might have through your employers. If you are self-employed, or your employer does not provide long-term disability insurance, at a minimum buy the coverage you need to pay at least your monthly mortgage checks. Look for policies that are non-cancellable and guaranteed renewable. This will keep the insurance company from raising the premiums or cancelling the policy.

Don't expect to find coverage for more than 70 percent of your income. But you can pay for riders that will increase benefits with inflation, and options that will help make up the difference if you can't return to as high-paying an occupation as you had before your disability.

LONG-TERM HEALTH CARE. One in five of us will go into a nursing home at some point. One in three of the nation's over-85 population now needs some kind of special help to get through the day or just out of the house.

The 85-and-older group will double in size by the year 2000, and the number of those who'll need some form of nursing-home care will skyrocket within the next 20 years.

What does this all mean?

It means that, like it or not, many of us will someday need some type of medical or nursing help in order to function. And to be able to afford this help, we will need some type of long-term insurance. Chart 11 can help you decide what coverage you need.

Everyone should become familiar with the cost of long-term health care and should be protected financially if and when the need for it arises. The statistics are enough to tell us that this is the only prudent thing to do.

If you are planning to obtain insurance against long-term health-care needs, here are some of the more important questions that you must answer for yourself before selecting a policy:

- Does this policy provide benefits for skilled care, intermediate care, custodial care or home care?

- What daily amount is paid for each of the above categories of care?

- How long will you receive benefits?

- Must you be hospitalized before you can receive benefits?

- How many days after you enter a nursing home must you wait to start receiving benefits?

- How long must you wait before you get benefits for pre-existing conditions?

- Does the company guarantee to renew the policy as long as you pay the premiums on time?

- Does the policy cover Alzheimer's disease, Parkinson's disease, and senility?

- Will this policy pay even if you're covered by Medicare or Medigap?

- What is the maximum age by which you may apply?

- Will the premium continue to be based on your age at the time of your enrollment?

- What is the maximum amount the policy will ever pay out?

- What is the cost of the coverage you want per month, per year, and over 10 years?

Sad to say though it is, there are insurance companies and agents who are unreliable or dishonest. You must be on the lookout for false representations of what a policy will provide in terms of long-term care, just as Medigap policies must be scrutinized.

Be especially wary of scare tactics by glib salesmen. They may be trying to push you into coverage that you do not need, cannot afford—or already have from someone else.

CHART 11

Are You Satisfactorily Covered for Long-Term Care?

- It is estimated that one in five Americans will spend some time in a nursing home.
- Estimated average confinement time is 2.5 years.
- Present average cost of a nursing home is $26,000 per year.
- An estimated 20% to 25% of the elderly are currently confined to their homes with regular care from others than relatives.

Use this checklist to appraise any (A) insurance policy or (B) other protection (a) you now have or (b) are, or will be considering adding:

1. If an insurance policy, how does "Best's" rate the insurer?
2. Does the insurance policy or other protection cover (A) "custodial"- and (B) "intermediate"- type nursing homes as well as (C) "skilled"?
3. Also cover (A) home health care agencies (service providers, supplies, and equipment) and (B) adult day care centers?
4. Insurer's "care coordinator" required to locate and approve (A) facilities and (B) services?
5. Exclusions for (A) existing conditions (B) pre-existing conditions (C) former conditions?
6. Exclusions for mental and nervous disorders, such as Alzheimer's disease?
7. To qualify for benefits: (A) Do you have to enter the nursing home directly or within a maximum period from hospital discharge? (B) Enter into a custodial or intermediate nursing home from a skilled? (C) Enter into home care or adult day center care from a hospital or nursing home?
8. How long is the "deductible" ("waiting," "elimination") period (when your benefits begin after confinement starts)?
9. How long will benefits continue: (A) maximum period(s) of confinement or (B) maximum dollar amount(s)?
10. If "discharged" from a confinement period, but resumed in the future: (A) New deductible period? (B) Prior confinement count toward maximum benefits?
11. What expenses are covered?
12. What expenses are not covered?
13. (A) Are benefits a fixed dollar amount for each qualifying day? If so, how much? (B) Or do benefits vary for different kinds of care?
14. Are benefits adjusted (fixed or variable percentage) each year for inflation? If so: (A) How much each year? (B) For how many years?
15. "Duplicate benefits": How do other plans you may have affect benefits of this policy or protection (other than a policy)?
16. Oldest age permitted to buy this policy or other protection?
17. (A) Guaranteed renewable or (B) "conditionally" renewable? (If conditions, what are they?)
18. What are the premiums or other costs? (Some premiums are a set amount with benefits and conditions the same for all. Others will have variable premiums based upon conditions (such as age) and benefits that you specifically select [such as deductible period, how long benefits continue, amount of benefits, and the like].)
19. Are the premiums you start with (A) fixed for as long as you continue to pay the premiums or (B) can they be increased if increased for all policyholders or holders of other protection (other than a policy)?
20. Are premiums waived ("waiver of premiums") while benefits are received?

Reprinted from SPARN 1/89

Look closely at pitches sent by companies that make it look as though their policies are being offered by the government or by some legitimate organization of senior citizens. The government doesn't sell Medicare supplement policies, and very few organizations do.

Do the same in connection with pitches for insurance that will cover you if you get a particular dreaded disease. The policies are offered on the basis that you probably won't, and, anyway your existing insurance covers not only the dreaded disease in question, but other diseases, illnesses, and injuries as well.

Don't fall for the phrase "No medical exam required." This does not mean that you will be able to get coverage even though you already have a medical condition. You almost certainly won't.

LIFE INSURANCE

Life insurance is not, of course, a favorite topic of conversation for many people. It's not even something most of us like to think about. It calls to mind one's own death or the death of a loved one. Who needs it?

You do, as you'll quickly realize when a death occurs, or when you think of what would happen to your family should something happen to you. Then, the wisdom of taking out a life insurance policy is recalled with gratitude and relief.

How much life insurance is enough? The checklist in Chart 12 should help you find the answer that's right for you.

If the death benefit amount is small, it can nevertheless see a grieving family through funeral expenses. If, however, it is substantial and it is handled wisely, it can see that family through the trials and tribulations of a lifetime.

Life insurance benefits are free from income tax. They may be spent or invested as the beneficiary sees fit. Life insurance in fact is the only asset many families can count on to protect them and see to their financial security should the breadwinner die.

Until recently, distribution of benefits has not been handled in the best of ways. When an insured person died, the life insurance policy's beneficiary informed the insurance company of the death, providing necessary documentation. The insurance company then issued a check for the full face value of the policy.

The problem is that shortly after the death of a loved one, most people are ill-equipped to make important and long-lasting decisions about the disposal of what can sometimes be hundreds of thousands of dollars. Grief can

CHART 12

Your Check List to Determine How Much Life Insurance You Need

Whom do you want to protect with your life insurance? ☐ Spouse ☐ Children
☐ Children from a prior marriage ☐ Parents ☐ Other: _____
To what extent do you want to protect them? ☐ Provide for their current lifestyle
☐ More modest lifestyle ☐ More affluent lifestyle
How long do you want to protect each? _____

Lump-Sum Benefits and Expenses When You Die		Income and Expenses (After Your Death) of Those Whom You Want To Protect	
Lump-Sum Benefits	Lump-Sum Expenses	Their Income	Their Expenses
☐ From health insurance for expenses of a terminal illness	☐ Cemetery plot (not prepaid)	☐ New working income (after taxes and pay deductions)	☐ Fixed expenses (household, utilities, transportation, insurance premiums, education, child care, pets, etc.)
☐ From your current personal life insurance coverage	☐ Funeral costs (not prepaid)	☐ From interest, dividends, net rents, etc. from assets owned by them (some of which may have even been inherited from you)	☐ Variable expenses (food, beverages, clothing, grooming, medical [unreimbursed], contributions, recreation, etc.)
☐ From your current employment and other group life insurance coverage	☐ Costs of an expensive terminal illness (not covered by health insurance)	☐ From your personal, employment, government, and other insurances and plans that pay in installments rather than in lump sums (see first column)	☐ Special: _____ _____ _____
☐ Death benefits from your pension, profit-sharing, deferred-income, and other plans	☐ Tax, probate, attorney, accountant, any other estate expenses	☐ Interest, dividends, or other income from investment of the amount left over, if any, after	
☐ From Social Security, veterans', and other government sources	☐ To pay your existing debts not collateralized or covered by redemption insurance		
☐ Other: _____	☐ Transitional funds to help tide your beneficiaries over as they adjust after your death		

☐ Other: _____

☐ Other: (deducting lump-sum expenses (second column) from lump-sum benefits (first column)) _____

Calculations

After filling in the check list above, you can prepare your worksheet, entering the dollar amounts for each item you checked.

- If your lump-sum expenses (column two) exceed your lump-sum benefits (column one), you need additional life insurance with lump-sum proceeds to pay the difference.

- If your beneficiaries' expenses (column four) exceed their income (column three), you need additional life insurance to provide the difference (from income paid by the policies, or from income resulting from investment of lump sums paid by the policies).

- The two items above show you need more life insurance. But you may be paying for more life insurance than you need if your calculations show significant excesses of both lump-sum benefits over lump-sum expenses and your beneficiaries' income over their expenses.

Redetermine periodically or when circumstances change substantially (such as children on their own and no longer dependent). Your periodic redeterminations should take into consideration keeping pace with increases from inflation.

cloud judgement and, even if it doesn't, many people just don't feel like tackling such decisions while bereaved.

A number of insurance companies, realizing that a grief-stricken family doesn't want to face such decisions, have in recent years created a new way of handling death benefit distributions. These new programs allow the beneficiaries to take some time in deciding what to do with the money. During the interim, the money earns interest at money market rates.

This kind of death benefit payment is called "access funds." About a dozen of the larger companies offer this option.

What's more, access fund money is always available. All the beneficiary needs to do is write a check to withdraw any part of it. The principal remains entirely tax free, though interest earned on it is, of course, taxable from the date of death.

Psychologists say that it may take as much as six months to a year for those who have had deaths in the family to get back up to speed. Only after you've recovered from the shock and are ready to move forward at your customary clip should you think about making important decisions about what to do with life insurance benefits.

Once you've decided, all you need to do to close the account is write a check for the full amount of the balance. You can, of course, leave your money with the insurance company for as long as you like. You may want to convert it into an annuity that will provide income for years.

SPENDING YOUR LEGACY—A BAD IDEA. There's a rider offered with some life insurance policies that allows the death benefit to be paid out ahead of time, to finance long-term medical care. But the plan is fraught with danger and probably should be avoided.

Many American families virtually go bust paying for long-term nursing care or a nursing home for a relative who has a paid-up life insurance policy that would take care of it all—if the relative were no longer living.

But now, the benefit can in some cases be paid out in monthly increments before the holder of the policy dies, with the balance paid in the normal death benefit fashion.

The disadvantage is that death benefits are exempt from estate taxes. Many are the widows who were able to pay those taxes, and thus hang on to the family home, because of a big life insurance payoff. Many are the students who were able to finish college because Dad—or Mom—had life insurance.

When considering the before-death option, there are several factors you should keep in mind:

- Why do you have life insurance? If it is to provide for your survivors, then the option of converting some or all of the benefit to long-term care isn't for you. If your family is well provided for, it is possible and in some cases maybe even advisable to take out a life insurance policy with the long-term care rider, solely as a guard against catastrophic medical bills. Why? Because the cost of the rider is much less than the cost of stand-alone nursing care insurance. If a policy is purchased with the idea of nursing care in mind, it will be there if needed—and if not, you will leave that much more for your survivors.

- The circumstances under which the payment is made. These can include long-term hospital care, convalescence, and nursing home or home nursing care.

- Your exposure to estate and other taxes. If you are otherwise well off, and have a substantial quantity of liquid investments that could, in a pinch, see to your care should a long-term health need arise, then this option probably isn't the one for you. Because a death benefit is not taxed, and because the rest of your estate is, better to concentrate funds in that benefit. If your situation is quite the opposite, and your family would have to sell their home to see to your care, this plan may be for you—but again, it would be best to take out an additional policy earmarked for such use, and if it isn't needed, so much the better.

- Your other life insurance and pension plans. Perhaps you have plans through your employer or labor union. If so, these could meet your survivors' needs. Now is the time to find out. Ask.

- The costs of medical care. Don't underestimate them. A friend recently sent me a listing of charges incurred during only a short hospitalization. They were astronomical, and the costs show no sign of going down or even leveling off. Most health insurance policies are designed for short-term stays, and even then the 20 percent policy holders are expected to pay can break the bank. Those policies run out altogether, in many cases, before the question of long-term care ever arises.

There are some statistics to think about: Of all Americans alive today, nearly 40 percent will spend time in a nursing home. The average stay is a little more than two years, and the average cost is about $25,000 per year.

Bear in mind, too, that government assistance is loaded with provisions that specify that the government, not you and not your family, will specify the circumstances of your care and, even then, will not always pay for the full care that you may need.

Before you even think of a plan offering pre-payment, you must determine whether your family can better afford to draw upon life insurance benefits now, to see to your care, or later, to see after your estate. In the majority of cases, life insurance is best left as life insurance.

6

INVESTING IN
THE '90s

Investing sounds so easy: All you need to do is buy when prices are low and sell when they are high—and collect handsome dividends in between. But thanks to the little variations on that theme, investing, for many people, isn't a sure thing. Remember: For every dollar gained, there's a dollar lost.

That doesn't mean that you can't invest with an enormous likelihood of profit. Armed with the facts, and sticking to the right philosophy, you can ride out almost any imaginable financial storm in fine style.

AMERICA'S ECONOMY
FACES THE '90s

THE UGLY SPECTER OF INFLATION. At the beginning of each recent decade, there has been talk of a "new round of inflation." During times of inflation, the value of money drops. It costs more for a given item or service. At the same time, interest rates rise, in anticipation that dollars lent today will be repaid later with dollars that are worth less.

The 1990s begin with a continuation of the longest economic expansion in American history. The economy has grown, inflation and interest rates have dropped dramatically, and unemployment has dropped so low that in some sectors of the economy there is actually a labor shortage.

This happy situation would, you would think, cause everyone to relax and enjoy the good times. Don't you believe it! Offering a variety of reasons, justifications, and theories, a broad spectrum of economic thinkers (and some cranks as well) have offered predictions of imminent economic downturn or even out-and-out collapse.

A return of the familiar "new round of inflation" is a big part of most of the theories.

The labor shortage is part of the picture. Employers have to pay more or else hire less productive employees. In some cases, they spend capital on new systems that allow the same number of employees to become more productive. All this costs money, which results in higher prices for the same goods and services—inflation.

THE ECONOMIC COST OF A LABOR SHORTAGE. This country is in the middle of a labor shortage, and the situation is likely to get worse.

Part of the problem is a decline in the number of people to fill entry-level jobs. The slack has been taken up in some areas by older people taking part-time jobs. Retired stenographers, for instance, increasingly do typing and other clerical work at home. Many companies, especially restaurants, are making a special effort to lure older Americans out of retirement.

Whenever there is a shortage of labor, there is an upward pressure on wages. The extent to which this takes place will determine the part it plays in any new inflation, which affects everyone.

Beyond that, costs, and therefore prices, are likely to rise in labor-intensive industries, less so in highly automated ones. Those companies that can take on new business without having to increase the number of employees are likely to do better than those whose marginal increase in trade requires a corresponding increase in the payroll.

The situation is not likely to get better anytime soon. You may have noticed that clerks, check-out people, and waiters and waitresses may seem less friendly or less informed than they seem to have been just a few years ago. The fact is that people who might have not been successful job applicants then are landing those jobs now, and the likelihood of being dismissed is smaller.

It spells happy days ahead for companies that develop ways of increasing productivity, allowing the same number of workers, expending the same effort, to get more work done. Companies specializing in automation systems face a bright future.

It means that companies that can adapt to a changing labor situation will rise to the top.

These things are important for you to consider in making investments, because they will determine the profitability of companies in the not-too-distant future. Find out the extent to which a particular company requires a huge labor contingent, particularly in lower-paying jobs, where the shortage is most acute. Find out how the company plans to deal with the problem, and whether the solution is likely to meet opposition from unions or elsewhere.

THE DEFICIT AND INTEREST RATES. If the government can find a way to reduce the budget deficit, some of the pressure on interest rates will be reduced. This would allow companies to invest more in productivity-enhancing machinery at lower costs, which in turn would relieve some of the inflationary pressure brought on by the shortage of labor. It's all tied together, and no one can predict with certainty how it will turn out in anything but the short term.

As 1989 drew to a close, the uncertainty grew because of the reordering of Eastern Europe. Changes there toward freer, market-based economies produced immediate speculation that the defense budget could be reduced substantially, in turn reducing the size of the federal budget and the budget deficit. This would require the government to borrow less, leaving more capital available at better rates for private investment.

But it quickly became clear that this was not a sure thing. For a start, the United States was not willing instantly to reduce the size of its armed forces, thus postponing a significant reduction in the federal defense budget. Second, it was by no means clear that the government would reverse its precedents, which means there's no way to be sure that the government won't simply spend the money for something else. Third, it wasn't yet known to what extent the United States would be called upon to inject capital into the newly free countries of Eastern Europe. Revolutions seldom take place when all is well. In the case of the surprising events of 1989, governments were toppled because they were on the brink of financial collapse. There is no way for anyone to know how much aid we will provide to these nations during the crucial decade ahead.

Enter yet another factor. This is the huge Social Security surplus that is expected to rise to nearly $200 billion by 1995. The government will do one of two things with it: Invest it to provide Social Security benefits to future retirees, or spend it.

What happens to this money will be one of the leading issues of the middle part of this decade, with shock waves that will carry well into the next century. If it is invested, it will inject a huge amount of cash into the economy, helping to reduce interest rates and make expansion possible. (It would, sadly, not be so good for the Social Security system, because the return on the investment would be low.)

Unfortunately, we are likely to see a generational war, as those who want lower taxes now argue against those who are entitled to Social Security payments in the future. How this struggle plays out will determine the fate of this huge surplus. Investors, both those seeking income at the time and those planning for retirement, will need to watch the situation closely.

THE WORLD STAGE

America's economic future is not determined solely by domestic politics and budget decisions. Broader national and global trends also influence the national economic picture. The maturing of the baby boomers, freer international trade, democratic trends in Eastern Europe, and technology's increasing capacity to develop new products (and make old ones obsolete) will all be important factors in the '90s.

MATURING BABY BOOMERS. About one-third of our population was born between 1946 and 1964. It pays to pay attention to companies and industries that meet their needs.

For example, just a few years ago, the baby boomers started to settle down. What happened? Housing demand peaked and real estate prices went through the roof all over America. Yuppies contributed to the growth of foreign car sales. As baby boomers had children (increasingly, just one), sales of baby food, diapers (especially disposable ones), and other infant products were robust.

This generation is now approaching middle age. They've bought their first house in many cases, and real estate values are stalled from a lack of new demand. There's a particular surplus of the sort of housing first-time purchasers buy; baby boomers are trading their condos and partments for bigger houses that will accommodate their families.

As they age, the baby boomers are saving more. And they're buying products associated with an aging population: cosmetics, building materials and gardening supplies, and life insurance, to name a few.

FREER INTERNATIONAL TRADE. Although sometimes obscured by events in Eastern Europe, the removal of trade barriers in 1992 among the 12 members of the Common Market will be a landmark economic event. Why should it matter to you?

Experts predict that, as a result of the removal of trade barriers, European economic growth will jump 7 percent, while its consumer prices drop 6 percent. That will make Europe an even more formidable competitor on the world economic stage. That means that European firms will get a share of the business American firms now count on.

Europe's not the only arena where trade barriers are falling. The U.S. and Canada recently agreed to phase out tariffs between the two nations over a 10-year period. And if Eastern Europe continues its trend towards greater democracy, look for the U.S., as well as other Western nations, to extend trade links to these nations to encourage continuation of this trend.

In the long run, it's difficult to tell if freer trade will open up markets, or result in a retreat to even greater protectionism. Countries raise trade barriers when they think they're losing at the free trade game.

In the short run, though, look for exports to rise worldwide. This will increase competition on all fronts. Low-cost producers will profit; inefficient producers that make products at higher cost will be in trouble.

EASTERN EUROPE. The political situation there could change at any minute. But the changes seen thus far have been breathtaking.

Keep in mind that these changes are the result of widespread dissatisfaction over the economic results that the Communist leaders have produced. Even if more restrictive regimes are installed, this dissatisfaction will not go away until the leaders do a better job of filling the needs of the people.

Also keep in mind that investment in Eastern Europe will not be easy. The new leaders are inexperienced, and the work force often isn't accustomed to the Western work ethic. In the Soviet Union, a huge, entrenched bureaucracy will make things difficult for Western companies. Topping things off, currencies in these countries often can't be exchanged for dollars, so it may be difficult for companies to get their profits out of Eastern Europe.

TECHNOLOGY AND NEW PRODUCTS. The advances in personal computers over the '80s boggle the mind. Computing power that literally filled a room a few years ago now can fit in the palm of your hand. Expect this trend to continue: Personal computers will compete with minicomputers (smaller than mainframe computers, but bigger than personal computers) to a greater degree than ever.

A growing number of Americans now use home computers for a variety of purchases, arrangements, and information gathering through on-line services. This means that they hook up their computers to the telephone line and by dialing a specific, usually local, number are connected with a huge computer offering information and services, and now advertising as well.

Despite some early false starts, look for on-line services to continue to grow in the '90s. Perhaps the best-known of these new services is called Prodigy. It's a joint venture between IBM and Sears, Roebuck, and Co. Unlike the earlier on-line services, Prodigy doesn't charge by the hour. Instead, customers—which the company calls "members"—have unlimited access to the service for a monthly subscription fee.

The most exciting and most potentially beneficial new communications technology involves something called "artificial reality." This promises to bring unprecedented change to the way we do things.

It works something like this: The user dons headgear that contains a small video screen for each eye and a small audio speaker for each ear. These are hooked to a computer, plus whatever peripheral equipment is needed for the application involved.

A computer program is run and the user is, in effect, someplace else. Turn your head to the left, and you see what is to the left of where you're "standing." Turn your head to the right, and you see whatever is "located" to the right.

By adding gloves or boots that contain computer sensors—or even by wearing an entire artificial reality suit—you can "pick things up," "walk around," even "fly." All while sitting or standing in your home or office.

Just as a mouse moving around the table top next to your computer can send the screen's cursor scurrying, artificial reality uses human senses and human actions to control computers and the things computers control.

The possibilities for this technology are endless. Artificial reality promises that any place or activity within human experience can belong to anyone. The potential for broadcasting and home entertainment is, obviously, enormous.

This dramatic new technology is already here in its simplest form. Like the computer revolution of the late 1970s and early 1980s, the pace of development will certainly be breathtaking. The abilities of the systems will rise and the prices will come down.

INVESTING TODAY

There may be no other aspect of our lives that has been changed by technological innovation more than communications. Laptop computers, cellular telephones, fax machines—items that were fantasies just a few years ago are now established features of our lives.

What does this have to do with investment?

As communication advances, the capacity to handle large transactions virtually instantaneously has increased. The October 1987 stock market crash resulted in part from huge stock transactions that simply could not have been accomplished before computerization. In fact, without the speed that computerization offers, program trading itself would not be possible; the program traders profit from minute, momentary discrepancies between markets, and they could not profit if there was a significant chance that, by the time they moved in, that discrepancy would have evaporated.

The stock market is just one example. Increased communications capabilities have permanently increased the speed at which transactions can occur. This means that all of our financial markets—and almost all of our investment alternatives—have become that much more volatile. Sharp price swings will become an increasingly commonplace feature of our economy.

That means you have to take this volatility into account when you plan to invest in any of the financial markets. You may choose to invest in a mutual fund—to pool your resources with other small investors to obtain access to resources that put you on an equal footing with the big boys. Or you may choose to go it alone, opting for maneuverability that large institutions, by their nature, cannot achieve.

But whether you pool your resources, or go it alone, be prepared for increased volatility.

RULES TO INVEST BY

In this era of frightening price swings, following tested investment principles will ensure that good sense, and not emotion, governs your investment decisions. Unerring reliance on a few simple rules will make sure that your investments represent security, which is what they're supposed to, instead of uncertainty and fear. Among them:

PICK INVESTMENTS FOR THE LONG TERM. Frequent buying and selling of stocks and bonds does little more than enrich your broker. Such profits as you might realize will be eaten up by commissions.

DON'T BE OVERLY GREEDY. Don't hold out for the few extra dollars you think you might receive by hanging on just a little longer. Stock prices can "top out" and head back down, sometimes steeply down, in a very short time. Very few people have the skill to buy at the very bottom of the market or sell at the absolute top.

PICK YOUR INVESTMENTS VERY CAREFULLY. While there will always be a temptation to indulge in swashbuckling market strategies, always remember that it's your future and that of your family with which you are gambling. Though the price of an issue may be set—for a little while, at least—by rumors and guesses, its value is found in careful study of the prospectus or annual report.

ONCE YOU'VE INVESTED, PAY ATTENTION TO THE THINGS LIKELY TO AFFECT YOUR INVESTMENTS. The last few years have shown that a healthy company can be all but killed by product liability issues, legislation, and changes in technology.

JUST AS YOU SHOULDN'T BE OVERLY EAGER TO BUY, DON'T BE STUBBORN ABOUT HANGING ONTO THE OC-CASIONAL LOSER. Again, there is an element of chance in the fortunes of even the best companies (or, for that matter, cities, if municipal bonds are among your holdings). There is a difference between keeping track of changing long-term prospects and joining a stampede. If you do the former, you won't fall victim to the latter.

LET YOUR INVESTMENT PORTFOLIO BE KEYED TO YOUR OWN FINANCIAL GOALS. There is no best way to invest, because each investor is different.

DON'T GET DRAWN IN BY THE EXCITEMENT OF LEVER-AGED BUYOUTS, HOT TIPS, AND THE LIKE. In a leveraged buyout, someone borrows against a company's assets to finance its purchase. Although the market today increasingly frowns on such debt-loaded acquisitions, they were the rage for quite a while. Many sought quick profits through insider information and hostile acquisitions. While the first part of the 1980s was a time when many fortunes were made through tricky stock maneuvers, the latter part of that decade involved big parts of those fortunes being given to defense lawyers and handed over in the form of fines. Yesterday's stock market hero, in several cases, became today's jailbird.

INVESTING IN VARYING ECONOMIC CLIMATES

For every dollar lost to inflation, a dollar is made. The old rule of thumb is that inflationary times are good for those who owe money but bad for those who have lent it, good for those who have inventory and bad for those who have cash. Which isn't to say there's reason to become overly alarmed, no matter what your position.

Some advisers tell their clients to put their money into high-quality, short-term bonds when there is uncertainty about inflation. Others suggest "parking" it in such investments as short-term Treasury paper. Here's why: Relatively high liquidity gives you the opportunity to take advantage of higher interest rates which are themselves a hedge against inflation, when they become available.

The conventional wisdom is that it's a good idea to invest in "stores of wealth," such as gold, in times of high inflation. But those who bought gold, instead of selling it, during the early 1980s are sorry now.

Gold can be a hedge against inflation, but the price of gold is determined largely by gold speculators, and when interest rates rise, it's less profitable for them to borrow money to buy gold. And the experience of the 1980s suggests that gold can be a terrible investment. Inflation aside, gold actually lost value during the '80s. (Silver was worse, losing nearly 85 percent of its value during the decade. If you factor in inflation, the picture for gold and silver is even bleaker.)

All else being equal, a much better hedge against inflation generally has been the purchase of a home. But this is not always so, and you should not depend upon the general rule for a specific situation you're considering. For example, values of homes dropped sharply in some regions during the later 1980s and early 1990s—houses in hard-hit oil, agricultural, and steel production areas, and co-op and condo apartments in major cities where building and conversion had created a glut. The outlook at least for the early years of the 1990s is moderate inflation, so home ownership would not benefit from this traditional hedge.

However, long-term home ownership can be a good hedge, because with it every tick upward in prices translates immediately into money you can use. Here's why:

Let's assume that you buy a $100,000 home with a $25,000 down payment and a fixed-rate mortgage. Then let's inject an interest rate of, say, 5 percent. At the end of the year, presuming your home is not in a neighborhood on the decline, it will have grown in value by about $5,000. That $5,000 belongs to you. It is an increase in the equity in your home. You can, if you want, borrow against it. What's more, the money you are using to repay your mortgage is worth less than it was when you borrowed it. You're repaying with cheaper dollars.

(This advantage will be less if you have an adjustable-rate mortgage, because the rate will rise as inflation rises, making ARMs less attractive if you believe inflation will rear its ugly head again.)

What about other securities? Surely they, too, are affected by rising interest rates and inflation.

That's true, but those effects can be tricky to predict. Rising interest rates limit capital expansion, so capital-intensive industries are likely to suffer. Those companies that have recently completed—or recently financed—expansions will do better. It becomes more important than ever to study stocks before buying them.

Rising Interest Rates: When interest rates rise, the value of bonds yielding at the old rates drops. That's why many advisors urge their clients to avoid long-term bonds, at least during times of uncertainty.

Social Security Surplus: How the $200 billion Social Security surplus is handled—whether it is invested or spent—will be an important element in determining the course of the economy.

If it is invested in government paper, it will drive interest rates much lower, providing a broader boost to business and industry, including consumer areas such as home sales.

If it is spent, some stocks will perform very well indeed. Obviously, which ones will depend upon how the money is spent. Possibilities probably include stocks of companies (and mutual funds specializing in such stocks) in infrastructures (highways, bridges, tunnels, buildings, and the like), environmental products and services, health care products and services, automation machinery, biotechnology, and computers (the government itself requires a lot of upgrading, particularly the IRS).

GOOD PROFESSIONAL HELP

Financial choices available to individuals have grown in number and complexity. These range from money market accounts at banks to variable annuities through insurance companies, and from stock options and indexes through brokerage firms to international, sector, option, index, asset allocation, and tax-exempt mutual funds. The diversity of choices (the above and many others) may make it more likely that you'll want the help of a professional financial planner.

The problem is in picking one. While the majority of financial professionals are honest, informed, and educated, there are enough crooks in the industry that you must make your choice carefully. The Council of Better Business Bureaus reports an increase over the last few years in complaints against investment advisers who, in fact, are nothing more than shills for one questionable investment or another.

Fortunately, events are combining to rid the industry of its worst elements. The Tax Reform Act of 1986 virtually outlawed tax shelters; many financial planners were in fact tax shelter salespeople, living off fat sales commissions that they received for selling tax shelters to their clients. With the demise of tax shelters, some of these financial planners have had to look for other occupations. As a result, the number of practicing financial planners has dropped sharply since 1986.

Increasing regulatory supervision promises to weed the field further. The Securities and Exchange Commission is considering requiring financial planners to register with it, in much the same way as stockbrokers currently do. Other federal and state agencies are examining ways to rid the field of those of easy ethics.

The International Association for Financial Planning (IAFP) is a professional organization. It and a similar group, the National Association of Personal Financial Advisers (NAPFA), exist in part to help police the industry, chiefly by making information available to individuals.

According to these organizations, there are certain things you should look for when shopping for a financial adviser.

First, determine the professional standing of the adviser. Those that are certified have undergone a lengthy and difficult course of study. Check also for professional affiliations, such as the Registry of Financial Planners, IAFP, and NAPFA.

It's a good idea to request references as well. A reputable planner will cheerfully provide them.

Inquire about the adviser's track record and investment philosophy. No matter how educated, intelligent, or personable a planner is, if he or she consistently loses money for clients, you should look elsewhere.

Find out the adviser's experience. Learn, too, what additional training the adviser has received and whether he or she is enrolled in advanced or refresher courses.

Not to be overlooked, too, is simply whether you get along with the planner you are thinking of hiring. A cordial atmosphere makes it easier for you to work with the planner who, after all, will be setting the course for a very important part of your life.

Then you should find out not only what the adviser charges for his or her services, but the way those charges are levied. An adviser who works for straight fees (such as those represented by the NAPFA) may have a different philosophy from that of one who works on commission.

The reason to be concerned about the manner of payment should be obvious: A planner who makes a lot of money from commissions stands to gain from a lot of transactions, while a fee-based planner is more likely to have you put your money where it can be allowed to grow quietly.

A financial planner disclosure form, such as shown in Chart 13, will help you find many of the answers you should seek.

Once that's all done and you believe you've found the kind of professional financial help you need, there's one more call to make. Check with the local BBB to determine if there are outstanding complaints against the adviser. While one or two resolved problems shouldn't necessarily be a warning sign, a long string of unresolved complaints are a strong indication that you had best keep looking.

When you're satisfied that you've found a planner you can work with, you can enter into a formal agreement, such as the one in Chart 14.

HOW TO USE A FINANCIAL PLANNER

After you've found a financial planner you're happy with, and you've made all the necessary background checks, it's time to sit down and map your financial future.

One of the first things you might want to do is drop a note to your lawyer, your accountant, and your insurance agent, introducing them to your planner. Send copies of these letters to the financial consultant.

These letters should not authorize the planner to act in your behalf. In fact, it's almost always a bad idea to give such authorization (known as a "power of attorney.") Instead, they should let these other professionals know that you'll be working with this planner or planning firm.

You can then review your tax and insurance situations with the consultant. He or she may make specific suggestions, or may want to talk with your agent or accountant. It's best to be present for these meetings.

If you have established your financial goals, it's time to discuss them with your planner, who can help clear a path to them. Particular investments and investment strategies will be suggested.

Your will and estate situation will be discussed, with suggestions for alteration where appropriate. Your employee benefits package, investments you already hold, and pensions to which you are or may become entitled will be on the table as well.

You should make a point of bringing up any areas of financial difficulty—too great a debt load, a problem with cash flow—because your planner can suggest solutions.

After this inventory of your monetary situation, a written plan will be prepared. It will make specific recommendations of ways to improve your situation. It will be tailored to fit you alone.

From time to time, you will want to meet with your planner to update your plan. This is because tax laws change, financial goals are reached (or abandoned for one reason or another), your employment or living situation may change, and the economy, too, is changeable.

CHART 13

Financial Planner Disclosure Form

11 questions to ask a financial planner *before* you sign them on to handle your money.

1. Does your financial planning service include:
   - ☐ A review of my goals.
   - ☐ Advice on:
     - ☐ Cash management and budgeting
     - ☐ Tax planning
     - ☐ Investment review and planning
     - ☐ Retirement planning
     - ☐ Estate planning
     - ☐ Insurance needs:
       - ☐ Life insurance
       - ☐ Disability insurance
       - ☐ Property/Casualty insurance
     - ☐ Other: _____
   - ☐ Other areas: _____

2. Do you provide a written analysis of my financial situation and your recommendations?
   - ☐ YES   ☐ NO

5. Is your firm registered with the Securities and Exchange Commission?
   - ☐ YES   ☐ NO

6. If "fee only," is your firm affiliated with a broker/dealer?
   - ☐ YES   ☐ NO

7. If "fee and commission," (or if affiliated with a broker/dealer), approximately what percentage of your firm's annual income comes from:
   - ☐ ____ % Fees charged to clients
   - ☐ ____ % Commissions earned from clients' purchase of investment products
   - ☐ ____ % Other (explain) _____

9. Will you furnish me with no-load (no sales charge) product alternatives, if available?
   - ☐ YES   ☐ NO

10. Do you or any member of your firm act as a general partner, or receive compensation from the general partner, of investments which may be recommended to me?
    - ☐ YES   ☐ NO

11. What is the average income in fees from a typical client?
    $ _____ (annual fee income divided by number of clients served)
    What is the average income in commissions from a typical client?
    $ _____ (annual commission income divided by number of clients served)

3. How is your firm compensated for the financial planning services you provide:

☐ Fees only (flat fee or hourly rate)

☐ Commissions only (from securities, insurance, etc. that I might buy from your firm.)

☐ Fees and commissions

4. If you charge a fee, what is it based on?

☐ An hourly rate of
$ _____

☐ A percentage based on _____

☐ A flat fee based on _____

8. If "fee and commission" or "commission only" (or if affiliated with a broker/dealer), what percentage of your commission income comes from:

☐ _____ % Insurance products

☐ _____ % Annuities

☐ _____ %Mutual funds

☐ _____ % Limited partnerships

☐ _____ % Coins

☐ _____ % Stocks and bonds

☐ _____ % Other _____

(explain) _____

To the best of my knowledge, the above statements are true and correct.

Name _____

Firm _____

Signature _____

Date _____

Prepared by:
The National Association of Personal Financial Advisors

CHART 14

Sample Agreement With a Personal Finance Professional

You will not have, nor need to have, a written agreement with every personal finance professional you use. Of those with whom you do have written agreements, they usually will provide you with the agreement they use. This may be prepared specifically by that professional for use with his or her clients, or it may be a standard printed form used by many practitioners in the same field. Content will vary by field and practitioner. You should review an agreement carefully and be sure you understand it and find everything acceptable before you sign.

This agreement is entered into (Date) by and between (Name and address of Professional/Firm), hereinafter referred to as "Professional" (in this sample agreement), and (Your name and address as Client), hereinafter "Client" (in this sample).

Professional is experienced in and agrees to perform the following services for Client: _____

_____

_____

_____

Client agrees to pay Professional for these services as follows:

Time period to render services: _____

Cost of services: _____

Expenses to be reimbursed: _____

Provision for variables: _____

Payments schedule: _____
Professional agrees to: explain to Client available courses of action and attendant risks; consult with Client in advance on any significant decisions; notify Client promptly of any significant developments; and answer Client's inquiries promptly.

Client agrees to make all reasonable efforts to be available and to provide relevant matter to Professional as needed.

Client may terminate this agreement, with or without cause, upon written notice to Professional. Professional shall return Client's matter to Client upon termination. Client shall be responsible to pay for services and reimbursable expenses rendered up to date of termination.

Professional may terminate this agreement for reasons permitted under the profession's code of professional responsibility.

This agreement contains the entire agreement between Professional and Client. It is binding upon them from this date.

_____   _____
Client   Professional

7
BALANCING YOUR
────── PORTFOLIO ──────

DIVERSIFY!

Mutual funds, at least those that deal aggressively in growth issues, wouldn't last very long if they only bought a few different issues. One or two of them would take a dive, and that would be that.

The power of mutual funds is in their diversification. They buy lots of different shares. Some of them perform; some don't. But overall, the well-managed ones make money.

You should think of your portfolio as your own little mutual fund. That's because you have a more demanding client than do the managers of mutual funds: you!

Mutual fund managers can always go someplace else and get another job if the fund goes kaput (which, it is to be cheerfully noted, very rarely happens). You can't. You have to live on a reduced diet instead.

When you look at your portfolio, you must think of yourself as looking at your future, your children's education, your retirement, and your hopes and aspirations. Your investments can bring those things happily about, or they can prevent them or make them far more difficult. You don't want to risk it all on just one or two investments or even one or two kinds of investments.

The importance of building diversity into your portfolio from the outset is illustrated by the fact that you want to move investments around only when you absolutely must. The reason is obvious enough: When you buy and sell, much of your profit is eaten up in commissions. Playing the market generally enriches your broker and no one else.

This isn't to suggest that you shouldn't sell when the need arises— but make sure the need has arisen! Those who succumbed to the silly and tragic panic of October 1987 lost a lot of money. Those who did nothing ended up recovering their losses and going on to new profits. The truly cool heads who bought right after the panic are now wealthy.

It's obvious, too, that setbacks in one place may well fuel advances elsewhere, which is yet another reason for diversification.

Remember: No matter how strong the company (or municipality) looks, no matter how promising its prospects, it is subject to the same quirks of fate as everything else is. It's only common sense to put those eggs in several baskets.

HOW MUCH RISK?

There comes a time in every investor's life where a decision has to be made: How much risk is acceptable?

Actually, here are several times in your life as an investor that you'll need to ask that question, and each time, the answer is likely to be different.

Risk is one of three interrelated factors involved in investments. The other two are market price and yield. If you know any two, you can pretty well figure the third.

For example, if you know that a particular stock, bond, or mutual fund share offers high yield at a low price, you can be sure that it's pretty risky. If you know of a high-risk investment and you know its price, you can fairly easily figure out what yield the market requires of it before driving its price still lower in order to achieve a yield that corresponds to the risk. Conversely, if you know the yield and the risk, you can calculate the price.

If you plotted these three factors on a graph, you would discover that the market is remarkably good at adjusting the factor it can control—price— to bring it into line with the other two. (The rules are temporarily suspended, along with sanity, when takeovers are rumored. Then nothing makes much sense, and fortunes are made and lost for no good reason whatsoever.)

What investments are riskiest? Which ones are least risky?

Treasury securities are the safest. Money market mutual funds are next in safety. Like U.S. government securities, they have a place in everyone's portfolio. They are followed by high quality corporate bonds and guaranteed or insured municipal bonds. These too are recommended.

Following, in order, are lower grade corporate and municipal bonds (though they can themselves in many cases be insured, making them, of course, safer).

It is only now that we get to the best of the blue-chip stocks, which are followed by the more speculative shares and bonds—right down to those that are extremely speculative and pretty much to be avoided. Stock options and indexes and commodities are the riskiest investments.

What you select will be based in part upon your objectives. Is one goal shorter-term, such as accumulating enough money for a down payment on a home? Is another longer-term, for example, financing college educations?

What types of investments generally might accomplish such objectives? For the example of financing college educations: Starting soon, you'll want investments that are relatively stable, to preserve your capital yet also produce higher income; if many years off, you'll want growth-oriented investments, to offset adverse effects of inflation.

If you lived through the Great Depression, or have relatives who did and who told you of its horrors, it's entirely understandable that anything that even remotely smacks of speculation gives you the shivers. But I'm here to tell you that there are times when you can afford to take more risk than is wise at other times.

When you are just starting out, for instance, you probably have more money, in proportion to your lower expenses and fewer responsibilities, than you are likely to have for many years.

This is when you should begin building a portfolio of very safe securities. But this is also when you can set aside part of your investment dollar for what are euphemistically called aggressive growth stocks. What this means is that you're going to take some of your money and put it into risky issues in hope of making a substantial profit. The purpose of the exercise is to build a good-sized amount of money to put into safer issues.

You can continue to afford to take some risks. The important thing to avoid is becoming addicted to risk. There is nothing like making a big hit on a speculative issue to make one feel invulnerable and omnipotent. Soon thereafter, it will cross your mind how much more you would have made if you had put everything you had into that one issue. Unless you quickly catch yourself, soon after that you'll probably lose everything. Don't do it—second guessing of that sort is like saying "If only I'd picked those numbers" after the lottery winner is announced.

As you grow older, your responsibilities, expenses, and income are likely to increase. You'll be socking away money in retirement accounts and in securities for your children's education—investments that should, of course, be quite secure. But as your wealth grows and it becomes clear that your needs and those of your family will be met, it is again possible to dabble in some of the riskier issues.

(A good way to do this is through a mutual fund that specializes in growth issues. The risk is spread out so that even if one company or another does poorly, the others will keep the fund afloat.)

Then, as you approach retirement, it's time to pull back a little, to assume a more conservative posture.

A final word about risk: Properly understood and carefully monitored, it can help you maximize your investment income. The mistake is made if you fail to recognize the risky nature of some investments, or become too fond of putting money—especially borrowed money—into risky businesses.

Asset Allocation: The term "asset allocation" became popular in the late 1980s. But the methodology has been around forever. It's just diversifying individual or mutual fund portfolios among different kinds of issues—mostly money market, bonds, and common stocks. (Some asset allocators also include options, indexes, going short, commodities, real estate, and precious metals.) The old-fashioned name for this is "balanced" investing.

By using the historical patterns of risk and return for these broad categories of investment, you can design a portfolio to earn the greatest possible return at the lowest possible risk. For example, according to Ibbotson Associates, between 1926 and 1988 risk for stocks was 20.9 percent, while the return (dividends plus price appreciation) was 12.1 percent. The risk and reward figures for bonds were 8.5 percent and 4.7 percent, respectively; for T-bills, the figures were 3.6 percent and 3.3 percent.

If a return of 3.3 percent was acceptable to you, you could simply hold T-bills. Your risk would be the lowest possible—3.6 percent. But if you wanted a higher return, you'd have to invest in other instruments and assume more risk. Let's say you wanted to earn 4 percent. Splitting your portfolio evenly between T-bills (earning 3.3 percent) and bonds (earning 4.7 percent) would accomplish this. But now your overall risk would be 6.05 percent, thanks to the extra risk you assumed investing in bonds. And if you needed such a high return that you needed to include stocks in your portfolio, your risk would really jump.

(How is risk measured? Professionals define risk for investment purposes as the "percentage standard deviation of annual return"; in other words, the amount that the actual return tends to vary from the overall return. This sounds complicated, but it really makes a lot of sense. Investments that can appreciate—or depreciate—sharply are, by definition, more risky than other investments that experience more moderate price swings; your chances of losing your money are greater with the former than with the latter. Standard deviation simply measures the size of the price swings.)

This is often combined with another old-fashioned approach, "market timing," so the asset allocators may switch and emphasize asset segments (reflecting their view of which way the market's going) more than balanced investors (who maintain approximate percentages of their holdings among money-market instruments, bonds, and common stocks).

YOUR INVESTMENT BUDGET

Will stocks, bonds, or other investments rise, fall, or remain stable? Like all other investors, you have no way of being sure.

However you may invest, you always should be aware of your risk temperament and tolerance. There's an old Wall Street expression, "Never buy beyond the sleeping point." What is your attitude toward risk? You want maximum safety; you don't want to risk any loss? Are you willing to speculate and take substantial risk of losses for possible maximum gains? Or do you fall somewhere in between?

Once you have determined your risk temperament and tolerance you can match these to investment securities choices (individually or through mutual funds).

Then relate your risk attitude and securities choices to the principal objectives of such securities, individually or through mutual funds (preservation of capital, more income, some income and some growth, long-term growth, shorter-term aggressive appreciation, tax advantages), and to your investment goals (funding a better lifestyle, a new home, college educations, your own business, retirement, etc.).

Dollar-Cost Averaging: Here's a simple way to hedge against jolts in the markets: Stagger your purchases through dollar-cost averaging, instead of investing a large sum all at once. You may not make the biggest possible score, but you won't take a big hit, either.

The shares, bonds, funds, and so on that you choose are only one dimension of diversification. Being diversified does not simply apply to what you invest in. It also applies to how and when you should invest.

Dollar-cost averaging allows you to diversify the prices at which you buy and sell. You may not always buy at the lowest prices, but you certainly won't end up paying unusually or artificially high prices, either.

How in the world can that be? Simple. When the price of those securities declines, you'll be able to buy more shares, bonds, whatever.

You don't believe it, do you? It sounds a little bit like smoke and mirrors—like the pitch from one of those scalawags I've spent years warning you to avoid. Okay, let's look at an example.

Let's say that you're interested in a stock or mutual fund that is selling at $15 per share. Three months pass, and the price drops to $10. Then, three months later, it's selling for $25, but then it drops again three months later to $20.

Okay. Add up the prices and you arrive at the cost of one share purchased at each of these times. You'll arrive at $70, which averages $17.50 per share. But guess what? You didn't buy it by the share. You bought it by the dollar.

You bought $1,000 in shares every three months. This works out to 66 2/3 shares at your initial investment, when the shares were $15; 100 shares three months later when they were selling at $10; only 40 shares at $40, in the ninth month of your investment plan; and, finally, 50 shares at $20. That comes to 256 2/3 shares. Divide $4,000 by 256 2/3. it comes out to $15.58, which is less than the average price.

Because, of course, your dollar went further when shares were cheaper. This meant you could buy more of them. When shares were expensive, you bought fewer.

Dollar-cost averaging is designed for conservative, sensible investors. After all, had you bought all your shares when they were $10, you would now have 400 shares. But at that point, the shares had been declining, and had they dropped to $5, you would have lost half your investment.

Conversely, had you decided that this was an up-and-coming stock (after all, it had gone from $10 to $25 in just three months), at the end of the year you would have $3,200 to show for your $4,000.

Roughly speaking (because distributions and dividends vary), this is how dividend, interest, and capital gains reinvestment works. The money buys as much as it can of whatever issues there are at their current price.

This technique can be applied to a variety of investments, even precious metals or certificates of deposit. But dollar-cost averaging is especially suited to the purchase of securities whose prices are somewhat volatile but tend to appreciate in the long run: stocks and shares in mutual funds.

Now comes an interesting question: If it works when you buy, what does it do when you sell? After all, that's when you are looking to get something above, rather than below, average.

And if you sell exactly in reverse of your purchases, you'll do just that. So you let the dollar value and number of shares switch places. Now, you sell a specific number of shares at each interval. When prices are higher, you'll get more money. It works.

Now comes the unhappy news—you knew there had to be some. This example has failed to take into account brokerage commissions. Obviously, a larger number of transactions translates directly into greater commissions.

If the stocks are very volatile, if you buy large numbers of shares, and if you use a discount broker, you can still achieve success with this system.

But its real beauty lies in the purchase of mutual funds. No-load funds don't charge sales commissions. Your brilliant market play can be untarnished.

WHAT PRICE LIQUIDITY?

Too much is sometimes made of the liquidity of investments. This may sound like heresy, but it's not.

Liquidity has its price. It is a component of the risk element of an investment: An investment is, or at least seems, less risky if you know that you can get out of it anytime you want.

In practice, when you want to is often the worst possible time to get out of your investments. If you are one of the many who unloaded shares in October of 1987, you probably wish today that it would have taken a week or two to get through to your broker. The safety of liquidity is often a mirage.

If you get into an investment that has proved to be disappointing over a period of time, by all means get out of it and put your money into something better. But you're foolish—and it's expensive foolishness—to try to respond to the day-to-day quirks of any of the securities markets. (The commodities markets are different. Fortunes are made and lost in seconds. That's why they are almost surely no place for you to put your money, as you'll learn in due course.)

The issue of liquidity of investments, the ability to get into and out of the market in a hurry, obscures and even goes at cross purposes with the reasons you invest. It is not important how quickly you can get out. What is important is picking good investments and sticking with them.

It is easy to wonder what many of the broadcast business reports and even some in the financial press are talking about. That's unfair in a way, because the very latest information that might signal trends is important. But when looking for trends where there may be none or inflating the importance of rapidly moving money around becomes of greater importance than measured investment carefully made, closely monitored, and pretty much left to grow, the emphasis isn't where it should be.

Investing isn't the lottery. It isn't a television game show. Sometimes it happens that a big gain is made, but it's almost always by accident.

Don't lose sight of your goals. They are why you invest. Make investments that you feel reasonably sure will bring those goals about. Unless something happens that shakes your confidence in those investments being able to do what you bought them to do, stick with 'em.

THE FINANCIAL SUPERMARKET

Among the hottest items in today's financial supermarkets are central assets accounts—with banks, brokers, savings institutions, and even insurance companies scrambling to offer you these all-in-one accounts . . . if you're fairly well off.

A central assets account consolidates your banking and investment accounts; offers you such brokers' features as trading in securities and margin loans; tops the package with such banking services as a checking account, access to cash, and a debit, credit, or charge card.

All central assets accounts automatically "sweep"—meaning they invest or transfer available cash into some type of interest-bearing account so that your money keeps working.

To keep you informed on all transactions and activities, you receive a detailed monthly statement.

Since 1977, when Merrill Lynch introduced the concept, cash management accounts have mushroomed in popularity. Not everyone qualifies for cash management accounts. A typical minimum initial investment ranges from $5,000 to $25,000 in cash, securities, or a combination thereof. In addition, you pay an annual fee—from $25 to $100—and possibly other monthly fees or service charges. You also may pay for the bank card.

To make the decision still more complicated, some companies now offer features such as free travelers' checks, electronic deposit of paychecks and government benefits, research reports, and access to networks of automatic teller machines.

Many accounts also offer a routine breakdown of expenses, and you can get a year-end, or even monthly, tax summary.

In shopping for a cash management account, consider:

- How often does the company sweep available cash? Some do so every day, no matter how trifling the amount; others do so weekly. And, at least one account sweeps small amounts at monthly intervals and large sums either daily or weekly.

- Most accounts offer a selection of three money funds for the sweep: A cash fund, a government fund, and a tax-free fund. Read the account prospectus carefully before you make a selection about which fund you want.

- Will your account offer full-service or discount brokerage? Does it matter to you?

- What kind of checking account will you get? Some programs limit the number of checks you can write every month; others place restrictions on the amount of the checks. Still others provide unlimited checking services.

You also may be able to tap into the loan value of the securities in your account simply by writing a check.

Note, though, that not all companies automatically return cancelled checks. If you want to retrieve a particular check, you may have to request it, and possibly pay a fee. If cancelled checks are part of your tax records, as they are with many people, this will be quite important to you and could, in fact, be the determining factor between two nearly equal accounts.

8

INVESTING IN
——— BONDS ———

When the stock market makes you uncomfortable (as it probably does sometimes and may do frequently), you can find a degree of stability by investing in bonds.

Bonds have a place in every well-thought-out portfolio. They come in almost every imaginable flavor and color: corporate, local, state, federal; short-term, intermediate-term, long-term; highly speculative, reasonably risky, and unparalleled in safety.

Bonds are loans, which means they differ from, for instance, stocks in that you can be fairly sure of their yield at the time you buy them. A company or local, state, or the federal government (or special authority thereof, such as quasi-governmental organizations that build roads, bridges, power plants, or sports stadiums) needs to raise money, generally for some sort of improvement to its physical facilities. It issues bonds, which are IOUs. You lend the entity a specific amount of money, and you are repaid at a specified time. Interest may be sent to you from time to time, or it may be collected when the bond matures.

That is the simplest explanation. Of course, nothing is simple anymore. As interest rates rise and fall, the value of your IOU—your bond—rises and falls as well. And as we shall see, interest rates today are more volatile than ever before.

The same holds true of inflation. If the rate of inflation comes close to or exceeds the yield of your bond, then its value drops, because a buyer could achieve a higher yield by putting his or her money someplace else.

To top it all off, many bonds are subject to early redemption. Let's assume that a project ends up costing less than was originally planned. (As

118

unrealistic as it sounds, this has actually happened.) The entity that issued the bonds finds itself with some money left over. It will pay interest on this money for 5, 10, 20 years—whatever is the term of the bonds. Of course, it doesn't want to do this. So it may pay off some of the bonds—give you your money back, with interest for the time the money was being used. Then you have to go out and reinvest.

Or perhaps the facility that was built has proved more profitable than projections suggested. Maybe the company was more successful than it ever had hoped. Perhaps everyone flocked to the new bridge or highway, despite the tolls. Bonds can be called and cashed.

Or interest rates could fall. The powers that be could meet and decide that it's silly to continue paying the high rate on these bonds, when they could borrow the money at a much lower rate elsewhere. What do they do? They issue a new set of bonds. What do they do with the money? They pay you off. Your bonds are redeemed. You have to reinvest, at a lower rate if you seek the same degree of safety, or in a riskier investment, if you seek the same yield.

Bonds, securities that seem positively boring compared to exciting things like stocks and real estate joint ventures, don't just sit there. They need to be chosen carefully and followed carefully as well.

BONDS AND INTEREST RATES. Just because the face value of the bond is $1,000—meaning that $1,000 was invested in the company—that doesn't mean that $1,000 is what you'll pay to own it. This is because bond prices rise and fall, though not as wildly as those of shares of stock. The bond's denomination, $1,000, is called "par." When the bond sells for less than its face value, it's said to be selling "below par." When the price is more than the face value, it is "above par."

Because the rate of return on bonds is fixed, the only way they can respond to a changing market is for their market price to change. The market, as you can see, adjusts prices to fit the prevailing interest rates. Imagine that you have a $1,000 bond that pays 5 percent. After you bought it, interest rates rose to 10 percent. In effect, the $1,000 bond paying $50 would be worth only $500 to a buyer in the market, to yield the 10 percent currently available elsewhere.

While the value of bonds decreases when interest rates rise, their value increases when interest rates decline. Suppose the $1,000 bond you owned paid 10 percent, and interest rates have now dropped to 5 percent. For every $1,000 you invested then, an investor now would have to invest $2,000 to receive the same amount of interest. The total value of your bond, principal plus interest, is therefore higher given current rates. This means that you can sell your bond at a premium, which will be the difference between the current rate and the higher rate your bond pays.

This model is not perfect; in the case of rising interest rates, the $1,000 bond wouldn't decline as much as our example states, because the face value still would be $1,000, which could be realized at maturity redemption. And if yields fail to keep up with inflation (which was raging throughout the '70s), people will demand even higher yields—or choose to spend their money, rather than invest it, figuring that prices for the same items would be much higher tomorrow.

The point is that the value of bonds rises and falls to remain constant with the prevailing yields of the day. This means that when the interest rates fall, the prices of existing bonds rise; when interest rates rise, the prices of bonds fall.

BOND RATINGS. Apart from interest rates, there are some other considerations that you face when looking to invest in corporate or governmental (non-U.S. Treasury) bonds. The safety of the bonds is tied directly to the financial strength and stability of the entity issuing the bonds. This means that while most bonds are a relatively safe investment—safer, for instance, than shares of stock in the same company—they are not free of risk. They do not carry the guarantees that bank-based investments do. So your research must go beyond a comparison of yields and maturity dates.

Fortunately, you have help. Ratings services—Moody's and Standard & Poor's—analyze the quality of bond issues and are constantly updating those ratings. Their analyses are available through your broker or, in all likelihood, at your local library.

Both Standard & Poor's and Moody's rate bonds using a letter code. The best bonds are rated "AAA." The second-best are "AA," followed by "A," "BBB," "BB," and so on. Because of the connection between yield and safety, the best bonds sell for more, all else (meaning the yield) being equal.

As is the case with other investments, you should not buy bonds so that you can play the market, which is to say, to buy and sell based on minor fluctuations in interest rates. In most cases, all you'll be doing is enriching your broker. Bonds are best purchased for long-term income, and a departure from this should come only when there are sufficient swings to make a change handsomely profitable.

The most important rule in investing is that you must diversify—have an investment portfolio that carries a variety of stocks, bonds, and other things. But because bonds sell in the $1,000 range, it is difficult to diversify sufficiently. There are ways around this. One is through bond-based mutual funds (see Chapter 10). The other is through bond pools set up by your broker where, through a much smaller investment, you can buy part of a bond.

THE INTEREST RATE
ROLLER COASTER

The Federal Reserve does much to determine interest rates, and therefore the availability of money, through manipulations of the interest rate it charges member banks for the use of money. When the rate is reduced, the Fed is making money more affordable to the banks, which can then afford to offer it at more attractive rates to their customers—all of which results in more money in circulation. The speed of money—its velocity, or the rapidity with which it changes hands—is just as important as how much of it there is to begin with. By putting more into circulation, though, the effect has been to speed up its movement, generally for the betterment of the economy.

But sometimes this energy gets wasted. All that happens is that the prices of things go up—inflation. The money simply becomes less valuable. The Fed's difficult task is to determine the extent to which it can feed money into the economy without overloading it to the extent that inflation surges upward. Conversely, in an effort to avoid inflation, the Fed can tighten the supply of money by increasing the rate so as to make money more expensive and less available. The higher rate then tends to slow the economy by its effects on other interest rates (and on financial analysts and commentators).

Apart from the effect that the Fed has on the money supply, interest rates are also determined by what the market thinks money is worth. Because safety is not really an issue with U.S. Treasury securities, the yields produced at Treasury auctions are seen as an important indicator of the price of money. In the case of many securities, however, this figure is difficult to arrive at, because there's no way of being certain to what extent the price of a given security is altered by considerations such as safety.

One of the most significant economic events of the '80s (actually, October 6, 1979) was the decision by then-Fed Chairman Paul Volcker that rampant inflation had to be stopped at all costs. This was done by fixing the supply of money; interest rates would be allowed to float according to supply and demand. Interest rates skyrocketed and became much more volatile than they had been.

(Also, bond prices—influenced as they are by interest rates—became much less predictable, experienced sharper variations in price, and, in short, became—in some hands, at least—vehicles for speculation.)

As a rule, and a very sensible rule if you think about it, long-term interest rates are higher than short-term rates. It is a premium paid to the bond holder for committing money for a long time, which reduces the investment's liquidity somewhat and gives the issuing agency or company money it does not have to repay quickly.

But there is another factor in the rates paid on government bonds: The market's predictions of inflation. That's because it would be silly to accept a 5 percent interest rate for, say, 10 years if the inflation rate is twice that. At the end of the 10 years, the investor would have lost, in effect, a yearly average of 5 percent in real terms.

When the "long bond"—the 30-year Treasury bond—yields less than shorter-term government securities, then, it means this: The Fed has raised short-term interest rates in the hope of stemming inflation, and the market believes it will work.

In 1989, short-term interest rates grew until they were higher than long-term rates. Economic figures, especially the producer price index, indicated that inflation was becoming a threat. The Federal Reserve Board, charged with defending the value of the dollar against inflation's erosion, planned and took action. This came in the form of making reserves less available, which is to say they raised the interest rate—called the federal funds rate—they charge to banks that borrow money from the Fed.

This caused short-term rates to rise. The reasoning behind this action is that when it costs more to borrow money, the economy slows down. When the economy slows down, there is generally a reduction in inflation.

(There have been exceptions. When there is enormous upward pressure on wages, for instance, a slowing economy can still experience inflation, a condition known to economists as "stagflation," which means a stagnant economy with inflation anyway.)

Many financial analysts will tell you that when there is an "inverted yield curve"—financialese for short-term rates being higher than long-term ones—a recession will follow. They point to historical examples, and to an extent they are right. This situation has, in fact, preceded recessions. But that doesn't mean—and it shouldn't be used to imply—a cause-and-effect relationship.

Why, then, does this seem always to presage a recession?

Think of the economy being pulled in two directions at the same time. On one side, the forces of inflation are pulling at the economic system. On the other side, recession is trying with all its might to pull the economy in that direction. When all is well, these pressures are about equal, and a healthy economy remains in the safe zone. The Fed acts as a kind of referee in this contest. When it sees one side of this economic tug-of-war getting too strong, it adds its strength to the other side in an effort to keep the economy in the safe zone. Its goal is to keep either side from winning.

The problem, historically, has been that it's difficult for the Federal Reserve Board to gauge the amount of help that's needed. So it has tended to give a mighty yank, pulling the economy not to safety but to the other side completely. Efforts to slow inflation have frequently dragged the nation into a recession.

This is a simplified description of the situation, but it explains an unusual, and at first blush alarming, state of affairs. The relationship between an "inverted rate curve" and recession exists only when the Fed over-compensates—when its enthusiasm for stopping inflation causes it to push too hard in the other direction, spawning a recession. It is like a physician giving too much medicine to a patient who, instead of being cured, dies from the overdose.

This time, the bond market believed that the Fed's medicine would work. Bond traders spoke in terms of a "measured response," meaning that this time, the Fed was giving just a little tug, reflected in higher rates for the moment but no adverse long-term effects. Thus, bond buyers were reacting to the current reality, but presuming that over the long haul it's pretty much business as usual.

In fact, a recession was avoided. Bond traders and institutional investors concluded that the Fed had refined its actions to a considerable degree, and this time would not use a steamroller to squash a bug. While the Fed is subject to change because its philosophy changes over time, the market decided that—at least this time—the central bank was able to provide just the right adjustment to achieve the desired effect.

Why should you care?

- First, it meant that the 1989 conditions were not especially good for borrowing money. The market was right; as the threat of inflation decreased, interest rates headed back down.

- Second, short-term investments in Treasury securities are a good value at such times. This is especially true if you deal with Treasury Direct.

- Third, it illustrates how the world is full of Chicken Littles, and sometimes it seems as though most of them have hung their shingles in the financial portion of town. It was heartening, though, to see everyone involved in the bond market and in the government act responsibly and do just what was called for.

HOW TO INVEST IN BONDS

As I said earlier in this chapter, bonds are best purchased for long-term income, and departure from this should come only when there are sufficient swings to make a change handsomely profitable. But because bonds have an element of value that is determined by interest rates, you should pay attention to the direction interest rates are headed when you are contemplating buying bonds.

The best time to invest in bonds is when interest rates appear close to their peak. Although even experts have trouble guessing turns in interest rates, they generally follow the economy. When the economy is growing rapidly, interest rates are usually rising. In a hot economy, with rising interest rates, the only time you want to invest in bonds are when you want to lock in an interest level for the long term by holding bonds until maturity.

Although bonds are more stable than stocks, they have their own unique risk feature in that their short-term value drops as interest rates rise. So the degree of risk you're willing to bear will determine your investment strategy in bonds. For minimal risk, look for long-term bonds that you're prepared to hold until maturity. When investing in long-term issues, double-check the call date, because many issues can be retired before they reach full maturity.

If you're willing to accept a somewhat greater degree of risk, you can seek to make a profit from falling interest rates by investing in short-term and intermediate-term bonds. The more time before a bond matures, the more its value fluctuates with changes in interest rates, so investing in short-term bonds minimizes the fluctuation in value interest rate changes will cause. Bond mutual funds are another alternative; their share price will vary with interest rates, too.

If you're confident that interest rates will fall, and you have capital available for speculation, you can invest in long-term Treasury bonds. Again, the more time before a bond matures, the more its value fluctuates with changes in interest rates; long-term bonds have the sharpest price changes (and the greatest opportunity for significant price appreciation).

You don't want to bet on falling interest rates through municipal or corporate bonds. Why? Because their value is not only a function of interest rates, but of their bond rating. If bonds are downgraded by the bond rating services, any price appreciation from falling interest rates could be wiped out. These bonds should be invested in only if you find their current after-tax yields attractive.

There are other issues that come into play when considering yield. For example, as discussed below, most people who are in lower tax brackets won't be able to take full advantage of tax-exempt bonds. It is very foolish to buy tax-exempts for your individual retirement account, because IRA income isn't taxed until you retire—at which time you'll probably be in a lower bracket. The same is true of Keogh plans, which are very much like IRAs for the self-employed.

CORPORATE BONDS

Because of their fixed rate of return, which can be counted upon except in the direst of disasters, corporate bonds are excellent sources of steady, reliable, predictable income. They are also typically safer than stocks by a degree or two.

Because they are a little more speculative (though just a little) than instruments such as bank certificates of deposit, they usually pay a higher return than CDs. Remember, there is a direct and corresponding relationship between risk and return. Your daily newspaper carries listings that are an easy way to compare various issues. For an explanation, see Chart 15.

The typical face value, or denomination, of a corporate bond is $1,000. This is the amount the corporation will repay when the bond matures, at a date specified on the bond itself. Under certain circumstances, the bond may be retired earlier, which is to say called in and paid off by the issuer.

(This knowledge could cause you to panic if you open the local newspaper to check the bond prices, because you will instantly imagine that prices have fallen terribly. Not so. There is a kind of agreed-upon shorthand that allows the final zero to be excised from the listing, so that a $1,000 issue will be listed as $100.)

ZERO-COUPON BONDS

If you're investing for long-term financial growth, you may want to consider zero-coupon bonds. Sometimes called "strips," they are excellent instruments for any goal that doesn't rely on income over the course of the investment, such as retirement or college.

Zero-coupon bonds pay all their interest at the end, when they mature. Interestingly, you are required to pay yearly taxes on this interest, even though you haven't received it (unless the bonds are part of an individual retirement account or Keogh).

Like government securities (described below), zero-coupon bonds are sold at a discount. That means you pay less than face value when you buy them, but redeem them at their face value. Because the interest payments are stored up inside the bond, and are constantly being reinvested at the

CHART 15

Corporate Bond Market Listings In Your Daily Newspapers								
52 Weeks			Curr.					Net
High	Low	Bond	Yld.	Vol.	High	Low	Close	Chg.
103	98	Smith Corp. 14s 91	14	75	101	100¾	101	+¼

Newspaper listings report the prior day's bond transactions on the bond exchanges and over-the-counter.

Corporate bonds typically are issued in $1,000 denominations, so you have to multiply the interest rate and the market prices and price changes by 10. Thus, the "14s" of Smith Corp.'s bond is 14 percent, which would be $140 annual interest on the $1,000 face value. Smith's "91" bond matures in 1991.

The "High[est]" and "Low[est]" prices at which the bonds traded are shown for the "52 [preceding] Weeks" at left, and for the day at right. The "Close" is the final trade price (101 = $1,010).

"Net Chge." is the change in price if any between the previous day's close (not shown) and the listing day's close ("+¼" = up $2.50).

"Vol." (Volume) is the amount sold during the day ("75" – 75 $1,000 face value bonds).

"Cur. Yld." (Current Yield) "14" is approximately 14 percent on 101.

bond's initial rate, the value of zero-coupon bonds fluctuates more drastically than most other bonds as interest rates shift.

MUNICIPAL, STATE, AND LOCAL GOVERNMENT BONDS

Cities, towns, villages, counties, states, and special authorities thereof also issue bonds (generically referred to as municipals). Their yield is free from federal income taxes, and state and local taxes as well, if you happen to live in the city or state that issued them.

Of course, the tax savings are reflected in the yield. We will discuss that more in a little while. To familiarize yourself with municipal bond listings in the newspaper, see Chart 16.

There are basically two kinds of municipal bonds: general obligation and revenue. You could probably figure out from their names the difference between them.

General obligation bonds are bonds that are paid from the issuing body's general fund, which is to say that interest and principal are paid from the taxes and fees taken in by the city, county, or state. They are backed by the

CHART 16

Municipal Bonds Listings In Your Newspapers*				
Debt Issue	*Coupon* %	*Maturity*	*Price*	*YTM* %
Municipality Authority Issue	8.000	11-15-Yr.	98⅞	8.10

"Debt Issue(s)" may include various types of municipal general obligation or revenues notes (shorter maturities) and bonds (longer maturities).

"Coupon %" is the coupon yield: the interest rate when the bond was issued. The "8.000" above is 8%, which was $80 on a $1,000 bond.

"Maturity" is the date on which the principal amount of the debt issue becomes due and payable. Also known as redemption date.

"Price" is the price at which the issue is currently trading in the market. For a $1,000 issue you have to multiply the price by 10; "98⅞" (98.875) would be $988.75.

"YTM" (Yield to Maturity) is the rate of return held to redemption including gain or loss from the current market price.

*Format of listings may vary in different newspapers. Most newspapers will carry these listings weekly instead of daily; and since there are so many issues, will only carry a representative number of issues. Some title the listings "Tax Exempt Bonds" instead of "Municipal Bonds."

full faith and credit of the issuing body, which means that the entire city, county, or state would have to go belly up to prevent the principal and interest payments from being made.

Revenue bonds are a little riskier. That's because they are repaid with money earned by whatever project the money was raised to finance in the first place. They're a little bit like an investment in a start-up business, because you don't really know whether the project will ever earn a dime.

Revenue bonds, however, are sometimes guaranteed, either by the parent governmental unit or by a corporation. Guaranteed bonds, being less risky, cost more than those that aren't.

This doesn't mean that revenue bonds are a bad idea. While there have been frivolous bond issues in which governments have built things that weren't needed (and in some cases brought the inefficiencies of government into competition with more efficient and therefore more profitable private business), such cases are by far in the minority. More often, revenue bonds build a bridge, toll road, or sewer project. People need to get to work, cross the river, and dispose of household wastes, so there will be income from these projects.

Perhaps as important is a consideration of the political situation in connection with a particular issue. If the need for a given project is hotly contested, the issuance of the bonds and, later, payment of interest and principal, can become a political football. For some reason, politicians love to speak of investors as some sort of criminals—people who deserve to lose their money. Fomenting war between the rich and poor is the stuff of which some political careers are made. It's never understood that many of the so-called rich got to be so by working hard and investing carefully. In any case, an issue of revenue bonds that is popular, well thought out, and generally believed to be necessary is always a better investment than one that has been the subject of hot dissension.

When municipal bonds are issued, which is to say when the government agency borrows money from you, the issuing body doesn't want to have to face a day when it has to repay all the money. So it takes out what amounts to an installment loan in the form of serial maturity. That's when some of the bonds mature in a year, some in two years, three years, and so on. The longer your money is tied up, the higher the yield will be.

Think of it in the same way you might think of an auto loan. You wouldn't borrow money to buy a car for, say, 36 months, with your payments for the first 35 only being interest and then, as the final payment, you would have to repay the entire principal. Serial maturity is the way governments borrow money on the installment plan.

Unlike corporate bonds, municipal bonds typically are issued in $5,000 denominations. Even those that have a lower face value are usually sold in $5,000 blocks.

You can also purchase zero-coupon municipal bonds, which offer the long-term advantages of zeros with the tax advantages of munis.

Safety—Your First Concern: About half a billion dollars in municipal bonds were defaulted on during the first six months of 1989. That represents about 1 percent of the munis sold during the same time.

While that statistic shouldn't send you rushing to your broker to unload your bonds, it is cause for concern. Most people buy municipal bonds at least in part because of their very high security.

Though it is possible to maintain virtually total security in municipal bonds, it will cost you. There are four ways of doing it:

PURCHASE YOUR BONDS VERY CAREFULLY. This means buying only the highest-rated issues. Because they are the safest, their yield is less. Triple-A bonds, as rated by Moody's or Standard & Poor's, are the best. Double-A issues are almost as safe at slightly better rates.

PURCHASE INSURED BONDS. These will yield one-eighth to one-half percent less than the same issues uninsured. But if for some reason the bond collapses, you will still get your money. When considering these bonds, though, take into account the price of the insurance over the life of the bonds.

YOU CAN ALSO BUY AFTER-MARKET INSURANCE FOR BONDS YOU ALREADY OWN. The cost depends on the bond's rating. Information is available through your broker. Again, consider the cost against the yield of the bond at maturity.

BOND FUNDS OFFER SAFETY THROUGH DIVERSIFI- CATION. Depending on the fund, and on its philosophy and staff, muni funds are generally quite safe, with the higher-yielding ones more subject to fluctuations. Again, investigate carefully before you invest. Most bond funds are "front-loaded," which is to say that you pay sales commissions and costs at the time of purchase.

You should consider adding municipal bonds to your portfolio for several reasons. First among them is the relative safety munis enjoy. Corporations come and go—and disappear down the great maw of corporate raiders. But cities are on a slightly more solid footing. They don't normally close up and go away. They collect taxes, which support general obligation bonds, and they engage in other projects, financed by revenue bonds—which depend on the success of the enterprise. And cities generally don't fail to pay their bills, despite the small but worrisome trend to the contrary.

Second on the list is the favorable tax consideration afforded the yield from municipal bonds. Some offer exemption from federal, state, and local taxes for all but those who face minimum tax exposure. Virtually all offer some tax savings. The effect, of course, is to increase the yield. This is some- thing you should know in detail about any given issue before you buy.

The third reason is less economic than philosophical. You may wish to finance projects that you believe are of public value. There is much to be said for investing funds in projects that you believe are worthy. Much of the country was so built.

But you mustn't let your wishes get ahead of your judgement; castles in the air are of no use to anyone. View offerings that fit your disposition as coldly as you would any other investment. If anything, you should hold your investment plans in local governments and projects to a higher standard. They tend to lag behind the cutting edge in efficiency.

The bottom line is this: Municipal bonds continue to be a fine investment in the vast majority of cases. The small default rate doesn't necessarily indicate a big trend. It should be, though, enough to get your attention. It suggests that you should evaluate your portfolio if you hold munis. It demands that you make your purchases carefully. Evaluate them with your eyes open. Compare them to similar offerings that have failed. Are the similarities important? Are the differences?

Finally, think of the place municipal bonds have in your portfolio. They shouldn't be adventurous. Save that small portion of your investment dollar for stocks. Bonds should be something you can count on.

The unusually high default rate among municipal bonds tells you that you must be especially careful to see that your bonds can, in fact, be counted upon.

Taxable Or Tax-Free Bonds? The idea of tax-free bonds—the idea of tax-free *anything*—sounds so good that you may be tempted to jump at it without really giving the question the thought it deserves.

First, you should know that tax-free bonds aren't always completely tax-exempt. You may still have to pay state and local income taxes on their yield. This depends on where you live and where the bonds were issued. And totally-exempt ("triple-exempt") bonds sell for more, of course, than those that are only federally tax-exempt. (To get an idea of the effective yields, look at Charts 17 and 18.)

If you live in a place that has no state or local income taxes, good for you. You don't have to worry about this. (Of course, triple-exempt bonds will still cost you more, even though you can't take advantage of all their provisions, because the prices will have been bid up by buyers in states where all the exemptions are of value.)

How do you determine whether the after-tax yield of a particular taxable bond is greater than the yield of a tax-free? In other words, how do you determine if you're a candidate for tax-exempt bonds?

It's simple. The first thing you must know is your tax bracket. If it's 15 percent, this means that 15 cents out of every dollar goes for taxes, leaving 85 cents, or $0.85. (This is Federal income tax only; you must add state and local taxes, if they apply, and subtract them, too, from your original dollar.)

Take the yield of the taxable bonds you're considering and multiply them by 0.85 (or whatever figure you've come up with). The yield of tax-exempts (or triple-exempts, if you've included all income taxes) must be higher than the figure you arrive at for there to be an advantage to your buying them.

CHART 17

Tax-Free U.S. Taxable Investment Yields

WHICH investment that you're considering will provide you with a higher *after-tax* return: that high-yield taxable investment or that lower-yield tax-free investment? Use the formula below to find out. But *keep in mind* that highest-yield shouldn't be your *only* —not even your primary—consideration. First and foremost is: is it a *good* investment?

$$\frac{\text{Tax-free investment yield}}{\text{divided by}} = \begin{array}{c}\text{Taxable investment} \\ \text{yield} \\ \text{you need to surpass} \\ \text{the federal tax-free} \\ \text{investment yield} \\ \text{in the equation at} \\ \text{left}\end{array}$$

(Tax-free investment yield divided by 1 minus your federal tax bracket*)

Here's an example of how the formula works:

$$\frac{\text{6\% tax-free investment yield}}{\text{1 minus a 28\% federal tax bracket}} = \frac{6.00\%}{0.72} = \frac{0.72}{} \overline{6.00\%} = 8.33\%$$

$$(1.00 - 0.28 = 0.72)$$

Thus, in this example, in a 28% federal tax bracket, you need to surpass an 8.33% yield from a taxable investment to get a better return than the 6.00% federal tax-free investment provides.

Too complex? Not really. *Let's work your example:*

$$\frac{\text{Tax-free investment yield: \_\_\_ \%}}{\text{Your federal tax bracket: \_\_\_ \%}} = \frac{\_\_\_ \%}{} = \_\_\_ = \frac{_____}{} = \_\_\_ \%$$

1.00 minus your tax bracket
% = _____

*There now are just three federal tax brackets: 15%, 28%, and 33%. You also may live in a location where you have to pay state and local income taxes. There are some investments that in addition to being free of federal income taxes also are exempt from state ("double tax-exempt") and local ("triple tax-exempt") income taxes. You can adjust the formula above for the bracket to represent your combined total of federal, state, and local income taxes.

That's of course with all else being equal, and all else seldom is. So you must consider the safety of the alternative investments, as well as the likelihood that they'll be redeemed before maturity.

It's clear, then, that the higher your tax bracket, the likelier that tax-exempt bonds are a good idea for you.

CHART 18

Representative Tax-Free Investment Yields Compared To Taxable Investment Yields									
Federal Tax Bracket	A Tax-Free Yield* Of:								
	4%	5%	6%	7%	8%	9%	10%	11%	12%
	Is Equivalent to a Taxable Yield Of:								
28	5.6	6.9	8.3	9.7	11.1	12.5	13.9	15.3	16.7

*Investments also exempt from state and local taxes would increase the tax-free yield.

This lesson hasn't been wasted on the market. In 1970, a little more than $10 billion in long-term, tax-exempt bonds were sold by states and cities across the United States. Less than 20 years later, the figure was nearly 10 times that high. Individual investors buy about three-fourths of those bonds.

An important thing to remember is that interest on locally issued municipal bonds is not only federal income tax exempt, but usually exempt from state and local taxes as well. These are the triple-exempt bonds mentioned above. The problem is, if you live in another state, they're not as good a deal for you. If the city issuing the bonds itself has a high income tax, then the price of the bonds will be driven up by residents of that city who purchase them.

Should tax-free municipal bonds be part of your portfolio? Probably—and if not now, later, when your other investment vehicles have shifted into high gear and you can enjoy not just the safety but the tax advantages they afford. When that happy day comes to pass, pat yourself on the back—you've done well. Buy yourself a cup of coffee. Then get back to your portfolio: There's work to be done!

But how do you know when that happy day has arrived? If you're certain of your tax bracket, use the formula described above. If not, consider these things:

If you can afford to put a good deal of money aside for savings and investment, you are probably in a high enough tax bracket to at least consider tax-exempt bonds. Look at the overall picture, especially if interest rates are fluctuating, as they have been wont to do in recent years.

For instance, a couple living in the state of New York, but not the city thereof, and making as little as $29,751 net taxable income on a joint return pays a combined federal and state total of 33.7 percent in taxes. A combined total of $71,901 puts them in the top bracket, 38.6 percent. The chances are good that you fall somewhere in between. If that's true, you'll be surprised when you run the yield on tax-free bonds through the test above.

There are some other features that might make tax-free bonds attractive to you. Different combinations of interest rates and maturities can be tailored to fit your present and anticipated needs. Before you pick a particular bond issue, talk with your accountant or your financial adviser, or perhaps your broker, to determine what's best for you. When, for instance, do you plan to retire? If your investments are likely to be the major part of your retirement income, you'll need to factor in just how far away retirement is. Are you investing in large part to leave a legacy to your heirs? Or are you looking to build wealth for middle age, or to send your children to the best schools? How much safety can you cheerfully sacrifice in order to realize a higher yield?

No, bonds aren't the placid investments they sometimes seem to be.

TREASURY SECURITIES—LENDING AMERICA MONEY

The safest investment you can possibly make is made by lending money to the United States government.

There is substantial concern, some of it justified and some of it not, about the federal government's budget deficit. Some doomsayers warn of bankruptcy for the United States. Although those who hold gold would be better off than owners of government securities if the federal government were to default on its obligations, it is easy to look at the history of government securities and that of gold. In the 1980s, gold lost more than half its value. Government securities continued to pay handsomely.

It is, of course, up to you to decide for yourself which is more likely to happen in the future. But it is safe to believe with reasonable certainty that the U.S. Treasury is not terribly likely to default anytime this decade. It certainly won't without warning. It makes no more sense to stock up on gold against this eventuality than it does to stock up on rifles and ammunition.

If the government were ever to default on repayment of a treasury security plus interest, you might as well tear up your money because it wouldn't be worth anything then, either. In short, before you would have to worry about your Treasury securities, you would have many other far more pressing concerns.

The United States Department of the Treasury issues, basically, three securities: bills, notes, and bonds. (There is a fourth issue, savings bonds, that we'll get to in due course.) Like other bond issues, these are listed in your newspaper, as explained in Chart 19.

Treasury bills, or T-bills, are short-term securities, maturing in three or six months or one year. Like other Treasury securities, they are sold at discount, which means that instead of making interest payments, T-bills are sold at a discount—face value minus interest. Then, on maturity, they are redeemed at full face value. The major shortcoming of T-bills, to most investors, is that the smallest denomination is $10,000.

Treasury notes are intermediate and mature in from one to 10 years. The longer-term issues (those with more than four years until maturity) can be purchased in denominations as low as $1,000. The shorter-term Treasury notes are sold with a minimum $5,000 face value.

Treasury bonds are the big guns. The shortest-term Treasury bond matures in 10 years; the longest bond collects interest for 40 years. They are issued in denominations of as little as $1,000.

You have probably noticed that no mention has been made so far of the yield of these federal securities. That's because no one knows the yield until they are sold.

They are sold at auction. A week before each auction, the Treasury announces which securities, which is to say their date of maturity, it plans to auction.

How are the yields determined?

Three- and six-month T-bills are auctioned every Monday morning (or Tuesday, if Monday is a holiday); longer-term securities are sold periodically, usually every few weeks. (To find out when the auctions will be, you may phone the Bureau of the Public Debt at (202) 287-4113. You will hear a recording listing the dates of upcoming auctions and the results of recent ones.) The yield you will receive is the prevailing price set at that auction. Bidders make their bids in terms of yield. The lowest yields that are bid take the prize. Generally, the longer the time until maturity, the higher the yield, with rare exceptions (such as the one discussed earlier).

From that point on, the market value of the particular issue varies according to market pressure. Treasury securities are pieces of paper that state that on a specified date the U.S. government will give the bearer a specified sum of money. The market determines how much that piece of paper is worth. It varies from day to day, especially in times of fluctuating interest rates.

T-BILLS AND THE SMALL INVESTOR. Individual investment in Treasury securities is booming—recently, individual purchases of T-bills have averaged $2.5 billion each week. In a late April 1989 auction, for ex-

CHART 19

U.S. Treasury Bills Listings In Your Daily Newspapers			
Maturity Date	Bid Discount	Asked	Yield
7-14	7.10	6.90	7.00

The yield for U.S. Treasury bills (which are known as "T-bills") reflect quotes set by major financial institutions. In the example shown above for the previous day's closing transaction, a one-year $10,000 T-bill with "Yield 7.00 (%)" would be purchased for the discount amount of $9,300. It would be redeemed for the $10,000 face value at "Maturity Date 7-14" (July 14). The interest is the $700 gain ($10,000 − $9,300).

Yields fluctuate in the trading market between issuance date and maturity date. "Bid," above, is what buyers are offering to pay to purchase. "Asked" is the price at which sellers are willing to sell. The "Bid" price above is $9,290 and the "Asked" price is $9,310. Actual trades may take place at any price between the "Bid" and "Asked" prices. In this example, the sale price is $9,300, which produced the 7.00% yield.

ample, individuals purchased $1.65 billion of two-year T-notes, up from $975 million at the same auction in April 1988.

Individuals like investing in Treasury securities because of their unparalleled safety and attractive yields; unlike your passbook account, you can expect Treasury yields to at least keep pace with inflation. And interest is free from state and local taxes, too (but not federal taxes).

Securities issued by the U.S. Treasury Department offer other advantages as well. They are extremely liquid, being freely bought, sold, and exchanged. Moreover, they are excellent collateral for a whole range of consumer and business loans. Stockbrokers will generally lend as much as 90 percent of face value, which allows investment strategies that normal margin accounts do not. All the while, the Treasury investment is making money, which serves as a hedge.

Treasury Direct: While it is possible for you to attend an auction and bid on a treasury security, it's unlikely that you'll do so. Buying and selling these securities has, until recently, been almost entirely the domain of brokers. But that has changed.

Investors who have as little as $1,000 can now open what amounts to personal accounts at their regional Federal Reserve Bank, thanks to a program the Fed phased in during the last three years of the 1980s.

It's called "Treasury Direct," and it offers some attractive features for those who would like to invest in government securities, but whose available cash has seemed to make it hardly worth the effort. Treasury Direct is just that—a path of direct contact between the individual investor and the great big U.S. Treasury, circumventing banks and brokers and the sometimes prohibitively high fees they charge.

The Treasury Department used to issue certificates, and they still do, but with Treasury Direct there is no physical security as such. Instead, the securities are entries on a ledger. This means there's nothing to transfer or store. Buyers don't have to work through a bank or broker; they can buy T-bills, notes, and bonds directly from the Treasury.

Transaction and storage fees levied by banks and brokers—which range from $50 to $125 per transaction—plus transfer fees of $25 or so, have all but priced the small investor out of the market. For instance, the first year's interest would be more than wiped out by fees alone were one to purchase a $1,000 T-note through the traditional channels. With Treasury Direct, there are no such fees.

There are a few complications. You must purchase your T-bill, note, or bond from the regional Federal Reserve Bank serving your area. Their operating procedures vary slightly, so it's best to call the regional bank near you and learn its particular quirks before you make a purchase.

Generally, though, here's how it works: The investor fills out a tender form, available from the Fed, specifying the number of securities to be purchased and whether the investment is to be rolled over—reinvested—at maturity. The T-bills, notes, and bonds are purchased at full face value as far as you are concerned, which means you must remit the full amount.

The investor must also provide bank account information, because the difference between the purchase price and the face value of the security—the discount—will be directly deposited by the Fed into the account you specify. This is not optional. The reason for all this is that you are, of course, buying something for which no purchase price has yet been set. That will happen at the auction, with your discount refunded to you. The lack of paperwork and the direct deposit are cost-reducing measures that allow the program to exist at all.

The tender form is all that's needed to open the Fed account. Payment must be enclosed. If the issue being purchased is a T-bill or a T-note with a term of two years or less, payment must be by certified or cashier's check. Personal checks are accepted for longer-term notes and bonds. In any case, it must be payable to the Federal Reserve Bank of your area.

Your tender form and payment should arrive before the auction; otherwise, it will be held until the following week's auction.

How soon after payment is the discount refunded under Treasury Direct? Usually within days. When yields have risen, though, the Fed has become busier, and in some cases it could take as long as two weeks. Again, the refund is made directly to a bank account you designate, so you need to check your balance to know exactly when it has been credited to your account.

Clearly, Treasury Direct is a great advantage to small investors.

Diversification: Higher interest rates and the lack of fees that effectively reduce the yield make Treasury Direct investments particularly attractive. But the high minimum investment reduces your diversification possibilities. T-bills require a minimum $10,000 purchase, with multiples of $5,000 above that. Treasury notes that mature in less than four years may be purchased in multiples of $5,000, with a $5,000 minimum. Notes for four years or more may be purchased in $1,000 multiples.

While safety is not much of a consideration, there are reasons why you might want to diversify among Treasury issues. If you're uncertain about the direction interest rates are headed (and if you're not, put down this book and go out and make a fortune!), then it's wise to hedge a little by buying a smattering of different maturities, generally in the medium ranges. You are not likely to squeeze every last penny out of your investment, but you won't be far off the mark, either.

There are ways around this. Your broker may have a program for splitting a high-denomination Treasury security among several investors (though unless there are many investors involved, selling your share of a Treasury issue can be more difficult than is selling the whole thing on the open market). It is also possible to buy into a mutual fund that deals exclusively in Treasury securities.

SAVINGS BONDS—THAT FOURTH TREASURY SECURITY

There is another security issued by the U.S. Treasury Department, and it is one of the best investments an individual saver looking for supreme safety over the long haul can make. It is, of all things, U.S. Savings Bonds.

Beginning in November 1982, the yield of savings bonds was tied to the rates paid on other government securities, to make the bonds more competitive in the marketplace. A floor rate of 6 percent was established, which means that Savings Bonds will always pay at least 6 percent. The rate is recalculated every six months, on the first of May and November. For the first six-month period under the new system, the bonds paid 11.09 percent. The low through the end of the decade was 5.84 percent, for the six months beginning in November 1986. (The 6 percent floor is for overall yield to maturity, rather than the semi-annual components that determine the final yield. It sounds complicated, and that's because it is.)

Savings bond maturity is nominally 12 years, based on the 6 percent minimum rate. When the rate is higher, the bonds will reach face value sooner.

The semi-annual rates serve chiefly as markers for buyers. They give a sense of where savings bonds stand among investments. The rate finally paid is an average of the semi-annual figures over the period the bonds are held. In this respect, savings bonds differ from other bonds in that the rate they pay is not fixed, and the only easy way to determine the value of a specific bond is to consult redemption tables, which are available for your use at any bank.

To get the full rate, the bonds must be held at least five years. This may seem a weakness, but in fact it is one of the great strengths of the savings bond program. For the first six months after purchase, the bonds may not be cashed at all. After that initial period, though, they may be turned in for principal plus interest based on a fixed scale keyed to the length of time the bond has been held. At six months, the rate is 4.16 percent; at five years minus one day, it is 5.75 percent.

The idea is that people can buy bonds and essentially forget about them. People who wouldn't normally save can do so, because they can't dip into those savings for six months, and by then they are likely to hold onto their bonds even longer.

Buying U.S. Savings Bonds is simplicity itself. They can generally be purchased through payroll deductions by filling out a simple form and giving it to one's employer. They are also available at banks. The Treasury likes to point out that they make fine gifts and can be purchased in other people's names for that purpose.

Unlike other government issues, one needn't have a lot to invest in order to buy savings bonds. They are sold at a 50 percent discount, which means that a $50 bond—the smallest denomination—can be purchased for $25. (One who so desires may purchase the largest denomination, $10,000, for $5,000.) And unlike other Treasury issues, the variable is the maturity date. They mature when they have doubled in value, which is based on the sale of other Treasury securities—even savings bonds are not unaffected by market pressures. They are certainly the safest place for a small investor to place his or her money, because they are backed by the U.S. Treasury.

Savings bonds offer tax advantages as well. They are federally tax-deferred, meaning that you are liable for no taxes on the interest until you actually cash the bond. The interest is state and local tax exempt.

Since the change in the program in 1982, which replaced a fixed interest rate with the current floating yield, savings bonds have been an investment competitive with other places the small investor might want to put money. Today, for example, one might expect about 5.25 percent from a passbook savings account, the traditional repository of modest nest eggs. To get much more with reasonable safety, one would need to purchase a $1,000, five-year certificate of deposit—which is out of reach of many people—or a high-grade corporate or government instrument, which purchase can be either complicated or expensive or both.

An additional advantage of savings bonds is that if they are lost or stolen, the Treasury will replace them free of charge.

All this convenience and safety does have its price, though, and that price is the lack of liquidity. Money invested in savings bonds cannot be touched for at least six months, and to get the full yield it must remain dormant for four and a half years after that. They are not traded on any exchange. On the other hand, they are free of commissions and fees.

U.S. SAVINGS BONDS AND COLLEGE TUITION. Beginning with this new decade, there's yet another important reason for you to invest in savings bonds. Under a new tax-law provision (that went into effect for EE Savings Bonds purchased after Dec. 31, 1989), you can buy bonds, let the interest on them accumulate, and if you can cash them in and use the money to pay for qualified education costs (chief among them being tuition), the interest on EE Bonds used in this way is tax-free.

By so doing, you have converted the taxable interest on the bonds into completely tax-free interest—thereby making an ordinary investment an extraordinary one.

The program only applies to U.S. residents 24 years old or older. You qualify for full tax deductibility only if your yearly adjusted gross income does not exceed $40,000 if single, or $60,000 if married. Tax deductibility is reduced according to a scale that phases deductibility out completely if your yearly adjusted gross income exceeds $55,000 if single, or $90,000 if married. Bonds purchased before Dec. 31, 1989, do not qualify for this special tax provision.

There is no dollar limit on the amount of savings bond proceeds that may be used in this way, but any amount above 80 percent of allowable expenses is taxable. In short, bond proceeds used to pay for tuition are tax-free up to 80 percent of those expenses and taxable beyond that.

The exemption applies only to tuition and fees, not to other items such as room and board. Your family income can determine the extent of your exemption as well.

If you plan to do this, and if your bonds were purchased before the effective date of the new law, and if your children are still more than five years away from college, then you should trot down to the bank with your old bonds right now, cash them in, and put the money into new issues that qualify. You'll have a little tax bite from the interest you've earned, but this will be more than counterbalanced by the tax savings later, even if your tax bracket has changed.

9
NAVIGATING THE
—STOCK MARKET—

The stock market during the 1980s was a lot like California in the 1850s—many fortunes were made, but those who weren't extremely careful were lucky to come out alive.

The '80s began with a lukewarm market in a soup of high inflation, ridiculously high interest rates, and a stagnant economy. Then, in the autumn of 1982, and pretty much thereafter, it began to boil. Investors who had shares and kept them are happy today.

After all, it wasn't so very long ago that the idea of the Dow Jones average of 30 industrial shares reaching 1,000 was simply unthinkable. More recently—in fact, as October 18, 1987—the idea of the Dow Jones average dropping more than 500 points in one day wasn't just unthinkable, it was unbearable.

Had you suggested in 1981 or even early 1982 that these things would happen, you would have been thought a crank or worse. Had you gone on to say that the market would be open for business the day following the 500-plus point drop, that two years later it would plummet more than 100 points with no long-lasting effect, and that at decade's end the Dow would be hovering between 2,500 and 3,000, they would have sent for a wagon to take you away!

Yet all these things happened, and much, much more. Enormous, independent companies merged. The financial equivalent of riverboat gamblers played the highest-stakes poker in history as they took over companies, or failed to take them over, without actually having the money to pay for them. The phrase "junk bonds" was a fixture on the evening news. Some genius financiers ended up in jail, and some healthy companies virtually committed

141

suicide to keep from being bought by speculators who were less interested in running them well than they were in breaking them up and selling the pieces.

Hello, 1990s! What have you in store for us?

CRASHING REALITIES

In the time since the stock market crash of '87, there has been a question that has to have at least crossed the mind of everyone who owns, or is thinking of owning, shares of stock: Can it happen again?

The answer: You bet it can. But if you're careful, as you should be anyway, you don't have to spend too much time worrying about it.

Following that unhappy period when an oversold and volatile stock market dove—the market tumbled for about two weeks, with October 19 being the wildest day—the markets have instituted reforms. The New York Stock Exchange will close after a 400-point drop. The Chicago Mercantile Exchange will close after less of a shift. A Presidential commission met and issued its findings. Computerized program trading, blamed for a few terrifyingly wild swings, has been reduced (although not eliminated).

Can these changes prevent a stock market nose-dive? Of course not. They can only slow things down a little in hope of calming the stampede. Bear in mind the chief rule of investing: Yield directly corresponds to risk.

The securities market has been somewhat disordered since about 1985. In the past, companies would normally buy stock and sell debt when stock prices were low. But lately many companies have bought stock at high prices, going into debt to do so. Why? So that corporate managements could stay in place rather than feel the boot of a highly leveraged takeover. In short, they've made themselves less and less attractive, in hope of preventing takeovers.

Wall Street insiders fear all this debt. Anything more than a twitch in the economy—a rise in short-term interest rates, for instance, such as might be brought on by a small economic downturn—could precipitate a credit crunch in which many heavily leveraged companies would have to service cheap debt with new, more expensive borrowing. This makes bankruptcy for these companies a real danger, and investing in such companies all the more risky.

This problem is compounded by

- Junk bonds, floated by those who would take over other companies and sell off their subsidiaries.
- Trading in market futures—though unlike the pre-crash practice, the

stock exchanges and futures exchanges now communicate—and the put and call options, which are the domain of the experts.

- The speed of computer trades of big accounts and the house accounts of brokerage firms.

All of these make the stock market a more volatile, and risky, place to be. And the more volatile the market—the greater the chance of sharp price swings—the greater the chance of a crash like the one we saw in 1987.

The inescapable conclusion is that the stock market can be a very dangerous place. Does this mean you should stay out? Not at all. But it does mean that you must follow some basic investment rules, about which more later.

Catastrophic Events—No Company Is Immune: The 1988 oil spill disaster in Alaska should stand as a stern warning to investors: No matter how solid a company, there can always be sudden and surprising events which can threaten share values over the short or long term.

The last decade saw a popular building product and a birth control device spell ruination for the companies that had achieved success with them for years. Product tampering and terrorism of other kinds took a financial as well as human toll.

An oil spill, such as the one in Alaska, has immediate and obvious effects, but there are also consumer boycotts, disruptions of directors' meetings, and other problems that couldn't be easily foreseen. And the stain will splash, to a lesser extent, onto other oil companies as well, in the form of more rigid legislation and increased regulation that applies to all. Without considering the merits of new rules and regulations, it can certainly be said that those things are expensive.

It can work both ways, of course. There can be sudden, spectacular discoveries or court rulings that greatly increase the prospects of a company. In pharmaceuticals, for instance, fortunes have soared for those who have found effective medicine for otherwise untreatable ailments. But there are also cases where a pharmaceutical product was found to be in some way hazardous or harmful years after it was determined to be safe. This can send a company's prospects— and its share prices—plummeting, at least for a while.

THE INSIDER TRADING SCANDALS

The investment world was shaken in the late 1980s by unprecedented insider trading scandals—Michael Milken, Ivan Boesky, Dennis Levine,

Martin Siegel, and many others—the shockwaves of which have yet to die down and probably won't for some time.

How and why did it happen? Probably because those involved were making and spending so much money, with attendant power, that they stretched the limits to make more money, cutting corners. The more corners they cut and got away with, making and spending still more money, they cut still more corners until eventually they were caught. The ones caught first, to get their charges or sentences reduced, squealed on others, and then these others informed on still others, in a spreading daisy chain.

The stakes became larger than they ever were, because large institutional investors play a much bigger role than they did in 1933, 1953, 1963, etc. In most cases they are using your money—in the form of retirement programs, mutual funds, and the like.

These institutional investors and some others as well are making big profits in certain cases from a particular source—takeovers. But from the viewpoint of American competitiveness, takeovers may have as many disadvantages as advantages. They scare bad management into working harder, but they also scare good management who have to worry about the magic quarterly bottom line. If it dips, the price of the stock sneezes, and it becomes worthwhile for a takeover artist to try to buy the company for less. End of job for our manager!

"Takeovers" are unfriendly. They've mostly been accomplished by leveraged buyouts ("LBOs"). The buyout usually is entirely in cash, at a price a steep premium over what the acquired company's stock has been selling for in the open market. Part of this cash has been put up by the raider (some of which may be from an LBO fund), but most is raised by issuing junk bonds secured by the assets of the target company.

Takeovers have put billions of dollars "in play." But these billions of dollars have not gone into enhancing companies and American competitive industrial capability.

"Takeover," in this case, is distinguished from a "merger" (or "acquisition") in that the latter is frequently done with both companies in agreement that it is a good thing.

The advantage of deals where the companies agree? First, they generally don't saddle the business with the amount of debt usually involved in hostile takeovers. Second, most of the managers are left in place (unlike in hostile takeovers, where senior management is usually shown the door). This permits greater continuity of management, and avoids the disruption companies face in wholesale management shifts.

If we were serious about doing away with the unfairness of insider advantages, we could bar—so to speak—some big takeovers that create the big insider opportunities.

Fortunately, the demise of the junk bond markets has dried up financing sources for takeovers that don't make much economic sense. In the next few years, expect the corporate raiders to concentrate on proxy fights (where they ask for shareholder support to replace the current board of directors with one that supports the raiders' aims) and not takeovers to win control of companies.

BASIC INVESTING RULES

As you can see, there are wild cards in the deck, and recently they've become wilder than ever before. How can you deal yourself a hand that has the best chance of winning?

There's no absolutely safe way to invest in stocks, but neither is the stock market a terribly dangerous place for those who pay attention and take the appropriate precautions. While sudden bad news can devastate a company, that doesn't mean it needs to devastate you. If you can avoid the temptation toward big, dramatic market plays, you can easily find sound, profitable investments in stocks.

What you need to do instead is follow the rules:

DECIDE UPON A STOCK INVESTMENT STRATEGY. Do you plan to "play the market?" If you do, you will be taking on a new, full-time job. More likely, you'll want to make careful purchases of stocks that you have decided are of good value, and then ignore day-to-day fluctuations in their prices as you hold them for the long run.

STUDY ANY COMPANY BEFORE YOU INVEST IN IT. Look at its assets and its exposures. For instance, many shares are trading at far below their book value, which means that the per-share assets are greater than the price of the shares themselves. This provides a margin of safety should a sudden drain on company assets come to pass, especially if there's no reason to expect future earnings prospects to decline.

MOST IMPORTANT, DIVERSIFY. Don't put all your money into one company or even one industry. A downturn in one field may not be a downturn in another. This may not maximize your income, but it will minimize your risk. You're looking for income or growth or both, but putting all your money in one hot stock is a gamble you probably shouldn't take. If you're a little less greedy, you'll be a lot safer.

CONSIDER OTHER WAYS OF INVESTING. Mutual funds that specialize in specific industries are available, and buying into their portfolios can provide added insurance against disaster striking any one company.

DON'T LIMIT YOUR INVESTMENTS TO STOCKS. By dividing your investment dollars among stocks or mutual fund shares, high-grade corporate bonds, government paper, and cash accounts, you can protect yourself against most eventualities, so that no unpleasant surprise for one company, industry, or market can leave you in a bind.

CONSIDER YOUR STOCK PURCHASES AS CAREFULLY AS YOU WOULD CONSIDER ANY OTHER MAJOR PURCHASE. When you buy a car, you don't look to sell it next week. If through some miracle its value shoots through the roof, wonderful. But that's not why you should buy a car, or a stock.

AVOID TRICKY MANEUVERS. Puts and calls are exciting, but they're for the experts who are constantly in touch with the floor, dealing with enormous amounts of money, and have the ability to move that money around very quickly. If you're left behind, you'll be crushed. Under certain circumstances, and with the help of a skilled and trusted adviser, it is desirable to use stock options as a hedge against a wildly fluctuating market. But it's not something to be done by amateurs.

REMEMBER THAT YIELD AND RISK ARE CONNECTED. Don't put more in speculative stocks than you can comfortably afford to lose. Those who took a flier before October 1987 are still nursing their wounds. Those who picked solid shares aren't feeling any pain, because those shares have continued to pay, and are again at or above their earlier levels. Those who kept a cool head and bought high-quality shares while everyone else was panicking did very well for themselves.

FOR THE SAME REASON, DON'T PANIC. If you've studied the financial reports of the companies you've bought, and have confidence in them, don't be swayed even by violent market swings. The companies that were solid to begin with will continue to be so. What the market does is of interest, but only of pressing interest when you choose to sell.

DO PAY ATTENTION TO NEWS ABOUT THE COMPANIES IN WHICH YOU INVEST. Rumors of takeovers can send share prices through the roof for no real reason. If you don't get too greedy, you can make some handsome profits, to be reinvested when things have cooled down a little. It's important, too, to follow what management is doing about such takeovers, because actions taken by a board of directors under siege can reduce the actual value of shares over the long term.

Despite the reforms adopted by the markets, stocks may well again plummet. But that should not be the concern of the investor who is looking for growth, income, and security for a family. Stocks well picked will provide growth, income, and security.

Which is not to say you should be complacent. In this day of wild takeover threats and wild responses, careful monitoring of the market and of the companies in which you've invested is essential.

NOT ALL SHARES ARE CREATED EQUAL

There are several different ways you can invest in a company. One way is to lend it money through the purchase of corporate bonds, about which more in Chapter 8. The others involve actually purchasing partial ownership of the company through shares of stock. But there are different kinds of stock.

Common Stocks: This is simply the purchase of a tiny piece of the company. As the company's fortunes rise (and, perhaps, fall), so does the value of your shares. Common stock is what you normally think about when you think of shares of stock.

Besides being the main form of stock, it is for most investors the best way to invest in the stock market. It offers both appreciation and dividends, and with the best stocks the dividends increase every quarter.

Common shares are traded at the major stock exchanges and over the counter.

Preferred Stocks: The name notwithstanding, these are not necessarily better than common stocks.

The "preferred" part of the thing comes from the fact that the dividends on these shares are paid before the rest of the distribution is divided among holders of common stocks. That sounds good, but it isn't always.

Preferred stocks normally have a fixed dividend. This can be good when times aren't so good, but they can reduce the yield of the shares, and therefore their value, during flush times. This makes them not quite a stock and not quite a bond.

In many cases, preferred stocks can be "called," which is to say the company can buy them back from you pretty much as it wants, whether you're interested in selling them or not. This is a lot like refinancing a loan; it's usually done when the company believes it can produce a new, lower-yielding issue.

Convertibles: These are preferred stocks (or bonds) that can be converted to shares of common stock. While they are not the best of all possible securities, they are not the worst, either, because they offer the potential advantages of common stocks, bonds, and preferred stocks at a somewhat reduced risk. As is true whenever risk is reduced, yield is also.

Under normal circumstances, convertible shares behave like preferred shares, with yields a little above those of common shares but below those of non-convertible preferreds.

Your biggest concerns when buying convertibles are the point at which they are convertible (which is tied to the price of common stock), and how long your option to convert lasts. If the stock must rise enormously before you can convert, and if it must do so within a year or so, there's a reduced likelihood that you'll be able to exercise your option to convert.

WHAT SHOULD YOU BUY?

Before you make your first buy order (and from time to time thereafter), you need to sit down and examine your financial goals. The stocks you want to buy, if indeed you want to put money in shares at all, will be determined by your situation and by what you hope to achieve. The securities you purchase will vary, depending on whether you are looking to put children through college, to pay for your retirement, to have income now, to have long-term growth, or to have somewhat risky quick appreciation of your investments.

Your financial situation—how much you are able to invest—will dictate some of your choices as well. For instance, if you have already established college funds for your children and a retirement fund for yourself, have enough ready capital to take care of any likely contingency, have built equity in your home, and hold a diverse group of high-grade investments, you may feel comfortable in going out on a limb a little for some growth issues, new issues, or other somewhat riskier stocks. These, of course, require more attention, but the effort can pay off handsomely.

If, on the other hand, you're just starting out and are trying to build a measure of financial security, risky issues are the last place you want to look.

What kinds of stock investments are available to you? First, let's take a look at the way a company's stock issues can be appraised:

Book Value: This is a criterion favored by many stock gurus, though it is to be noted that stock gurus come and go like television sitcoms: What is popular one year may flop the next. In short, book value is how much money stockholders would receive for each share were the company to be liquidated. Of course, that is not especially likely to happen (though it has been the basis of some hostile takeovers in recent years, many of which pushed share prices beyond book value). Still, it does provide a measure of security to know that shares are selling below what they would bring if the company closed its doors.

Additionally, shares selling for less than book value are more likely to be targeted for buyouts, especially if the company has been run for years by someone who is likely to retire soon.

In order for book value to have any real meaning, though, you must take a close look at the company's annual report. Your first step is to take the total value of the company and subtract its debts. Take what's left over and divide it by the number of outstanding shares, and you have the company's value per share. (This does not, of course, have anything to do with the amount the company has earned—or lost. It says nothing about it as a moneymaking enterprise.)

Ah, but you mustn't stop there. You must look and see in what form the company's value is. Obsolete plant and equipment may be carried on the books at a value somewhat higher than the amount the company could reasonably hope to realize from its sale.

Some equipment and locations are unsuitable for use by anyone else, which could reduce their value. This is especially true of high-tech companies. It is not their fault; the pace of technology is so rapid that much expensive equipment is virtually obsolete when it is delivered, and if the company actually manufactures high-tech devices, frequent and expensive retooling can make the company's book value difficult to appraise.

If, on the other hand, the company's holdings are in real estate that has appreciated nicely, book value can take on added meaning, especially if the property is not carried on the books at its full appreciated value.

Earnings Per Share: This is to the revenue side of the company equation what book value is to the physical plant. It is simply the amount of money the company makes per share of outstanding stock.

To calculate it, take total revenues and subtract expenses, including debt service and taxes. Divide what's left by the number of outstanding shares. (You don't actually have to do the arithmetic yourself; the figures are published in the annual report and in Value Line and other investment information services.)

The earnings per share number is not the dividend, by the way, unless the company is undergoing no expansion or investment, in which case there are many more questions you want to ask before you buy any shares! Generally, a substantial part of the earnings will be put into company growth.

In any case, stocks that are most likely to appreciate over time are ones that have a solid history of growth, as measured in increased earnings per share over the years. There are exceptions, of course, such as companies that have made breakthroughs or that provide materials or goods that are of increasing importance.

Price/Earnings Ratio: This is an excellent tool for determining the relative market value of a particular share. It's calculated by dividing its current selling price per share by the dividend it has paid over the last year.

The P/E ratio can be a measure of the perceived safety of a given stock, there being a direct relationship between risk and yield. If the P/E ratio of a stock is, for instance, 15, it may mean that the market believes the investment is so safe that investors are willing to accept what has for the last year amounted to a $6\frac{2}{3}$ percent return. (It may also mean that the company suffered a one-time, sudden downturn, and that its fortunes are expected to improve.)

If the P/E figure is a low 5, on the other hand, it means that it is so risky that no one will touch it unless they can reasonably expect a 20 percent return on their investment.

Both of the examples cited are extreme, but they demonstrate how the price/earnings ratio reflects the market's opinion of the company. The figure is of most use when compared with that of other issues you are considering.

MAKING THE APPRAISAL. While annual reports are an important resource in determining the value of shares, there are others you should look at. The standard among these is Value Line, which provides the history of a company's securities going back several years. Standard & Poor's and Moody's also provide services that can help you determine the quality of companies and their offerings.

It's useful to compare the performance of a stock that interests you with the performance of other stocks in the same and similar industries, and with the market as measured by market indices. Don't be overly alarmed if the shares haven't kept pace with the Dow Jones Industrial Average, because this index measures the performance of very high quality stocks—the "blue chips." The Standard & Poor's 500 is a more realistic benchmark for most stocks.

PROFITING FROM GROWTH. The profit you realize by owning shares of stock comes in two forms: dividends and appreciation. While the two are related, they are not utterly tied together. The distance between the two increased enormously in the late 1980s, when the amount of money a company made sometimes had nothing to do with the selling price of the stock.

Dividends are the portion of company earnings the board of directors decides to distribute to shareholders. It almost goes without saying that this should be more than you would expect from other, less risky investments; otherwise, there would be little point in putting your money in stocks. Over the years, well-chosen shares have paid investors handsomely. Boards of directors are loath to reduce or—even worse—eliminate a quarterly dividend payment. It reduces investor confidence and usually results in an immediate tick downward in the share price. A number of companies have paid dividends continuously for many decades. There are a handful that note that they have paid higher dividends each quarter for decades as well.

Appreciation is growth in the value of the share itself, which is to say the amount for which you can sell it. Much money can be made here, but it is here that most individual investors get into trouble. That's because it is here that get-rich-quick fantasies are acted upon. It is the domain of the wild tip, of phrases such as "double overnight," and so on. Those phrases, rumors, and tips almost always involve companies you've never heard of until now. They never involve the blue chip, investment-grade issues. This should tell you something.

While it's a good thing, and something that should be sought, appreciation is terribly misunderstood. You may wish to play the market in hope of making a killing, but you do so at your own peril.

Here's a quick rule of thumb to employ in choosing growth stocks: Try to pick those that will increase in value, as opposed to those that will increase in price. There's a difference. The value of a stock is the strength of the company, the way it is managed, the continuing usefulness of its goods and services, and an economic situation that will allow the company to prosper.

The price is based somewhat on those things, but there is more. The price is determined by market pressures. In recent years especially, the prices of shares have often had little to do with their value. Prices have just as frequently been based on buyout rumors, unrealized market projections (that came from market analysts, not from the companies themselves), a herd mentality that has resulted in stampedes time and again, and the infernal program trading in which computers use all sorts of criteria to buy and sell big blocks of shares with little regard as to their value.

The value of a share is the thing to look at because it is the only thing that has any meaning in the long run, and the long run is what you should be looking toward when you invest. Over the course of time, as the value of a share increases, the price will surely follow.

(Again, if you own shares and the prices of them have risen beyond what you believe to be their value, go ahead and sell, and put the money into shares where the price is lower than or equal to their value. In the volatile current market, this is a real consideration. But remember to figure in brokerage commissions and taxes when you sell, because they can greatly reduce what seems at first like an enormous profit. And don't try to take advantage of every short-term spasm in the market.)

SHORT-TERM SPECULATION— HIGH-STAKES POKER

There are several issues that offer the potential for vast profit with little investment. That is everything good there is to be said about them. They are a minefield. Even the mine detectors of the professionals don't always guarantee safety. The amateur can lose the entire investment quickly with these.

These are options of various sorts. With them, you don't actually own anything except the right to purchase a certain number of shares at a certain price within a certain period of time. Utterly speculative, they are a bet placed on the performance of an issue. They deal solely with its short-term price fluctuations.

Warrants: Often offered with, and tied to, a new stock issue, these grant the right to buy additional shares should the price rise by a certain amount before the warrants expire. After a period of time, the warrants can be traded separately.

If the shares skyrocket, then the warrant can be exercised and everyone is happy. During the price rise, the value of the warrant rises also, allowing its sale at a profit. But if the stock just sits there, the warrant is of little value until it expires, at which time it becomes of no value at all. No one is going to purchase the privilege of buying a share at $20 if there's little likelihood it will rise above $17 before the privilege is withdrawn.

Puts: Traded by themselves, puts are options that allow the seller to realize a specified price for shares during a specified period of time.

Let's say you expect a certain stock to drop in price. You buy a put— the right to sell—a number of shares at a price near the current market value. The stock price does indeed drop. You buy shares at the new, low price and sell them at the higher price specified in your option. (More often, you will simply sell the option at the difference between the current and the option price, saving you the intermediate step.) You've made as profit the difference, minus the price of the option and brokerage fees. Or . . .

You expect the stock to drop in price, so you buy the put for whatever number of shares. The stock doesn't drop in price. In fact, it goes up. Finally, the option expires. You are now out the price of the option plus fees. You have gotten no dividends, because all you've owned is the right to sell something you don't yet own at some future date. When that right expires, you have nothing.

Calls: On the flip side of puts, these allow you to purchase a specified number of shares at a specified price before a specified date.

Let's say that this time you expect the price of a given stock to rise. You could make some money by investing in shares, but you're just so sure about this stock that you can taste it. You want to really make money on this one!

So you take enough money to buy a handful of shares and, instead, you buy a call option on hundreds of shares. Then, sure enough, the stock heads for the moon. You buy the shares at the lower price specified in your option— or sell the option for the difference in prices—and realize the profit from hundreds of shares from a very small investment. That's how it is supposed to work. It doesn't always; otherwise, no one would sell the options.

More likely, the stock doesn't head for outer space. It may appreciate a little, and with some luck you'll break even. Or it will just sit there. Or it will drop. And you're out the whole bundle. Instead of owning a handful of shares, you own nothing.

Index Options: These are tissue-thin securities, made of smoke and mirrors. They are a bet on broad market performance, pure and simple.

Just as one might bet on a football game, a horse race, or the cards in one's hand, one can, through index options, bet which way the market will go.

Like those other kinds of bets, it's possible to win a bundle or lose the whole investment. Unlike the others, everything in between is also possible.

As in stock options, index options may be purchased as either puts or calls, depending on what you believe the market will do. If it does as you expect, you win. If it doesn't, you lose.

There is a useful purpose for index options, though. Properly used, they can serve as an insurance policy for your portfolio. If you fear a market decline, you can purchase a put option, which will allow you to recover your loss if the market does decline. If it doesn't, you're out the price of the option, but have a portfolio that has increased in value.

This sounds like a wonderful idea, and for those who make a point of following the market so closely that their predictions are frequently correct, it is. But remember: Yield and risk are always connected—the market cannot be fooled, at least not for long. Things you do to reduce your risk will reduce your yield. Add in the fees, taxes, and your time, and you'll find that reducing your risk to zero will actually cut into your capital. That's why the most cost-effective way of reducing risk is by careful investment in a diverse portfolio.

Selling Short: The first person to successfully sell a stock short probably grinned like a Cheshire cat for weeks. A well-executed short sale is a neat trick.

It is risky, but in many ways selling short is no riskier than buying shares. Still, it sounds scary.

Simply put, selling short is when you sell shares that you don't own in hopes of replacing them later with shares purchased at a lower price.

You believe that a stock is likely to drop in price in the very near future, that its price is temporarily too high or that the company will make an unhappy announcement of some sort. So you borrow a number of shares from your broker. You sell them, putting the proceeds in your money market account, where they'll be safe.

The price of the shares drops. You buy back the shares at the new low price, and give them back to your broker. You pocket the difference, minus fees, commissions, taxes, etc.

If your best guess isn't accurate and the price doesn't drop or, worse, it rises, you still have to buy back the stock and replace it, only this time you lose, just as you lose when shares you own drop in value. The difference is, you don't have to pay for all the brokerage action when shares you own drop a little.

An anecdote: A reporter in New York a few years ago sought to track the performance of stocks recommended on a popular television program. He discovered that the stocks rose several points in price on the first trading day following the program, but then rapidly declined to their former levels.

He decided to conduct an experiment. He opened an imaginary account, based solely on shorting shares recommended on the program. From a beginning of $5,000, he had more than $22,000 after a single year.

(He published his results, so it doesn't work that well anymore, now that it's widely known.)

YOU AND THE ANNUAL MEETING

When you own shares in a company, and therefore part of the company, you have a right—albeit usually a very small one—to participate in corporate decisions. This means that you can take part in the company's annual meeting, and can vote on corporate decisions according to the company's bylaws. When you receive your notice of the annual meeting, you will also receive a proxy form that will allow you to assign your voting rights to an officer of the company. This can be essentially a pro forma matter, but that's not always the case. This is another reason why you should pay close attention to your stock investments, read the annual report, and so on. There can be corporate intrigue afoot that can affect the value of your investment.

(A good indicator of such intrigue is found when the directors—or their opposition—begin taking out full-page advertisements in financial newspapers, making ugly claims about each other and begging for your proxy. You had best find out what's going on, and vote your shares the way you think is appropriate.)

Annual meetings are usually fairly boring events. There can be fireworks, but even then they are seldom marked by dramatic behavior and inspired oratory.

In any event, as part owner, you have a say in what happens to the company, and you should exercise it. Today's market climate frequently involves an attempt to take over the company. If, after hearing the arguments of those wishing to seize control, you believe they could run the company in a better, more efficient, and healthier manner, then vote with them. If, after hearing those arguments, you decide that they are there for a quick killing, and if you're happy with the stock's performance under the current regime, vote against the raiders.

PICKING A BROKER

Unless you happen to own a seat on one of the exchanges—and, actually, even then, because you may want to trade issues not listed on that exchange—you will need a broker. But what do you look for? What do you need?

There are more choices of brokerages available to you than ever before. This has simultaneously made it more likely that you'll find the broker who's right for you, and made the process more confusing.

Just a few years ago, you were limited to the big national houses and the somewhat smaller regional ones. These offered (and offer) services beyond merely taking and executing your order. For instance, they will suggest investments and investment strategies, making your broker a sort of financial planner. The full-service brokerages often have libraries of investment reference material available for your use as well.

But because brokerages make their money by commissions, you may find that full-service brokerage houses urge you to be a little more active in buying and selling than you would otherwise be. And because you are probably not one of the company's bigger investors, with millions to throw around, you may come to feel as though you're being shuffled off to an extremely junior dealer. (In defense of junior members of the firm: They have access to the same information as everyone else in the brokerage house. More and more, recommendations are made by senior analysts, on whom the broker's reputation rests. They also want very much to succeed, so their enthusiasm may compensate for a lack of experience.)

Then came the discount brokerages. These offer substantial discounts in commissions, but they don't give you investment advice or some of the other features you may have come to expect from a full-service house. Instead of a particular person to handle your account, you will deal with whoever answers the telephone when you call to buy or sell. Still, they are the way to go if you're confident in your own investment decisions and are willing to do the necessary homework, without having the options narrowed down for you. They are also a good idea if you already employ a financial planner (especially one who receives no commissions).

Some banks now offer discount brokerage services. Some brokerage houses, in turn, offer services traditionally provided by banks. The lines have blurred. But with a little research, and perhaps a little experimentation, you should be able to find a perfect fit for your situation.

YOUR BROKERAGE ACCOUNT. Your first account should (and probably will) be a cash account. This means that you must pay for your purchases within seven business days.

There are a number of variations on the theme, just as there are with a bank account. These include joint accounts, for purposes of a seamless continuation of the account in the event of death; assignment of accounts to family trusts or "living" trusts; and the like. These considerations are not to be overlooked, and should be discussed not only with your broker, but with your financial planner and lawyer as well.

A cash account is the way to get your feet wet. Because you have to pay almost at once for the shares you buy, you can't risk more money than you have.

You will be asked whether you want your stock certificates sent to you or kept, either in your name or in the name of the brokerage, at the brokerage firm. While there is a certain pleasure in being able to hold and look at your stock certificates, it's usually a better idea to leave them at the brokerage. (It's nice to look at money, too, but you probably wouldn't—and certainly shouldn't—keep your money in a box at home!)

At the same time, you can arrange for automatic reinvestment of dividends—a good idea. This is most easily done through a money market account of the sort that is offered by most brokerage houses. This means that your dividends will be earning dividends of their own and, in due course, you will be able to move money to and from this account for other securities purchases. Because many of these accounts offer the same privileges as a negotiable order of withdrawal (NOW) checking account, you may want to keep much of your working capital in this account as well. (See Chapter 10: Investing in Mutual Funds.)

Then you place your order. You may do this initially when you open your account at the brokerage office. It's a good idea for you to be there for your first order, because it will allow you to see how the system works. Frequently, you'll see a brokerage worker type your order into a computer. It then appears on a screen in New York, Chicago, or elsewhere. A floor trader is told to make the offer to buy at the price you've specified. Presuming that you've offered the current market price, you will receive confirmation of your purchase in minutes. You write your check, and that is that. You'll receive confirmation of the whole event in writing in a day or two, by mail.

Thereafter, you'll phone in your order. Depending on the kind of brokerage house you're dealing with, you'll either talk with one of several brokerage employees or with the trader who usually handles your account. (If you employ a financial planner, he or she may handle some of these dealings for you.) In most cases, you can wait on the phone for confirmation; in any case, you will probably be called back with confirmation in a few minutes—certainly by day's end. When you receive your confirmation in the mail, you must mail your check at once. Settlement day, the day when the money changes hands between the buyer's representative—your broker—and the seller's representative—his or her broker—is five business days following the transaction.

The procedure is pretty much the same when you sell shares. You'll phone the brokerage and say you wish to sell a certain number of a particular share at a price you specify. If you choose to sell at the market price, you will receive confirmation almost instantly.

A useful stratagem for times when the market is getting a little wild, or when you have heard of rumors about a particular stock that are likely to drive the price up, is to establish a price at which you would be willing to sell. (Be sure to consider the brokerage fees and taxes you'll pay on the profits when arriving at the price.) Then phone your broker and say that if the stock reaches your specified price, you'll sell.

After things cool down, you can use the same money to buy more shares of the same stock, or you can buy shares of something else. In the mean time, invest the proceeds in your money market account. When people are eager to pay ridiculously high prices based on rumors and get-rich-quick ideas, there's no reason why you shouldn't oblige them.

In any case, the proceeds of your sale will come due to you on settlement day, and will be disposed of according to your wishes. The best place to put them, unless you wish to purchase other shares at once, is in your money market account at the brokerage. You may, of course, have a check mailed to you, but then it's not an investment anymore, until you invest it again.

MARGIN ACCOUNTS. If the road to Hell is paved with good intentions, one of the leading access ramps is papered with margin accounts. For it is here that you can lose more than you own. A margin account allows you to buy stock using borrowed money. If the margin requirement is 50 percent, as it is in most stock transactions, you can in effect purchase twice as many shares for the same amount of money. This allows you to realize twice the dividends and appreciation for the same amount of money invested. It also allows you to lose twice as much should the shares drop in price.

What's more, the money you borrow from your broker to finance the other 50 percent of your purchase does not come for free. It is usually a point or two above the prime rate. This, of course, drastically reduces the effective yield of your shares.

When shares bought on margin drop in price, your equity in the shares drops as well, twice as quickly as it would if you owned them outright. When your equity reaches about a third of the value of the shares, you will receive a margin call. This means that you must ante up more money or the brokerage will sell the shares. If the shares are sold, your paper loss becomes a very real one.

When you buy securities on margin, which seems like and is a contradiction in terms, they must remain at the brokerage and be held in the brokerage's name. You must additionally provide $2,000 in cash or twice that in securities. The shares that you buy are collateral for the loan you receive to buy them. You will also be required to sign an agreement allowing the brokerage to lend your shares to other brokers or to other accounts, or to borrow money on. As a practical matter, this is unlikely to affect you.

The crash of 1929 proved the lack of wisdom in letting people buy huge blocks of shares for pennies on the dollar. The margin requirements are now much higher, and it would take a true catastrophe to put your margin account into the red. It's far more likely that you'll merely suffer a tremendous, crippling loss. Chart 20 graphically illustrates this.

It should be clear that a margin account is something to be entered into with extreme caution. It is not the best idea for most people.

DISPUTES WITH YOUR BROKER. When choosing a financial planner, you are able to look at his or her track record and investment philosophy. You will be able to find out if, for instance, a prospect has led a string of clients inexorably toward bankruptcy. You will then be able to look elsewhere.

Sadly, this is not true with stockbrokers. Over the course of time, ones that engage in out-and-out crookedness, or who are totally incompetent, will be found out and driven, one way or another, from the industry. But . . .

No matter what your securities broker does or fails to do with your account, no matter what it costs you, chances are you can't take him to court. That's because virtually every brokerage agreement signed in this country contains buried in the fine print a clause that requires binding arbitration in the event of a broker-customer dispute.

But the situation may be undergoing a change. State legislators and U.S. representatives have considered a number of measures that, when and if

CHART 20

Effects of Buying Securities or Mutual Funds "On Margin"**

Buying on margin (that is, leveraging your investment) can increase your gain—as shown in *Illustration 1*. But it also can magnify your loss—as shown in *Illustration 2*.

(1) Favorable Results—Your Investments Grow In Value

You Buy for Cash:
You buy securities or mutual funds for $5,000 cash. No borrowing. The $5,000 investment represents your net worth of this investment.

Net Worth $5,000   Total Value $5,000

Five years later the value has doubled, to $10,000.

Net Worth $10,000   Total Value $10,000

You Buy on Margin:
You buy $10,000 of the same securities or mutual funds on 50% margin. You pay $5,000 cash and borrow the other $5,000 with the investment as collateral.

Net Worth $5,000
———
Debt $5,000

Total Value $10,000

Five years later the value has doubled: the $10,000 is now worth $20,000. You've done 23% better than you would have done if you'd only bought for cash.*

Net Worth $11,543
———
Debt $8,457

Total Value $20,000

*Here's why: Your net worth would be $11,543, which is $1,543 more than the $10,000 result if you bought only for cash. $1,543 is a 23% greater gain on your original $5,000 cash investment. The $11,543 net worth is a result of the gain in value to $20,000, less the $8,457 of your debt, which consists of the $5,000 you borrowed and of $3,457 accumulated interest (which for purposes of this example is compounded annually at 12%).

**Similar effects are possible with investments other than securities or mutual funds—such as mortgaging real estate.

approved and upheld by the courts, would strike down the arbitration clauses.

The securities industry uniformly opposes such legislation. Depending on who's talking, the industry reasons are either what's best for everybody or almost unconscionably self-serving.

The arbitrators are usually provided by the National Association of Securities Dealers, which says the issue is important to anyone who has an agreement with a broker, especially those who have margin accounts, which

CHART 20 *(continued)*

(2) Unfavorable Results: Your Investments Decline In Value		
You Buy For Cash: You buy securities or mutual funds for $5,000 cash. No borrowing. The $5,000 investment represents your net worth.	Net Worth $5,000	Total Value $5,000
Five years later the value has declined 10%, to $4,500. Your loss is $500.	Net Worth $4,500	Total Value $4,500
You Buy on Margin: You buy $10,000 of the same securities or mutual funds on 50% margin. You pay $5,000 cash and borrow the other $5,000 with the investment as collateral.	Net Worth $5,000 ————— Debt $5,000	Total Value $10,000
Five years later the value has declined 10% to $9,000. But the $5,000 you invested now has a net worth of only $543.*	Net Worth $543 ————— Debt $8,457	Total Value $9,000

*Here's why: The 10% decline in value reduced the $10,000 to $9,000. Of this $9,000, you owe $8,457—the original $5,000 you borrowed plus the $3,457 accumulated interest at 12%. Your net worth is $543.

In an actual situation, your net worth would have dropped below the usual 30% margin maintenance level, and you would have received a margin call to put up more cash or additional securities as collateral.

Note: Situations described do not take into consideration commissions, other charges (except for interest on the borrowed money), or taxes.

virtually always include the arbitration clause. This has led to the criticism that industry-supplied arbitrators are likely to side with industry insiders. The response has been that the industry is so competitive now that it is eager to see justice done and to police its own. The debate rages.

Indeed, even if laws are passed and upheld that allow you to take a broker to court, in most cases you'll probably choose arbitration. There's little reason to pay a lawyer several thousand dollars to attempt to recover an amount not much more than that.

Clearly, it is an issue that will become more important as time goes on. In 1986, NASD arbitrated only 1,587 broker-client disputes. That number nearly tripled in the following two years.

A HAPPY CLOSING NOTE

You're in the attic, going through a nearly forgotten trunk or box of papers, and out drop some old stock certificates. Maybe they're for the Fisk Rubber Company or a company called Marconi Wireless Telegraph. They're nicely engraved, maybe something you'd like to hang on the wall.

You've never heard of the companies, though, so surely they're not worth anything as securities, right?

Wrong! In the examples above, Fisk Rubber Co. later changed into Uniroyal. Marconi Wireless Telegraph became a little outfit called RCA which, a few years ago, became part of another little outfit called General Electric.

There can be big money in those old stock certificates. Frequently, though, they're found after the death of a relative or in other circumstances where determining their origin isn't easy. The certificates are nice to look at, but the company name is unfamiliar. You have no idea whether you've found valuable securities or just pretty pieces of paper.

How do you find out? Actually, researching old stock certificates is enjoyable, a lesson in the ways companies come and go, gobble up other companies, or get gobbled up themselves.

The first thing to do is pop into the nearest library and look for a book called *Capital Changes Report* in the reference section. This will very likely tell you what happened to the company that issued the stock certificates— whether it changed its name, merged with another company, or whatever.

If you have no luck, the next stop is your stockbroker. Chances are, your broker won't be very encouraging, because the majority of old stock certificates are worthless as securities. But there's a chance that your broker has a curious streak and a taste for adventure, and if so, there's a good likelihood that the brokerage's resources will be able to illuminate the fate of the company.

If you still can't determine anything about the stock certificates, there is one final step you can take, and that is to contact a company that specializes in tracking down the companies that issued old securities.

Don't be put off by what appears to be bad news involving a company. A number of companies that seem to have folded turn out, further research will indicate, to have been resurrected later. And, even a company's bankruptcy doesn't necessarily mean that a security it issued is worthless because money is frequently set aside to pay off bond- and stockholders. Though this may amount to only a few cents on the dollar, it's worth looking into.

What this means is that if you discover the company went bankrupt, you're not at a dead end. You need to find out what happened as a result of the bankruptcy and who handled the distribution of the company's assets. The same is true of a company that went out of business. Its assets had to be disposed of in some way; it's up to you to find out how.

Conducting such a search, while time-consuming, is fascinating. There's real excitement as you gather each piece of the puzzle. In some cases, solving the riddle becomes more important than whether or not the stock or bond is worth any money.

Even if it turns out that those old stocks and bonds have no value as securities, that doesn't mean they're worthless. Many are collector's items. Their value as art objects depends largely on how they look. Elaborately engraved certificates are things of beauty, popular with memorabilia collectors. Among the most valuable are stock certificates from old railroads, with their romanticized pictures of locomotives. Aircraft company and airline certificates are popular with aviation buffs, though most of these are valuable securities. And so on.

The best way to determine their value to collectors is to look at publications aimed at hobbyists. If you're sure that the certificates have no value as securities, and you can't find any indication of their value to collectors, it's always a good bet to take a few to a swap meet or collectors' convention. Price them at far more than you think you'll ever receive, and bargain. You'll then begin to get a sense of the market value, and can price others accordingly.

10
INVESTING IN
—— MUTUAL FUNDS ——

Total assets and diversity of mutual funds grew enormously during the 1980s. Not only did more people invest directly into mutual funds, but they indirectly invested through retirement plans, such as IRAs, 401(k)s, 403(b)s, SEP-IRAs, Keoghs, and so on. Overall, performance of mutual funds was good, and individual investors felt the funds' professional management afforded them equality, considering the increasing institutionalization of investing driving out individual investors.

In addition to professional management, mutual funds offer diversification and convenience, and during the 1980s offered an increasing range of new types of funds such as in sectors, international, option, index, asset allocation, tax-exempt, and more.

Mutual funds should continue to expand and grow in the 1990s.

Simply put, a mutual fund is a professionally managed pool of investments used to buy a range of securities that, it is hoped, will advance the fund's stated goals. Those goals range from rapid growth to steady income to capital building.

They offer the investor the advantages of professional management along with diversification that keeps any one issue from causing a disproportionate loss. The latter is of special interest to you if you have relatively little to invest. Here's why: For you individually to purchase a few shares of a number of different issues would probably cost more than you want to invest. But beyond that, the percentage of your investment that would go to sales commissions would be very high; the stocks or bonds would have to do quite well before you would even break even.

Due to the immense popularity of mutual funds, it is now possible to find one that specializes in almost anything. It is possible to build a good portfolio through diversifying among a handful of mutual funds: one, perhaps, that specializes in government securities; a money market fund; one that is in blue-chip stocks; and perhaps one that aggressively tackles the growth issues.

Thanks to SEC rules instituted in the late 1980s, it is now easier to shop for a mutual fund. And shop you must before you buy any shares in a mutual fund.

The rules provide:

- That no shares may be purchased before the investor has received a copy of the fund's prospectus.

- That all fees be stated on a standardized chart, making it easy to compare funds.

- That the fund make available to investors, again on a standardized chart, the fund's past performance.

How do you pick a mutual fund that's right for you?

Because mutual funds are pooled investments, you need to become familiar with the pros and cons of those particular types of investments. So the first thing you may want to do is familiarize yourself with the chapters in this book that deal with those various kinds of investments, for many concerns carry over into the mutual funds that buy and sell them.

Then, you must decide what you want the fund to do, beyond "make me a lot of money." Are you looking for rapid growth of capital? Or somewhat safer, steady income? (Bear in mind that the terms "growth" and "income" can be misleading, for both kinds of funds offer automatic reinvestment of dividends. The difference is that a growth fund looks for securities that are likely to appreciate, while an income fund looks for securities whose strength is in the dividends or interest they pay.) Maybe you are looking for tax-free growth.

Begin shopping for funds. Follow their performance over several years, through swings in the market. A widely quoted and largely meaningless statistic is which funds performed best over, say, the previous year. Far more important is how the fund has done over the last five years.

The size of the fund is increasingly of importance. If a fund's assets are less than about $75 million, it can be thought of as small. Its size gives it some mobility advantage over its more ponderous cousins, but the smaller the fund, the more it is subject to size-related dangers. A chief one is that, with fewer investors, a handful of investors with many shares could pull out of the fund and cripple it. Being smaller, such a fund must either charge more per share in fees in order to pay for top-notch management, or try to get by with second-string managers. If it has have been small for many years, you must look carefully to see why it hasn't grown; new small funds have little in the way of track records by which they may be measured.

The fund's leverage position is of interest as well. Many funds do not borrow money for investments at all, while some buy heavily on margin. The risks here are the same as they would be in your own accounts: You can realize more of your investment in dividends or appreciation, but you can more easily lose more of your investment if the securities you've purchased on margin drop in price. You must consider to what extent you're comfortable with a fund that invests on margin.

Remember that while mutual funds diversify to insulate themselves from bad news about a particular company, they are still subject to the factors that affect the broad market. The more aggressive funds will be more volatile. This is not a criticism. It's simply a fact.

Fortunately, many companies offer mutual funds specializing in several different areas with different investment philosophies. It is an easy thing to move your holdings from one to another as the economic and financial climates change, and as your investment goals mature.

Another advantage to mutual funds is that they allow you to become a player in the markets usually reserved for the big guys. For example, some investments—notably T-bills—require a $10,000 investment. You may not have that kind of money to throw around or, if you do, you may not want to put that much in one place. Instead, for a tenth of the amount you can buy into a mutual fund that has extensive holdings in those securities.

Mutual funds also give you automatic reinvestment of earnings and, if you use your fund shares as income producers, automatic withdrawal. A monthly or quarterly statement keeps you abreast of your account's activity, making record keeping simple.

It may also be that you simply don't want to do the homework necessary to pick individual issues for your portfolio. It may even be that your luck in choosing securities has been so bad that you're hesitant to go back into the market. Much of this worry can be relieved by buying into a high-quality mutual fund.

Pick out a few funds that seem right for you. Send for their prospectuses. (Many funds will send you one if you telephone; some even have toll-free numbers for this purpose.) All else being equal, a fund that has been in business a long time is better than one that hasn't. Look at the management fee, and look at a different fund if the fee is much above 0.5 percent of the net assets of the fund. Check also to see if there are more redemptions or if more new shares have been sold. You want a fund with the latter. See if there is a redemption fee. The presence of one isn't necessarily a red flag, but you should remember that this will be subtracted from your yield. (See Charts 21 and 22.)

Find out the sales fee, which is typically less than 3 percent for no-load funds. (Load funds are sold by stockbrokers. They require payment of a commission, but they have no sales fee. In either case, they reduce your yield, but the longer you hold your shares, the less per year is the effect.)

Find out, too, how much it costs to get in. The customary initial investment is $1,000, but this varies somewhat from fund to fund. Just as important is the amount required for additional investment. For many funds, this is $250. Because you will probably want to put additional money in the fund, you will want to find one that allows this in amounts convenient for you.

Once you're satisfied that you've found the right fund for you, go ahead!

NO-LOAD FUNDS

Because no-load mutual funds carry no sales commission, there is no particular reason for stockbrokers to sell them (though some do). Instead, you have to seek them out yourself, do your own research, and make your choice.

This is an area where a good financial planner can be a big help, because the planner is likely to be up-to-date on the best mutual fund investments.

You can save thousands of dollars by not having to deal with fund salesmen or brokers. But the trick is to know what you're doing. Here are some suggestions:

- Choose a "pure" no-load (no sales charge) fund. With a little research, you can save 8.5 percent or more by not paying a sales commission. That adds up to a hefty sum over a period of time. With a no-load, 100 percent of your money is put to work for you.

- Do not be put off by performance fees. These are essentially a bonus paid by the fund to its managers when the fund shows capital gains. Obviously, a manager is going to do his or her very best if it means he or she stands to be rewarded for success. (One can only ponder that this philosophy, broadly applied, could do much for productivity in general!)

- If you prefer a 12b-1 fund (one that allows the management of a fund to deduct a certain percentage of your investment for distribution costs), select those funds that have a maximum annual 12b-1 fee no larger than 0.25 percent of assets.

CHART 21

Guide to Income-Oriented Mutual Funds

Virtually all mutual funds pay some dividends—from their net income (interest and dividends they earn from their portfolio holdings, less the funds' expenses and management fees). But dividend yield is slight for equity (stock) funds whose primary objective is long-term growth or shorter-term maximum capital appreciation.

The other types of mutual funds, below, vary in their income orientation. Those whose yield is the highest also are the riskiest—investing mostly in "junk (low-quality) bonds."

You may need income from your mutual funds to supplement your other income because of your lifestyle or because you're retired. However, if possible, you also should try to invest for some potential long-term growth (as well as necessary current income) to offset the eroding effects of inflation. But not to such an extent as to risk preservation of your capital, which is paying you needed dividend income.

When applicable, you also should determine which will yield more net income to you: higher-paying but taxable dividends vs. lower-paying but tax-advantaged dividends.

MONEY MARKET MUTUAL FUNDS
(Unlike the other types of income-oriented mutual funds below, the prices of money market funds do not fluctuate.)
- GENERAL MONEY MARKET FUNDS (they generally invest in money market instruments of domestic and foreign issuers, including: CD's, bankers' acceptances, and time deposits of financial institutions; short-term commercial paper, notes and bonds of corporations; and bills, discount notes, and other short-term obligations of government agencies and other issuers).
- U.S. GOVERNMENT SECURITIES MONEY MARKET FUNDS (debt obligations issued or guaranteed by the U.S. government or its agencies).
- TAX-EXEMPT MONEY MARKET FUNDS (short-term debt obligations of municipalities).

BOND FUNDS
(In addition to the categories below, some bond mutual funds are classified by the lengths of maturities of bonds they specialize in: "short-term"—generally less than 3 years; "intermediate-term"—generally 3 to 10 years; "long-term"—generally 10 years or longer. Some diversified bond funds may invest in debt issues of foreign governments and corporations. Some specialize in foreign issues.)

U.S. Government (safest of all investments):
- U.S. TREASURY SECURITIES FUNDS (bills, notes, and bonds).
- U.S. GOVERNMENT SECURITIES FUNDS (Treasuries plus debt issues of other U.S. government agencies).

Municipals (bonds and other debt issues of state and local municipalities or their specific projects; interest is exempt from federal tax, and also state and local taxes if investor lives there):
- BETTER-QUALITY MUNICIPAL BOND FUNDS (quality as graded by independent rating services, such as Standard & Poor's and Moody's).

CHART 21 *(continued)*

- LOWER-QUALITY MUNICIPAL BOND FUNDS (as graded or unrated; lowest-quality known as "junk bonds").
- INSURED MUNICIPAL BOND FUNDS (slightly lower yield, because of the cost of the insurance, for the extra safety).

Mortgage (and Other Asset) Backed (securities collateralized by pools of mortgages):
- GINNIE MAE FUNDS (mortgage pools via Government National Mortgage Association [GNMA], known as Ginnie Mae).
- MORTGAGE SECURITIES FUNDS (Ginnie Mae and other government and commercial mortgage-backed securities).

Corporates (bond and other debt obligations issued by corporations):
- BETTER-QUALITY CORPORATE BOND FUNDS (quality as graded by independent rating services, such as Standard & Poor's and Moody's).
- LOWER-QUALITY CORPORATE BOND FUNDS (as graded or unrated; lowest-quality known as "junk bonds").

Zero coupon (government and corporate bonds issued at a deep discount from face value, with interest accumulated to maturity; you could stagger redemptions to produce accumulated interest by investing in zero coupon funds with various targeted maturity dates).

BOND AND STOCK FUNDS

- CONVERTIBLES FUNDS (preferred stocks and bonds convertible into shares of common stocks).
- BALANCED FUNDS (common stocks, convertibles, preferred stocks, bonds, money market instruments).

EQUITY INCOME FUNDS

- EQUITY INCOME FUNDS (higher-yield dividend-paying stocks).
- DUAL-PURPOSE FUNDS' INCOME SHARES (the other shares in dual-purpose funds get the appreciation).
- INCOME AND GROWTH FUNDS (more income plus some growth).
- GROWTH AND INCOME FUNDS (more growth plus medium income).
- INCOME-ORIENTED SECTOR FUNDS (such as sector funds specializing in utilities or real estate or other fields usually higher-yield).
- OPTION INCOME FUNDS (options for income rather than appreciation).
- MIXED INCOME FUNDS (high-yield stocks, options for income).

It may be that you choose a particular fund because it is part of a group of funds, allowing you to switch from one to another whenever you choose. If so, find out what fees are involved in doing so. Remember, too, that capital gains go on the books any time you do this, making you liable for income tax on those profits.

For a detailed listing of fees, see accompanying "Mutual Fund Fees" chart.

CHART 22

Types of Mutual Funds*

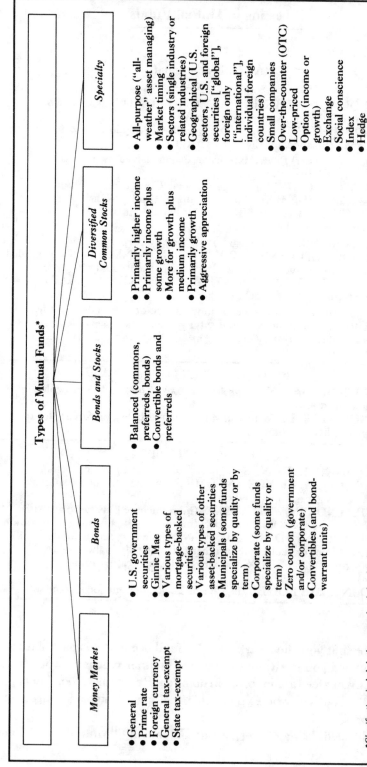

Money Market	*Bonds*	*Bonds and Stocks*	*Diversified Common Stocks*	*Specialty*
• General • Prime rate • Foreign currency • General tax-exempt • State tax-exempt	• U.S. government securities • Ginnie Mae • Various types of mortgage-backed securities • Various types of other asset-backed securities • Municipals (some funds specialize by quality or by term) • Corporate (some funds specialize by quality or term) • Zero coupon (government and/or corporate) • Convertibles (and bond-warrant units)	• Balanced (commons, preferreds, bonds) • Convertible bonds and preferreds	• Primarily higher income • Primarily income plus some growth • More for growth plus medium income • Primarily growth • Aggressive appreciation	• All-purpose ("all-weather," asset managing) • Market timing • Sectors (single industry or related industries) • Geographical (U.S. sectors, U.S. and foreign securities ["global"], foreign only ["international"], individual foreign countries) • Small companies • Over-the-counter (OTC) • Low-priced • Option (income or growth) • Exchange • Social conscience • Index • Hedge

*Classifications include both open-end and closed-end mutual funds. *Objectives, investment strategies and tactics, and risks* will vary among individual funds within the types.
In addition to bonds, some *bond funds* also invest in bills, notes, debentures and other debt securities. Many *common stock funds* also include small holdings of bonds, preferred stocks and "units" (which may comprise warrants attached to bonds). Portfolios of *diversified common stock funds* also may include small holdings of bonds, preferred stocks and units. Holdings of *specialty funds* are primarily in common stocks (or issues related to stocks, as in the case of option funds).

MUTUAL FUND FEES

Virtually all mutual funds charge management fees, below. Some funds charge some of the other fees below.

Fees	*For*
LOAD	Sales commissions on your purchases of funds that charge these fees. Many of the load funds are sold by stockbrokers. The maximum load usually is 8.5 percent of your investment. *No-load* funds do not charge a sales commission. Many of the no-load funds are sold by the mail. Most load funds as well as no-load, or low-load funds (below) do not charge a fee on re-investment of dividends and capital-gains distributions into additional shares.
LOW-LOAD	These funds charge less than load funds in sales commissions, generally up to 3 per cent.
MANAGEMENT	These fees are charged for administration of a fund and management of its investment portfolio. They average about one-half of one percent of average total assets during the year.
PERFORMANCE	This type of fee is based on how well a fund has performed compared to a yardstick such as a specified stock-market index. Most funds don't charge performance fees.
SWITCHING	Such fees may be levied by some funds when you switch all or part of your holdings from one fund to another of the same management company.
12b-1	Fees, typically one-quarter of one percent of average total assets during the year, charged by some funds for advertising and marketing.
RETIREMENT	Fees, usually $10 per account per year, charged on IRA, 401(k), 403(b), IRA-Rollover, SEP-IRA, Keogh, and other mutual-fund retirement accounts, charged by some funds.

CLOSED-END FUNDS

Closed-end funds are mutual funds that are initially offered with a certain number of shares available for sale. Unlike open-end funds, though, the number of shares in a closed-end fund never varies. The shares are therefore not completely tied to the holdings of the fund. They are also subject to the vagaries of the market.

This means that the shares can be sold at a discount, which is to say, for less than the holdings they represent; or at a premium, meaning for an amount greater than the sum of the parts.

They are traded like shares, through stock brokers, with commissions paid. When they become available and sell out within a year or so, and you buy into them, you are almost certain to lose money.

The reasons that buying into a new closed-end fund is a very easy way to lose a lot of money are fairly simple:

- Buyers pay hefty commissions to brokers who sell them, typically 7 percent of the investment. This already puts you in the hole, because for every dollar you invest, you are actually only investing 93 cents. The rest you are giving away.

- Because closed-end funds are not especially popular (in part because they are little publicized), they drop in price almost at once and trade at a discount, below the value of the underlying securities.

On the other hand, you can make money in closed-end mutual funds. Here's how:

- Don't buy a new issue. For every one that rises to sell at a premium, there are many that languish in discount land.

- Even more important, never buy at a premium. Funds that invest in the securities of a single foreign country, for instance, often sell for more than their assets are worth. Maybe their value will rise to match the price of the fund shares, maybe not. It's not a chance you want to take.

- Be skeptical of bond funds with high yields. That's because the yield is only part of the story. The other part is the fact that the bonds themselves could be dropping in value, offsetting some or all of those impressive yields. Your principal could actually drop to the point that you've lost money.

- Look for funds selling at a deep discount. The share prices may rebound, and beyond that you may think of the securities backing the fund as the fund's "book value."

Closed-end funds also offer few of the advantages of an open-end fund. Buy with caution.

MONEY MARKET FUNDS

The chances are that your first mutual fund purchase will be shares in a money market fund. In effect, these offer all but one of the benefits of interest-bearing bank and checking accounts with substantial improvements as well.

The one benefit that they do not offer is the safety of government insurance. But because they invest in a very high quality portfolio, heavy in government paper, high grade corporate bonds, and bank certificates of deposit, they are generally very safe.

(To be completely fair, it should be noted that the fund owns these issues, not you. You own shares of the fund. This means that, if through mismanagement or criminal behavior, something happens to the investments, you could be left out in the cold. It isn't likely, but it is possible.)

On the other hand, money market funds, like most other mutual funds, are utterly liquid. They offer check-writing privileges, though there may be some restrictions on the number or amounts of the checks you may write.

Their yield is generally much higher than you would receive through any other account offering such convenience.

What's more, you can have such an account at the brokerage with which you deal. Then the proceeds from sales of securities can be instantly deposited in the fund, making sure that your money is always earning. This also makes it easy to move money around, from one issue or fund to another.

Money market funds invest in short-term securities. In fact, the newspaper listing of a given fund will carry the average maturity of issues held by the fund. This can be of importance when interest rates are volatile, as they have been in recent years. Why? When rates are on the decline, it's good to be in a fund whose holdings don't mature for a while. That means that the fund will continue to enjoy high rates for a relatively long time.

When interest rates are edging up, it's good to be in a fund whose issues mature soon, so it can buy newer, higher-yielding securities.

Typically, a $1,000 investment is required to join. The rules of the different funds vary. Some require that checks written against account holdings reach a minimum amount.

Bear in mind also that the yields of money market funds vary, depending on their holdings. While the genre is considered safe, some funds invest in issues that are safer than the portfolios of other funds, though, of course, the yield on these funds will be lower.

You may also purchase tax-free money market funds, which are federally tax-exempt. Depending on where you live, you may be able to buy triple tax-free fund shares, which are exempt from all income taxes. Like other tax-free securities, these trade at a premium that takes their tax status into account. So they are an especially good investment only if your tax situation calls for them.

BOND FUNDS

Just as there are many different kinds of bonds, there are many different bond funds, which roughly correspond. They range from the very secure funds backed exclusively by U.S. Treasury issues to fairly speculative ones that buy and sell the bonds of risky and fairly insecure companies. (The latter are still safer, though, than some of the highly aggressive stock funds, which buy shares of these companies.)

The important thing to remember with bond funds is that they typically yield several percentage points above the corresponding money market funds, because they invest money for the longer term. But because they buy longer bonds, they take more of a hit when interest rates climb for any sustained period of time.

And, there being no tax-free stocks, you will find tax-free funds among this group. There are funds that deal only in federal paper; funds that, as described above, deal only in mortgage-backed bonds; and those that are exclusively municipal–either very safe guaranteed or high-yield non-guaranteed–and high-yield corporate bonds.

Of course, as always there's a correlation between the degree of risk and the degree of yield. The riskier the fund, the more closely you will want to look at the fund's track record. Pay special attention to times when things in the market as a whole were shaky. This will tell you whether the fund managers were quick to recognize the trouble and fly to higher quality securities. (Of course, if the fund is operating under different management now, this datum will be of limited utility.)

When buying into a bond fund, it's very important that you understand the philosophy employed by the fund, because you might otherwise be saddened by lower yields than you had hoped for or, conversely, surprised when higher risk than you're comfortable with makes itself apparent.

The way to check is simply to determine the ratings of the bonds they buy. Bonds carrying an "A" or higher rating, as specified by Moody's or Standard & Poor's, can generally be considered to be safe; those with lower ratings—"BBB" in the Standard & Poor's lexicon, "Baa" in Moody's and below—may be thought of as speculative. This applies to both municipal and corporate bonds. For an expanded discussion, see Chapter 8.

Within the municipal bond funds are ones that are triple tax-exempt. If you're at all familiar with municipal bonds, you'll know that this can be quite a trick.

That's because a bond is exempt from federal, state, and local income taxes in only the place where it was issued (and in places where there is no state or local income tax, but they are scarcely a good value in those places, because you end up paying for a tax advantage that you get for free anyway).

This means that such funds must be limited to the individual state or, in some cases, the individual city. If you live in a city that has a lot of outstanding paper, and if the city seems to be in pretty good shape fiscally, and if it has an income tax, and if you need the tax advantages . . . then they are a good idea for you—if you can find them. Obviously, these funds are limited in number and scope and serve limited markets.

You might also want to consider what is called a target fund. This is a fund that buys bonds maturing a specified number of years down the road. They are less volatile than funds that invest in many different maturities, with the bonds held to maturity. These are a good vehicle for long-term growth, and can be part of, for example, a college education portfolio.

Another way to achieve the same end is to buy into a zero-coupon bond fund. These funds invest in securities that do not provide periodic interest payments, but receive the interest in one lump sum at the bond's maturity. This makes them ideal for investment toward a long-term goal. Some are backed by government securities and are extremely safe, while others are backed by corporate zero-coupon bonds and therefore offer higher yields for a slightly greater risk.

Corporate bond funds are by definition a little more speculative than government bond funds. Of course, they also typically yield more. These can specialize in particular industries or types of industry—high technology or utilities, for instance—and can be quite safe or quite risky. Again, the track record and prospectus will fill you in.

At the fringe of all this are the truly speculative funds. They are not for the faint of heart. Nor are they for people who don't already have more than enough money someplace else.

The managers of these funds take big risks in hope of big gains. They buy heavily discounted paper from shaky corporations, junk bonds issued as the result of or in hope of financing takeovers, and other issues that you would be foolish to buy on your own.

You may still be foolish in even investing in such a fund. But at least you have the advantage of a professional staff that is making the fund's choices carefully within the fund's philosophy. And it's always possible that the right combination will be hit, and the fund will return an astonishingly high yield.

If you are lured by such a fund, just make sure you don't put the rent money in it. These funds are strictly for money you can afford to lose.

GINNIE MAES—BIG SECURITY, SMALL INVESTMENT

Despite the extreme uncertainty about the direction interest rates are likely to take, Ginnie Maes remain a popular investment. Are they a good idea?

Ginnie Maes are the securities issued by the Government National Mortgage Association, created a little more than 20 years ago by Congress to sell off FHA and VA mortgages. Because both principal and interest are protected by the U.S. government, they are extremely safe. They offer the highest yields of any government-backed security.

Here's how they work: The investor purchases a Ginnie Mae certificate from a brokerage house or a bank for a minimum of $25,000. Then each month the investor receives a check for a portion of the principal plus interest—which is usually about 0.5 percent below the going rate for commercial mortgages. Simple enough, if you have $25,000 to invest and the self-discipline not to spend the principal when it is returned to you.

Hey, wait a minute! $25,000? Just hang on. Fortunately, through the wonder of mutual funds, you needn't have $25,000 to invest in these securities.

It sounds good. But Ginnie Maes are not without their risk. For instance, the value of a Ginnie Mae certificate can plummet if interest rates rise. Because of this, they are best for those who are not looking for high liquidity. Of course, conversely, their value can rise if interest rates drop. In this respect, Ginnie Maes, like bonds, have a value irrespective of principal plus interest, which makes them a chancy proposition for those who require high liquidity.

It is possible to buy older certificates that have been paid down, at market prices that reflect the interest they bear. These are good for those who find Ginnie Maes ideal, but who want to invest something less than the full $25,000.

Ginnie Mae certificates are excellent for those who seek a monthly income—such as retirees who have received a lump-sum benefit they wish to distribute over a period of years.

Those who want the safety and high yield of Ginnie Maes but who have less to invest and who want a little more protection from interest rate fluctuations should consider Ginnie Mae mutual funds. Why?

- Shares in Ginnie Mae mutual funds can be purchased for as little as $1,000.

- Principal and interest or just principal, if monthly income is the goal, can be automatically re-invested by the fund, eliminating the temptation to spend it.
- Re-investment cushions the effects of changes in interest rates, because the principal is put back into Ginnie Maes at the newer rates.
- Ginnie Mae funds, like other kinds of mutual funds, are professionally managed.

Ginnie Mae mutual funds do have some disadvantages, though:

- There is slightly higher risk. Because the fund, not the investor, technically owns the Ginnie Mae, the investor is one step removed from the government guarantee of principal and interest.
- Share values rise and fall with interest rate fluctuations. This can be moderated, but not eliminated, by reinvestment in the fund.
- The costs involved reduce your yield. Sales charges range from about 2 to 6 percent. Management fees run another 1 or 2 percent. Some funds base their charges on a sliding scale; the longer your money remains in the fund, the less the charge will be. The charge is levied when the investor withdraws from the fund.

Not surprisingly, most investors choose Ginnie Mae funds over outright purchase of the certificates. But there are dozens of funds. How do you choose the one that's best for you? Fortunately, the new SEC rules covering all mutual funds make shopping much easier.

Before investing in any Ginnie Mae fund, get the prospectuses from several. Consider the features that are important to you. For example, you will want to explore the liquidity of your investment. Some funds offer checking privileges. Others do not. And some base their fees on the amount of time your investment remains in the fund.

Find out about automatic re-investment. Is there a charge for this service? Likewise, explore the fee structure. A back-end loaded fund would be ideal for those who intend to leave their money there for a long time.

Compare the funds' returns. These, too, are standardized.

You will also want to consider the fund's legal standing. If there are lawsuits pending against the fund, for instance, you will want to consider the wisdom of investing there. Such information must be included in the prospectus.

Similarly, you can buy into mutual funds that specialize in mortgage-backed securities guaranteed by the federal government (Fannie Maes, Freddie Macs) and commercial guaranteed mortgage pools.

MIXED FUNDS

From considering your own portfolio, you know there are advantages to having holdings in both stocks and bonds. When stocks look as though they are headed for a rough time, you can head for the relative placidity of the bond market, with its consistent yields and low (by comparison) volatility. Then, when the sun shines brightly on the stock market, you can go back into stocks, along with a world of variations on the theme.

There are some mutual funds that do the same thing. Some deal exclusively in preferred stock and convertibles, which are securities that have some of the attributes of both stocks and bonds. Others hold a range of common stocks, bonds, and preferreds. They are medium in risk, medium in growth, medium in income.

STOCK FUNDS

There is no law that says stock funds may buy only shares of stock, and many diversify from time to time into other corporate issues. That is of no real importance; what is critical, instead, is the philosophy behind the fund.

The first of these philosophies calls for a concentration on income. The fund's managers are less interested in the stock growing in value than they are in a low price/earnings ratio. Of course, because you can reinvest the dividends from shares in the fund, such an investment can be a vehicle for long-term growth. Your tax situation will play a part in determining whether this is a good idea for you.

The second philosophy is one where the managers are looking for growth in the value of the stock itself. Such funds are likely to invest in companies that show great promise but aren't quite big money makers just yet. These stocks might pay a dividend or they might not. Because this has little to do with the philosophy of the fund, it really doesn't matter. A concern here is that such companies are among the first to be affected in a broad market downturn, so you might need to strap yourself in for a rocky ride.

The third of these philosophies is a combination of the first two. While the idea of this kind of mix may seem good at first, experience suggests that the result is the best of neither world. It is possible to buy into funds that tend to favor one of the philosophies or the other. You may decide that if your philosophy favors a mix, you might just want to buy into a good fund of each type, rather than a hybrid.

The final major type of stock-backed mutual fund is the riverboat gambler or gunslinger of fund investments. It's the fund whose managers go in for the big, quick killing. Called an aggressive growth fund, these guys take big risks in hopes of making big money. In times when there are more dollars than sense in the marketplace, these funds can do quite well. But they are terribly volatile, because it doesn't take much bad news to send the shares bought by these funds into a nose-dive. Of course, the value of your holdings in the fund is determined by the fund's holdings, which means that your investment is at risk when things do not go well.

If you insist upon taking on risk, it's better to do it through an aggressive growth fund, because you at least have the edge you get from professional managers. Still, they are certainly not for everybody. In fact, they're certainly not for most people. Unless you have money that, again, you can afford to lose, you should stay away.

As a small percentage of a very broad-based portfolio that is heavy in much safer investments, they do have a place.

SPECIALTY FUNDS

Unlike funds that deal exclusively or nearly so in a particular kind of security, specialty funds deal in a particular industry or in some of the more arcane securities. As the 1980s drew to a close, for instance, the best performing fund was one that dealt in companies that stood to gain from changes that had taken place in Germany.

It is possible to invest in funds that deal in market futures, in rare coins, in precious metals and gemstones, in art-related companies, in real estate, in just about any investment you can imagine.

Or perhaps you would like to invest in several mutual funds, but do not want to (or feel you lack the skill to) decide which ones would be best. You can invest in funds of funds. As their name implies, these are mutual funds whose holdings are in other mutual funds. One concern with these otherwise interesting investment vehicles is that management costs tend to be somewhat higher than they are for the individual funds themselves.

A variation on this theme is the all-purpose fund. This is like a fund of funds, but in this case the fund does all the investing itself. It invests in everything. It takes diversification to its logical extreme. That, as a rule, is good. But it takes a lot for granted, because there are certain to be losses, and some of the investments made by these funds are ones where the losses can be truly heroic.

The fact is, it is now almost impossible to think of a way of shuffling the deck without finding a fund that deals only in those cards. For instance, you can buy into:

- Option funds. These invest in stock options and are, therefore, based on pure speculation. You can get these as income producers or as growth funds.

- Index funds. These literally buy a stock index. Whatever the index does, the fund does.

- "Conscience" funds. These are funds that don't invest in companies that kill whales or baby seals, pollute the environment, or eat non-union lettuce. They do invest in companies that seek to improve the environment and otherwise do good deeds. The drawback is that these things do not necessarily make money.

- International funds. If the trend of the last part of 1989 and the first part of 1990 continues, these could be big players in the years ahead. They allow you to invest directly in foreign companies. This has always been a chancy thing, because some countries have the ugly habit of nationalizing industries that show signs of making money. Or political conditions suddenly can make a local economy very rough. The local potentate can be suddenly transformed into the local impotentate, taking with him a kindly attitude toward business. But in times when things are becoming more placid, these funds could thrive.

- Regional funds. Like international funds, these invest in foreign companies, but unlike international funds, they pick a particular part of the world or a particular country. The huge successes of a fund, cited above, that invests in German companies is just one example of the growth and income possibilities that these funds offer in the coming years, as the world moves closer to becoming a global community.

- Global funds. These are similar to international funds, but they have a component of U.S.-owned companies. Broadly diversified, they are less likely to take a big hit from this revolution or that typhoon. They do call for the investor to become more familiar than most Americans are with the international economic scene— something that all by itself very nearly justifies the investment.

- American regional funds. These are the internal version of regional funds. They might concentrate on investments in a particular state, certainly on ones of a particular region. If you think you know where domestic growth will be, these funds are a way for you to invest in your beliefs.

- All-weather funds. These funds play the market. Skilled (it is hoped) market managers follow the trends and the technical market cycles and move money from one kind of security to another. Ideal in concept, all-weather funds are as good or as bad as the people making the decisions. Special study of their track record under the current decision makers is critical to investment in them.

Whatever fund investment you choose, there is an art to withdrawing money from it. To help you determine the way that's best for you, see Chart 23.

HOW TO BUY

Open-ended funds are bought and sold by the sponsoring companies. The process is straightforward, though as I mentioned, the law requires that you be given a prospectus before you may invest.

After your initial investment, you will probably want to put more money in the fund from time to time. The fund will let you make additional investments in increments smaller than your original $1,000. These smaller amounts can be as little as $100.

The first thing you should do is arrange for automatic reinvestment of dividends, interest, and capital gains. Because the fund is very liquid, you will have access to your money, but with automatic reinvestment, your income has income of its own.

You may then wish to consider various investment strategies. One, for instance, might call for investment of a specified amount per week, no matter what individual fund shares cost. Another might call for the purchase of a specified number of shares irrespective of their cost. Yet another might call for a given investment each month, with your profits offsetting some of that investment. Some months, when things have gone very well, you may find that your profits and capital gains are nearly as great as the amount you would have invested. In other months, you might need to put a little more in the kitty.

You may wish to divide your investment dollars among several different funds. By watching the market, you may decide that some or all of this month's contributions should go into long-term bonds. Or stocks might look good to you. Perhaps things are unsettled and the money market account is the answer.

Decide what your investment objectives are and find funds to fit them. If you are conservative in your investment strategy, you should invest primarily in fixed-income, equity-income, or growth-income funds. If you are willing to take more risk, invest in a growth fund. If you are truly daring, invest in an aggressive growth fund.

No matter what your investing style, allocate a major percentage of your

CHART 23

A Withdrawal Plan for Mutual Funds

Most mutual funds have programs allowing shareholders to receive regular automatic payments from invested principal and/or dividends and capital gains distributions. Such programs can be particularly helpful to supplement your other retirement income.

This guide indicates how long your accumulated investment will last during retirement if the percentage rate of withdrawal each year exceeds the mutual fund's percentage of average annual rate of return. (The average annual rate of return is equal to the per-share increase in net asset value, plus reinvested dividends and capital gains distributions.)

If your mutual fund's rate of return exceeds your withdrawal rate, your capital will never be depleted.

Your investment is worth $150,000. The fund's average rate of return is 10%. If you systematically withdraw 11% each year, your principal will last 25 years—the number of years found at the intersection on the chart of the 10% return and the 11% withdrawal.

A Withdrawal Plan For Mutual Funds

Rate of Annual With-drawal	Average Annual Rate of Return on Your Mutual Fund Investment													
	1%	2%	3%	4%	5%	6%	7%	8%	9%	10%	11%	12%	13%	14%
	Number of Years Your Money Will Last													
15%	6	7	7	7	8	8	9	9	10	11	12	13	16	21
14%	7	7	8	8	8	9	10	10	11	12	14	17	22	
13%	8	8	8	9	9	10	11	12	13	15	17	23		
12%	8	9	9	10	10	11	12	14	15	18	24			
11%	9	10	10	11	12	13	14	16	19	25				
10%	10	11	12	13	14	15	17	20	26					
9%	11	12	13	14	16	18	22	28						
8%	13	14	15	17	20	23	30							
7%	15	16	18	21	25	33								
6%	18	20	23	28	36									
5%	22	25	30	41										
4%	28	35	46											
3%	40	55												
2%	69													

assets into a core of mutual funds that you can hold long-term through both bull and bear markets. These are generally conservative funds, or perhaps more aggressive funds that go to cash when market conditions are uncertain or adverse. Diversify. Under no circumstances put more than 25 percent of your assets into the most aggressive growth fund.

Sector funds are funds that invest in one segment of the economy, such as technology, energy, health care, or leisure. These funds are for sophisticated investors only. In order to make sector investing profitable, you must have an independent opinion of the investment merits of the sector (examining past performance is not enough); you should monitor these investments constantly; and you must pick the right time to move in and out of different industries.

Read the prospectus. You must, by law, receive a prospectus before you invest in any fund. It will tell you the investment philosophy of the fund, allowable investments, and fees. Look carefully to see if the fund lists a 12b-1 fee. It usually will be in the section entitled "Management" or in the section immediately following, sometimes entitled "Distribution Plan." Next, check the table entitled "Net Share Income and Capital Changes" for the fund's expense ratio. If the expense ratio (the total of the management fee and other charges) is more than 1.85 percent, do not buy the fund.

Do not buy solely on the basis of recent past performance. There is no guarantee of a repeat. Where possible, use long-term (five to 10 years) over short-term track records as criteria for selection.

Check the management and portfolio manager. Is there continuity of management? Was the record achieved by the present staff?

What additional services are offered? Are you allowed switching by telephone within a family of funds? Telephone purchases or redemptions? Check-writing privileges?

Seek advice from outside sources on no-load funds. Find the best performers and get reports on timely developments.

Most important, time your purchase carefully. Even the best-managed, most conservative mutual fund will be rocked by adverse economic changes. When you feel sure the stock market is about to top out, don't buy shares of a stock-backed mutual fund. If it looks as though interest rates are going up, it's silly to buy into a fund that invests in long-term bonds.

You are safe in investing in either, though, after the change has taken place, because the share prices will have adjusted downward to take them into consideration.

One of the greatest strengths of mutual funds, and one of the greatest joys in owning shares in them, is that you are working with a portfolio much broader than you could possibly hope to achieve yourself. The decisions you make are not unlike those made by the big institutional investors. And like those investors, you have professional managers working to carry out your wishes.

Not bad for only $1,000 up front per fund, is it?

MUTUAL FUNDS AND IRAs

Mutual funds are an excellent investment vehicle for retirement savings.

If you own a mutual fund as part of an individual retirement account, Keogh, or 401(k) plan, your profits are tax deferred (though, of course, you do not have access to the money until you are 59 1/2).

By investing your retirement money in a mutual fund, the growth is magnified. Because it is not taxed now, either more of it can be reinvested or, better still, you can afford to invest more of it. In addition, the amount you invest is tax-deferred up to a certain point as well. It is like a gift from the government. Cherish it—such gifts to investors are few.

Of course, because you already are enjoying big tax savings, it would be very foolish to put your retirement money in tax-free or tax-advantaged mutual funds, because you would be paying a premium to duplicate advantages you already enjoyed.

The idea is worth discussing with your financial advisor.

NOT-QUITE FUNDS

There are a number of investments you can make that share many of the characteristics of mutual funds without actually being mutual funds. Some are worthy of your consideration.

Unit trusts are similar in some ways to closed-end funds, but they are far more straightforward. Here's how they work: You buy a unit, which is a share, in a portfolio of bonds that has been assembled. Once all the units are sold, that's it—no more units are offered.

Because the portfolio is fixed, so is the yield. The bonds mature, the money is divvied up, and everybody goes home richer.

Generally, units sell for $1,000, though you may be required to buy more than one unit. They are purchased through—and sometimes sponsored by— brokerage houses. Units may be sold, but that is not the purpose of a unit trust. A zero-coupon unit trust can be a good vehicle for long-term growth, particularly if you are lucky enough to buy into one at a time of high interest rates. Tax-exempt unit trusts and single-state unit trusts (which can offer triple tax exemption) are also available.

You may also be interested in a real estate investment trust, which does much the same thing with a property or group of properties.

Limited partnerships were once popular because they allowed passive losses to offset active income. But no more. Now, their losses can only offset passive losses, which makes them less attractive as a tax shelter. Now you only want to invest in ones that actually plan to make money!

11
YOUR HOME–NO LONGER
–A SURE INVESTMENT–

After decades of steady increases in home values, a house, co-op, or condo is no longer the sure investment it once was. Some markets have already gone soft. In other places, the rate of growth is declining.

In the worst cases, families have sought home equity loans only to find out that even though they had been paying toward their mortgages for years, their equity was now less than zero—they owed more than their home was worth.

The problem comes from many directions. First, the speculative buying frenzy of the late 1970s and early 1980s drove the prices of many homes past their actual values. Many buyers saw homes as the ultimate hedge against inflation, and many purchased beyond their means, hoping that inflation would continue, thereby increasing their equity.

(Equity is the percentage of your home you own free and clear, as opposed to the amount encumbered by a mortgage. Suppose you buy a home for $100,000, taking out a $75,000 mortgage. Values increase by 10 percent. Your home is now worth $110,000, but you still owe the bank only $75,000. Your home equity has increased by $10,000. But if home values drop, your equity is reduced correspondingly. The amount you owe the bank remains constant.)

Second, the savings and loan crisis resulted in more real estate in many parts of the country being placed on the market, and when supplies increase, prices drop.

Third, in some areas prices have risen so high that would-be buyers have been priced out of the market. This is a particular problem in the Northeast, especially in and around New York City.

Surprisingly, the one area in the Northeast where the market had grown

186

was in $1-million-plus luxury homes. Realtors in New York and Connecticut reported that the palatial mansions in the suburbs were selling more quickly, and at higher prices, than they did when the rest of the market was booming.

Fourth, some areas that looked very promising a decade ago have had terrible economic downturns instead. Workers, now unemployed, have had to sell their homes, or those homes have been foreclosed upon. But in regions of economic decline, there are no new workers to buy the homes, so the market prices plummet.

Finally, there are fewer buyers. The 25 to 34 age group, which includes most first-time buyers, increased 74 percent between 1969 and 1989. This increased demand was a major factor in propelling home prices. That 25 to 34 group will decline by 15 percent over the '90s. Demand by first-time buyers can be expected to decline as well.

The result has been that some homeowners find that their equity is much less than they hoped for, and in worst cases they actually owe the bank more than their house is worth. If they can still afford mortgage payments, and if they like living in their home, this can present a problem only on paper, and perhaps they do not even notice the decline in their home's value.

What a shock they will receive, though, if they try to take out a second mortgage, or are counting on the value of their home for retirement security or their children's education!

What's the forecast for the '90s? Expect slower appreciation—roughly keeping pace with inflation.

The lesson is to buy your home carefully and with an eye toward the future. You do not any longer have the luxury of assuming that your home will increase in value.

ALL REAL ESTATE IS LOCAL

The smart buyer can find a home that is not only a good place to live but a good investment as well. Regional considerations come into play here. Growing areas will experience more growth in home prices than will those in areas where the general population and economy is shrinking.

How does this affect you? That depends, of course, on whether you are selling or buying—or are simply a homeowner who is rightly concerned.

In any case, you should look for trends in the area where you own a home or are considering buying. Questions you should ask:

- What is the economic situation in the area? If employment is steadily growing and industry there is secure, your home investment is likely to be secure also. This is not always the case, as witnessed by the Texas oil boom followed by the Texas oil bust. In areas that experience diversified growth, though, this is a good measure.

- What is the recent history of home sales in the area? Are homes remaining on the market for an extended time? Are sellers accepting far less than their asking prices?

- What is the foreclosure rate in the area? A high foreclosure rate means a shrinking local economy, an overpriced market, or both. Nationally, the foreclosure rate nearly doubled in 1988 and 1989, and there was little evidence the trend would reverse.

- Is the number of houses on the market shrinking or increasing? A decreasing number is a good sign, because it means homes are being bought. It also means the supply is limited, which tends to keep prices high.

- What is the industrial outlook for the area? If major companies are making big purchases nearby, especially for labor-intensive operations, homes will come to be in demand. Before you buy, though, determine how much this anticipated demand has affected the price being asked for the house now. Conversely, if office and other commercial vacancy rates are high, you may have missed out on the boom. This can result in good values, but remember, the owners expected their homes to be a good investment, and they may have unrealistic asking prices. Swallow hard, bid low, and bargain.

- Those who have lots of land and less house are in better shape than those who have a big house on a tiny lot. Houses can always be made bigger. Land cannot.

- If you're selling, get appraisals from at least three brokers. Be realistic. If no interest is shown after your home has been on the market for a month, consider reducing the price.

There's one big factor that influences real estate sales that isn't local—interest rates. Real estate sales are highly dependent on interest rates. When interest rates rise, more and more consumers—especially first-time buyers—are priced out of the market, and still more will have to settle for less than they would have been able to buy just a few months earlier. And these buyers already face a shortage of suitable homes, which is likely to drive prices still higher.

THE PLIGHT OF THE FIRST-TIME BUYER

A smaller percentage of Americans now own homes than was the case just a few years ago. In 1985, almost 66 percent of American families owned their homes; by 1989 only a little over 63 percent did. Young families—those in whom the breadwinner is under 35—have eschewed home ownership for one reason or another at an even more alarming rate.

Decreasing affordability is a key culprit. Affordability is the relation between what you make and what you can afford to pay. If you're seeking to pay for a new house with 10 percent down and a mortgage covering 90 percent of the purchase price, you can afford to buy a house that costs a little more than twice what your family earns each year.

The gap between what first-time buyers can afford to pay, and what sellers are willing to take, is unprecedentedly high. The average first-time home buyer cannot afford to pay the median price for a home in most markets, and the situation is likely to become even more acute, at least for the first few years of the new decade. In the late 1980s, buyers of their first homes were paying between 75 and 80 percent of the median price in their area for a home.

Why this affordability gap? Real estate brokers and dealers reported a shortage of starter homes in more than half the markets. An even larger number of real estate agents said it was more difficult to find a good starter home in recent years than it was even five years before.

HOW BUYERS CAN MAKE THE MOST OF THE MARKET

With the soft housing market ("overbuilt" is how the experts describe it) expected to continue for some time, there are opportunities to buy more home than you thought you could afford.

You can make your dollars go further by deciding to buy in the late autumn or winter. That's because the spring and summer are the peak times for home purchases. The market—like the weather—being a little hotter, the prices gotten are higher. The other two seasons are better because both buyers and sellers are more relaxed in the cooler weather, it is easier to shop, you won't have to deal with hurried real estate agents, and sellers are eager to unload homes that have probably been on the market since spring.

Auctions: Auctions because of bankruptcy or foreclosure are well established. But auctions are becoming an increasingly popular marketing tool for real estate.

Thanks to the soft real estate market, houses can remain unsold indefinitely. Auctions bring together buyers and sellers in a short period of time. Although sellers may not get the price they wanted, they do get the market price. And buyers can save as much as 50 percent over the original asking price.

Keep in mind that just because a property is sold at auction, it may not be sold to the highest bidder. When property is sold on a reserve auction basis, sellers have a set period of time (usually 48 hours) to accept or reject the bid. But property sold on an "absolute" basis goes to the highest bidder, regardless of the size of the bid.

Fixer-Uppers: One answer to high home prices might be to look for a "fixer-upper." This is a house that will send you seeking help from one of the television shows that teaches you how to restore a home to a pristine condition—because it won't be pristine when you buy it.

You should look for a home that, despite its need for a coat of paint, new flooring, and perhaps a new appliance or two, is structurally sound. It is a home in which the repairs you make will increase its value virtually dollar-for-dollar, turning sweat equity into home equity.

How do you find such a house? Actually, it's not all that difficult. There are some virtually everyplace—even in developments that are fairly new. The reason they're easy to find is that they are difficult to sell, so they remain on the market for quite some time. People generally want to be able to move into their new home without having so much as to clean the oven or wipe out the refrigerator. They do not want to buy a home that requires a lot of work to make into a place where they'd be proud to entertain visitors. Often, they don't want to buy a home that only needs a good cleaning and a little fixing here and there.

There is no hard and fast rule for determining the price you should offer for such a home because circumstances vary. Sometimes the seller believes the home, or the property under the home, is worth more than it actually is. If the house has been on the market for some time, the owner may well have been disabused of such notions by now, and may simply be looking to unload it. That is the seller you're seeking.

How do you find someone desperate to sell his or her house (which real estate agents call a "motivated" seller)? Look for the flags they're waving! Look in the real estate classified advertisements in your newspaper. You'll see phrases such as "moving—must sell," "divorced," "job transfer," and the like. This tells you that the sellers are motivated to unload the thing pronto.

Be extremely careful that your "fixer-upper" does not need major structural work. Your contract should be contingent on a thorough inspection by a building inspector of your choosing. Refinishing the floors is troublesome enough—pouring a new foundation is more project than most home handy-persons care to undertake. Make sure the inspection covers the building's structure; its plumbing system, including the septic system or sewer; electrical system; and heating, cooling, ventilation, and air conditioning system.

Look at other, similar homes in the same area, to see what is being asked for them. A local real estate agent should be able to give you a sense of the actual sale price of homes of the sort you're considering; the local county clerk certainly can, though the research is a little more difficult than it is when you use a real estate agent.

Employ the other research tools that you would use in buying any house to determine whether the market in the region is a strong one, or whether today's value is likely to be higher than tomorrow's.

Check with your insurance agent for the construction replacement cost in the area. This should confirm your other research.

A MORTGAGE TRICK WITH A BIG PAYOFF. Homeowners who can spare a few extra dollars each month can save thousands of dollars on mortgage costs. All you have to do is add a little extra to your monthly payment. Let me give you an example:

A homebuyer takes a $100,000, 30-year mortgage at 10 percent. Each monthly payment will be $877.57. At the end of 30 years, when the mortgage is retired, the homeowner will have paid back the $100,000 principal—plus $215,929 in interest. (To get a graphic sense of all this, see Chart 24.)

But if that same homebuyer pays an even $900 each month—an additional $22.43—the loan will be paid off nearly four years earlier, and the total interest paid will be $182,256, or an interest savings of $33,673.

Think of it: For payments totaling $7021, paid out in small monthly bites, you can save nearly $34,000.

Here's why this works: Mortgages are front-loaded. In our example, the first payment the owner would make on that new home would be $877.57. Of that, $833.33 would be interest. Despite parting with nearly $900, the buyer would have exactly $44.24 worth of house to call his or her own.

At the end of three years, the happy homeowner will have paid $29,744 in interest, but the principal itself will have been reduced by a meager $1,848. That amount is the owner's equity in the home. In fact, it is not until the 23rd year of this 30-year mortgage that interest payments and amortization payments (repayment of the principal) are even equal, and it is 23 years and seven months before you own half equity in the home!

CHART 24

Figuring Monthly Mortgage Payments

Use the table below to calculate monthly mortgage payments.

A. Select mortgage term   _____
B. Select mortgage interest rate   _____
C. Consult table. Find intersection of year and %   _____
D. Divide your intended mortgage amount by $1,000   _____
E. Multiply C by D.
    This is the total monthly payment covering principal
    and interest   _____

Interest Rate	Mortgage Term			
	15 Years	20 Years	25 Years	30 Years
10%	10.75	9.66	9.09	8.77
11%	11.36	10.32	9.81	9.52
12%	12.00	11.02	10.54	10.29
13%	12.65	11.72	11.28	11.07
14%	13.32	12.44	12.04	11.85
15%	14.00	13.18	12.81	12.65
16%	14.69	13.91	13.58	13.45
17%	15.39	14.67	14.39	14.26
18%	16.10	15.43	15.17	15.08

It's scary. But that is how mortgages work.

The beauty of paying a little extra each month is that it does two things:

- It applies to the principal, directly increasing the buyer's equity in the home. That means it can be borrowed against, should the need for a second mortgage arise.

- Because it applies to the principal, it reduces forever the amount of interest. An additional $22.43 paid in the first payment alone reduces interest by $67.29 over the life of the loan.

Let's see what else happens when you pay that little extra $22.43 each month.

At the end of 36 months, you will have saved $130 in interest. You will also have gained $937 in additional equity. The point at which interest and amortization payments become equal will come in the third month of the 19th year. Eight months later, your home equity will for the first time be more than half of its value.

That's a substantial savings, for the price of a family outing once a month to a fast-food restaurant. If you can afford a little more, you can make out like a bandit:

- If you add $50 per month to your payment, for a total in this example of $927.57, you will pay off the mortgage seven years early, at a total interest savings of $60,333. Your interest and amortization payments equalize in 16 years, and you own half your home in 17 years. At the end of the third year you will have already saved $289 in interest, and your home equity will be $3,937.

- If you can budget and discipline yourself to pay an extra $100 each month, you will be astounded by the savings. You will pay off your home in slightly over 19 years at an interest savings of $90,511. Half equity will be reached in 13 years and eight months, and your interest and amortization payments will match each other after 12 years, four months. At the end of three years, you will have saved $578 in interest, and you will have built $6,026 equity in your home.

It is almost like a savings account that pays 10 percent.

Q: But wouldn't these savings be even greater if I paid them all up front, in the form of a bigger down payment?

A: Of course. This can be taken to the extreme—if you pay cash, you will have no interest payments and the time it takes to repay drops to zero. What this is, instead, is a way that homeowners can realize truly enormous savings by investing a little more in their homes each month than they absolutely must.

Q: But does my mortgage contract allow this?

A: Most do, but it is worth checking to make sure. It's a point to consider when shopping for a mortgage. If your current contract includes a penalty for early payment, check to see if it specifies a percentage below which your overpayments are welcome. Some, for example, do not allow payment of more than 15 percent of the principal during the first two years. All the examples above are well within that limit. In any case, it's worth checking with your lender if you already have a mortgage.

Q: Since mortgage interest on my family home remains fully tax-deductible, how will this affect my tax picture?

A: Because mortgages are front-loaded, it won't have much effect on your taxes for the first few years, because the interest portion of your payment still remains high. The long-term tax picture is more difficult to predict, for political rather than financial reasons. And because you are increasing your equity at an accelerated rate, you will have greater options no matter what the tax picture.

HOW SELLERS CAN MAKE THE MOST OF THE MARKET

Four people out of 10, according to a recent survey, discovered upon applying for a home loan that they did not qualify. That meant that tens of millions, hoping to realize the dream of owning the roof over their heads, could not. They were locked out of the market.

This sounds discouraging, doesn't it? It probably sounds more than that if you're one of the many who can't afford to buy a home, or if you're one of the many who thought your home was sold, only to learn that because no mortgage was available, your home is back on the block.

If you're trying to sell a home, your prospects are bleaker, even, than those of the buyer who otherwise can't get a mortgage.

The problem is due to several factors:

- Home prices that got too high in some regions.
- There is a glut of available housing in those regions that are now experiencing an economic downturn.
- The savings and loan crisis has greatly increased the available housing stock on the market, again chiefly in depressed areas.
- The high down payment that is usually required, typically 20 percent of the purchase price. According to a Harvard-MIT study, more than four-fifths of those in the 25-to-34-year-old bracket—a crucial home-buying demographic—can't afford the down payment, even though they can make the monthly mortgage payments.

What are buyers and sellers to do? Arrive at a meeting of the minds.

Be much more flexible and imaginative in negotiating the deal, say a sampling of real-estate agents and brokers from several states in the Northeast, South, Midwest, and West. There are several strategies that can be employed to bring about successful, though unorthodox, deals.

WARRANTIES. A popular selling tool is the existing-home warranty. For a small amount, generally under $500, a homeowner can provide what amounts to a year's service contract for the heating, air-conditioning, and other major systems in the home. The National Home Warranty Association says such a warranty causes homes to sell much faster and for a better price. The buyer, though, would be well advised to look closely at the warranty to determine whether it covers the most worrisome items in a home he or she is considering. Often, a warranty sounds better than it actually is.

(New home warranties are another matter. While the appliances and utility systems in your new home are covered by their individual guarantees, you will want additional assurance that the roof won't leak and the basement won't fill with water.)

LEASE OPTIONS. Often, if a home has been on the market for some time, both the seller and buyer might consider this route, with a portion of each month's rent applying toward the down payment in the event the option is exercised. This allows a buyer to build what amounts to equity in a home he or she does not yet own. It may be possible to negotiate a deal where the lessee does restoration and repair work on the home, under the owner's supervision, with the value of the improvements applying to the purchase price.

PRE-FORECLOSURE PURCHASES. Lenders do not like to engage in costly, expensive foreclosure proceedings. It is sometimes possible, especially in areas where the market is especially weak, to arrange to take over the payments on a home.

MORTGAGE INSURANCE. You may be able to get, or assume, an existing FHA or VA mortgage or, in some cases, you may be able to get private mortgage insurance which will reduce the size of the down payment.

You may also be able to contract for the deed of the home. In this situation, you make payments over a specified period, which are installments toward the down payment. Once the payments are made, you have the right to buy the home at a price negotiated at the time the contract was arranged. While this system offers a way to sell—or buy—a home that has stagnated on the market, it is vulnerable to abuse, and the contract should be carefully negotiated by skilled real-estate lawyers for both parties.

OWNER FINANCING. If a sale contract is arrived at that seems satisfactory in every other respect, you may consider becoming the lender of last resort. This may involve a higher than market interest rate but be more flexible as to the down payment. This requires that you be completely educated as to the prospects for the housing market in your region. More than one owner provided a mortgage that resulted in a default, only to discover that home values had dropped and there was no hope of recovering the difference. While the borrower is responsible for the difference, collecting it can be problematic, to say the least.

LAST RESORTS FOR SELLERS. Your home has been on the block for some time, and there still are no serious offers. You feel terrible. You're sure you'll never sell.

Don't be discouraged. In some parts of the country it takes longer to sell a house than in others. The market's fluctuations can affect the time it takes to sell, but those fluctuations may be only temporary. There are a lot of factors outside your control that can determine, to some extent, your chance of selling quickly and profitably.

But if there is no sign of improvement after several months, you may want to take some action on your own in hopes of moving things along.

One thing you might do is bite the bullet and consider cutting the price. When you cut the price of a home you are trying to sell, it is almost as though it were appearing on the market for the first time. There are reconsiderations all around. Real estate agents are more eager to show it, because the chance of closing quickly, and thus having to spend less time per dollar of commission, is enhanced.

(More and more agents are refusing listings for overpriced houses. In fact, if real estate agents think your asking price is too high, they may not devote much effort to selling it; if their chances for a commission are low, working to sell the house isn't worth their time.)

Don't be shy about thumping the tub for your house. Even if your home is listed with the local multiple listing service, even if you have advertisements running in the newspaper every day, still do everything you can to make sure everyone you know, and those you don't know but happen to meet, are aware that your house is for sale. Make sure everyone in your neighborhood knows. Perhaps they have friends or relatives who would like to live nearby. Perhaps they have older parents who should move closer.

Don't forget free bulletin boards at supermarkets and other public places. If yours is a college town, there are sometimes clearinghouses for information on homes that are available, because the population in such communities is quite high.

Above all, don't panic. If your house has been on the market for some time, you are likely to receive ridiculously low offers for it from people who figure you are probably fed up with the whole business and will accept their offer, just to get out from under a house you want to sell.

In fact, unscrupulous buyers sometimes act in tandem. One goes to a seller's house, looks around, and makes an insultingly low offer. A day or two later, the buyer's confederate comes by with another low offer, but one that's a little higher than the first one. Some sellers, detecting what they believe is a trend and fearful that it's the last, best offer they will receive, accept it.

Just remember this: You bought the house, didn't you? Sooner or later you will meet up with someone who sees what you saw in the house—someone who will offer for it what it's worth.

WHAT ARE IMPROVEMENTS WORTH? You may be overpricing your home because you want back every penny you put into home improvements—a deck, perhaps, or a pool; finishing the basement, or adding the extra bedroom. But few home improvements pay for themselves, and many—such as decks and pools—can actually detract from the resale value of your home. (See Chart 25.)

Wait, a pool? Reducing the value of a home? It sounds unlikely, but it's true. That's because a swimming pool is real work, unless you're willing to have it become an algae-filled cement hole in the backyard. The maintenance and upkeep costs are high. What's more, families with young children are fearful the toddlers will find their way to the pool when no one is watching, with tragic results; news reports tell us those fears are not unfounded. There can be liability problems as well. Above-ground pools are considered an eyesore by many and are viewed unfavorably by buyers.

Modernized kitchens and well-installed fireplaces are among the very few improvements that enhance the likelihood of your selling your home at a price that reflects the work that's been done. They add to your home's value and make it more attractive to prospective purchasers.

Some "improvements" can really hurt the likelihood of a resale. For example, it used to be extremely popular to transform the garage into an apartment for the kids. The chances of finding a buyer who is looking for such an arrangement, though, are slight. It's far more likely that a buyer will think of a garage as a place to put one or more automobiles.

Avoid going overboard with stylish—for the moment—finishes and wild paint schemes. Stucco walls, phony brick, and Tudor planking, added on after the fact, can cause the value of a home to plummet. An acquaintance was able to buy a fine home in a good neighborhood at a very low price,

CHART 25

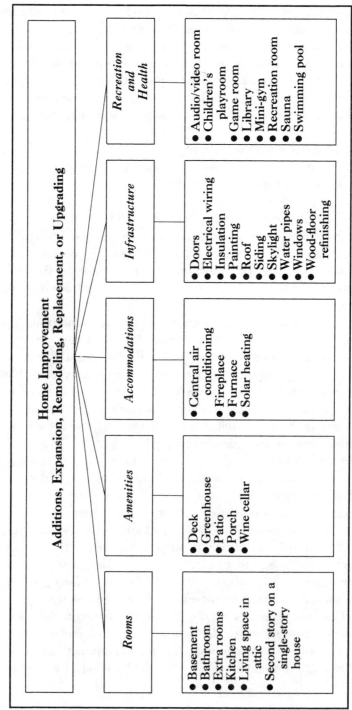

Home Improvement
Additions, Expansion, Remodeling, Replacement, or Upgrading

Rooms
- Basement
- Bathroom
- Extra rooms
- Kitchen
- Living space in attic
- Second story on a single-story house

Amenities
- Deck
- Greenhouse
- Patio
- Porch
- Wine cellar

Accommodations
- Central air conditioning
- Fireplace
- Furnace
- Solar heating

Infrastructure
- Doors
- Electrical wiring
- Insulation
- Painting
- Roof
- Siding
- Skylight
- Water pipes
- Windows
- Wood-floor refinishing

Recreation and Health
- Audio/video room
- Children's playroom
- Game room
- Library
- Mini-gym
- Recreation room
- Sauna
- Swimming pool

because its owners had seen fit to cover its beautiful exterior with plastic clapboards. The first thing my acquaintance did on moving in, of course, was to have the clapboards removed and a coat of paint applied—for far less than the difference between what he paid and what he was prepared to pay had the plastic siding not been there to begin with.

FIX IT UP. If the way to buy a cheap house is to buy one in need of a little paint and plaster, the way to keep yours from becoming a cheap house is to apply that paint and plaster before you sell.

It may not seem to make much sense to you—after all, the new owners may not have tastes identical to yours. They may want a different color of paint or a different kind of wallpaper. It doesn't matter. People will pay extra for the feeling that they are moving into a fresh, clean, sturdy home. They almost always overestimate the costs involved in simple repair and redecoration. Redecorate in conservative colors, keep the lawn manicured and the bushes trimmed, and make it look as though the home has been cared for.

In fact, you might want to visit a garden supply store and get a few plants, flowers, and small shrubs to give your home a homey look.

Walk through the house and check out the electrical plates, doorknobs, cabinet knobs, drawer pulls, towel racks in the bathrooms, and so on. Those that aren't up to par should be replaced (you can get the materials at any good hardware or building supply store). Clean the dead bugs and accumulated dust out of both outdoor and indoor light fixtures, and make sure all the sockets have working bulbs in them. A few dollars and an afternoon's work spent sprucing up the little things can make a big difference in the impression the place gives prospective buyers.

After you've gotten your home to look the way you think it should, put it to the test. Ask a friend or neighbor—one you can trust to be honest with you—to look the place over, walk through it, and give you their impressions. Ask what they like about it and, especially, what they don't like, because those are the areas that need your attention. Perhaps you've grown accustomed to the odors from a cat or dog so that you don't even notice them anymore. Prospective buyers aren't accustomed to those odors and don't aspire to become accustomed to them. If there are smokers in your house, it could be that the stench of years of accumulated smoke blinds would-be buyers to the home's strong points. If either of these things is the case, give the house a thorough airing, and banish pets and smokers to the outdoors, or have them temporarily take up residence elsewhere.

It may well be that you have become so much at one with your home that the impression your house gives has you indelibly attached to it. If so, go ahead and pack the collection of swizzle sticks from hotels all over the world. Take down the framed family pictures. Allow buyers to imagine themselves living there.

There is another thing you might want to do: Reconsider whether you really want to sell. If by now it is clear that you won't realize what you imagined you would for your home, just staying put might be an option.

Many homeowners today are improving rather than moving. Understand at the outset, though, that the chance of recovering your investment should you again decide to sell is slight. Such improvements should be undertaken when you want to make your home a nicer place for you to live.

In fact, if you go too far—overimproving to the extent that your home now looks out of place in your neighborhood—you can have new and real difficulties when it comes time to sell. Your neighbors are likely to become less friendly as well.

THE RENTAL OPTION

It is, of course, part of almost everyone's plans to one day own their home. But sometimes it makes no financial sense to do so, at least not right now. And some families will be a better position to buy a home a few years down the road.

The answer, for the time being, is to rent.

To determine if renting makes financial sense, you should compare an investment in a home—costs versus likely gains—against other investments. How much could you earn elsewhere on the money you'd have to commit to the purchase of a home? And how much more would your out-of-pocket costs be if you bought than if you rented? It could well be, especially in depressed areas or during a time of uncertainty in home prices, that you can receive greater safety and a better yield putting your money someplace else and renting.

(For example, I know of a situation in one Eastern city where two people live within a block of each other. One lives in a co-operative apartment building, which is to say he owns his apartment. The other rents. The apartments are virtually identical, and were built at about the same time by the same builder. The co-op owner's maintenance fee—the fee paid to the co-op association each month for maintenance of the building in general and common areas—is actually slightly more than the rent paid by the fellow living in the rental. The co-op owner must also make a mortgage payment each month. He's counting on his equity in the apartment being worth something. The renter is socking away his cash in high-grade bonds and several good mutual funds. What he owns will certainly be worth something—in fact, it already is.)

If you do decide to rent, keep in mind the tax aspect if you're selling your current house. Unless you invest your profit from the sale in another home ("primary residence" in tax jargon) within 24 months, you'll have to pay tax on that profit. If paying rent rather than a mortgage makes more sense for you economically, renting out your old home, rather than selling it, may make more sense taxwise.

TAKING ADVANTAGE OF THE WEAK RENTAL MARKET.

Apartment vacancies in many parts of the country are expected to be unusually high for the foreseeable future. The reason is the "birth dearth," which is another variation on the baby boom theme. The country got overbuilt to provide housing for that huge demographic lump. But the baby boomers didn't have as many babies of their own as might have been expected, so now there are fewer young people—the majority of apartment renters in most places—than there are apartments in which to house them.

As you might expect, this has resulted in a renter's market in many parts of the country. The chief exception is those areas where there is rent control, which reduces or eliminates any incentive to build apartment buildings. This means that apartment prices will always be at their highest price limit, and even then there won't be enough to go around. (Why would anyone enact rent control then? Because there are more renters than there are landlords, so rent control makes good political sense. History has taught us that when economics and politics are at odds, politics wins.)

The high vacancy rate in many parts of the country means that, as a tenant, you may be able to negotiate a lease on more favorable terms.

Your chances of success are better if you're dealing with an individual landlord rather than a giant management company. When you sit down to negotiate, you will probably be handed a printed lease, and may not be aware negotiation is possible at all. Take your time. Read the lease. Take it home and read it again, and if there are parts you are not sure you understand, have a lawyer explain it to you. The expense now is better than an expensive surprise later. You are not obligated to take or leave a deal just because the landlord has presented you with a lease. If you don't push for what you want, you certainly won't get it. You may not anyway, but it's worth the effort of finding out.

Take the money you've saved, and invest it in something that will perform for you.

12
INVESTING IN
——REAL ESTATE——

Scarlett O'Hara's father taught her that land is the only thing that lasts—the only investment that you can count on. He said it somewhat more poetically, but that was the gist of it.

Although Gerald O'Hara's words still have a germ of truth to them, today's world is more complicated. Like everything else, real estate investments must be entered into only after intensive study and with great caution. Over the years, real estate has come to suffer from many of the shortcomings of other investments, ranging from swindlers to external economic forces to prices driven artificially high by rumors. "Swampland in Florida" is popularly synonymous with sharp dealing; the farm crisis of the mid-1980s stands for hopes that boom times would continue—as does the depressed market in parts of the oil patch.

Expensive real estate acquisitions have become the domain of limited partnerships, which are the real property equivalent of mutual funds. And like mutual funds, some are excellent while others are doomed to failure for one reason or another. Unlike mutual funds, limited partnerships are not closely regulated, though there is a body of law that protects the wise.

Like any other investment, real estate investments can perform wonderfully, just okay, poorly, or end up costing far more than they're worth.

And like other investments, there is no way of being certain your real estate investment will succeed. But there are ways to maximize the likelihood that your real estate dollars will be dollars well invested.

RESIDENTIAL OPPORTUNITIES

A home in the country can buck the trend in residential properties and be a remarkably good investment. Some of the best land and country home values can be found just outside the circle of properties whose prices have already gone through the roof (and where, in many cases, they are already on the way back down). A number of experts believe that property three or four hours from a major city offers tremendous investment potential, particularly if you're prepared to hold it for some time.

Only a few years ago, the average distance most Americans would travel to a weekend retreat was about 100 miles—the distance they could typically travel in two hours of driving. But today it's twice that. The key is affordability.

In addition to distance from a major city, other factors influence land and country home values. These include the scenic quality of the area, the quality of the housing stock, and, in some cases, whether the property itself can produce income. Working farms, especially those set up for breeding high-quality livestock or horses, are at a premium—in part because of their real value as investments, and in part because of the images of the landed gentry that they invoke.

Other factors being equal, prices are a lot more likely to rise in areas near little storybook communities than they are in areas where the homes are poorly constructed, of undistinguished architecture, or merely look out of place.

Rural land prices in general, after having bottomed out in 1986, are back on the rise. In some parts of the country, farmland that sold for as little as $350 per acre in 1960 is selling for 30 times that amount now—and selling well. Rural properties have thus far been fine investments, and there's no indication the end is in sight. What's more, they're still inexpensive enough that individuals of average means can afford them.

FORECLOSURE BARGAINS. If you are in the market for a house as an investment property, it's wise to consider buying a foreclosed home. Depending on where you live, this can be a real option that deserves serious consideration.

If the thought of hunting for a foreclosed property makes you feel like some kind of vulture, bear in mind a terrible fact: Foreclosures are at record levels. Many of the economic factors cited elsewhere have driven people to over-extend themselves, to buy more home than they could afford, or simply to presume that times were going to become better than they ultimately came to be.

Regional variations are at the heart of this "homesickness." Foreclosures are not unheard of in the Northeast, but the general economic decline of the early 1980s caused a much deeper problem in the so-called energy belt (Texas, Louisiana, and Oklahoma) than in other distressed areas where housing also had been overbuilt.

Known as an "REO" in the industry, a Real Estate Owned property is a property that has been foreclosed and is currently owned by a mortgage investor who wants to sell it. The most common sellers of these properties: the Federal Housing Agency under the Department of Housing and Urban Development (HUD), the Veterans Administration, Fannie Mae (a private corporation that is the nation's largest investor in home mortgages), and such lending institutions as savings and loans and commercial banks. Now that push has come to shove among the savings and loans, there are likely to be some real bargains due to the enormous supply of homes in places where the demand is low.

Information on availability of foreclosed properties in your area can be obtained from any of these institutions. Properties are also often advertised in local newspapers, sold through local real estate brokers and agents, or offered at auctions. Fannie Mae even has a toll-free number you can call to obtain a free listing of properties in any community where Fannie Mae owns such a mortgage. The number is 1-800-553-4636.

Due to the huge supply of foreclosed homes at the beginning of this decade, it's no surprise that there was a steep jump in foreclosed homes sales. Figures from HUD show that business is still buzzing: In 1986, HUD's foreclosed home sales totaled about 39,000. That figure surged to 52,000 in 1987. A department official reports that HUD expects to sell close to 70,000 foreclosed properties in 1988.

Your main reasons for considering purchase of a foreclosed property will certainly be the price and attractive financing terms. In most cases, lenders are as eager to get rid of these properties as you are to buy them.

Caution: While the setting is right for a great deal, be careful. Promises of great bargains should be viewed skeptically. You are dealing with a complex subject and talking about substantial amounts of money. You're not just buying a house on the market, so you must be especially sure about all documentation.

Make sure there is a clear title to the property and that all liens on the house have been satisfied. Foreclosure laws vary from state to state. Some states have a set period in which the original owner has a right to buy back the property after it has been foreclosed. Check it out. You don't want to be negotiating for a house, then find out the original owner has the right to buy back the property.

Carefully inspect the house you want to buy. Look at it top to bottom before you make a bid. Bring in an expert to evaluate its condition. Know in advance whether the home requires simple cosmetic improvements or substantial repairs. Figure out those costs and consider them when you negotiate price.

Investigate the neighborhood. Find out how long the house has been vacant. If the entire neighborhood is distressed, or if the whole area has been overbuilt or is overpriced, you could be asking for trouble. You want to invest in a stable development, where perhaps just one family got in too deep and was unable to meet the payments on the home, not into a totally distressed community.

Don't assume you are getting the bargain of a lifetime just because it's a foreclosed property. Banks obviously have a vested interest and try to get what they can for such properties. The same is true of other lenders. Particularly in auctions, prices can be bid up quickly.

THE TIME SHARE DISAPPOINTMENT. You may remember all the hoopla a few years ago about time share resorts.

It certainly sounded wonderful: For a relatively small investment, you could buy a share of an apartment in a popular resort area. You would have use of the apartment for a week or two each year. And, you were often as not led to believe, if ever you wanted to sell your share, you could probably realize a capital gain. What a great idea! An investment you could enjoy at vacation time!

Owners discovered that they don't necessarily want to vacation the same place year after year. Maintenance fees continued to rise. Sometimes other owners left the property in less than perfect condition.

So the owners have decided to sell. What they've discovered is that there's no convenient way for them to do so at all, never mind at a profit. To begin with, many developers offered no provision for resale of units. This is easy to understand, because there's little profit in it, when they'd rather sell new developments.

This has led to a second industry in the form of time share resale brokerages. But a dispute has developed between the brokers and the developers—who see the brokers as competition. To make things worse, the brokerage commissions can run to 35 percent or even higher.

Needless to say, in a typical time share it's highly unusual for the seller to recover his or her initial investment. Brokers say that the average seller realizes only about two-thirds of the original investment on resale.

Selling your own time share is difficult but possible. It requires expenditures for advertising and, if you do not live near the resort, some difficulty in showing it. Other owners of your unit will not welcome the intrusion of prospective buyers during their week there. A worst case would involve you having only your week each year in which to try to sell.

(One strategy that has worked for some has been to sell the week to other owners of the same unit. In fact, there are all kinds of ways that you and other owners can work together to attempt to sell. This may reduce the problems, but it won't eliminate them. Selling your time share isn't an easy task.)

This immediately suggests several things to owners who wish to sell and would-be buyers:

- If you can sell your time share privately, you will be able to offer it at a lower price and still realize more money, because of the size of commissions.

- If you are looking to buy, there are certainly bargains available, simply because the market is flooded.

- If you are looking to buy into a new development, it's very important that you find out what resale services are available—and at what cost—before you sign anything. Make sure you get it in writing.

- Carefully consider your reasons for buying. Ask if you really want to vacation in the same place each year. Think, too, about whether you will be able to vacation during the assigned week each year. You won't just lose flexibility as to the place of your vacation; you'll get stuck with a time to vacation also, unless you can arrange swaps with other owners.

- Unless you're extremely lucky, you will not turn a profit on a time share, so you should think of it as a leisure or entertainment purchase and not an investment. A developer who tells you that your time share has great investment potential may well be violating the law—such practices have been the subject of a continuing investigation by the Federal Trade Commission.

BUYING FOR PURE INVESTMENT

There are three honest ways you can make money in real estate:

1. Buy land or buildings that are likely to appreciate. Wait for them to appreciate. Sell them.

2. Buy land or buildings and rent or lease them to residential or business tenants.

3. Buy land or buildings and improve them so that you can either sell them for more than your total investment or rent or lease them for far more than you would have realized from the unimproved properties.

Just about everything else is a variation on one of these themes. It is in the variation that things can become incredibly complex.

But for the moment, let's just deal with the basics. The value of real estate is affected greatly by economic changes, inflation and regional economic downturns in particular.

Most of you are familiar with the crash in real estate in oil industry states that occurred when oil prices fell. But this scenario, in less drastic fashion, has played out all over the country at one time or another. When the space shuttle exploded, for example, the space program was slowed considerably for a number of months. Workers were laid off. The impact on the economy of the area around Cape Canaveral, and on real estate prices, was noticeable.

Beginning in the late 1970s, home prices began skyrocketing. They kept climbing, with no end in sight. Now, with the beginning of a new decade, it has become apparent in the Northeast and in some other regions that prices may have gone just a little too high. Many people who want to buy homes are being priced out of the market. The supply of high-priced homes exceeds the demand for them, which means the prices come down or the homes go unsold.

The same holds true for the kind of residential buildings that frequently draw investors. In parts of the country where the demand for co-operative apartments and condominiums was almost beyond belief, it has slacked a little. Clearly, investors are losing money on some kinds of real estate. To get a closer look at the bottom line, see Chart 26.

When you seek to invest in some kind of commercial structure, you truly need professional help. It is difficult to appraise the factors that determine the worth of the property, which include such elements as the business or businesses located there now, the turnover rate, certainly the location (and whether new development will suddenly take it off the beaten path), and its suitability for other uses than the one it currently has.

It can no longer be assumed that real estate does nothing but grow in value.

BUYING INVESTMENT PROPERTY. It's clear by now that you need to do more research when buying real estate than you do when making

CHART 26

Calculating Mortgage Payments to Achieve a Desired Rate of Return on a Cash Investment in a Real Estate Property

1. First calculate the amount of debt you can handle while still realizing the desired rate of return on your investment:
   A. Cost of rental-income building $280,000
   B. Cash that you're considering investing 80,000
   C. Mortgage that would be required $200,000
   D. *Desired percent return on cash investment of $80,000*   12%
   E. Present gross rental income from this building $54,000
   F. Less: Present operating expenses* and allowances
          for rental delinquencies and vacancies 16,000
   G. Present net operating income .... $ 38,000
   H. Less: 12% return desired on cash investment of $80,000   9,600
   I. Net amount that you would have available for debt service
        (paying mortgage and interest) .... $ 28,400
   J. Divide the net amount that you would have available for debt service ($28,400) by the mortgage required ($200,000):

   $$\frac{\$ 28,400}{\$200,000} = .142(14.2\%)$$

   K. The result in this example, 14.2%, is known as the *annual constant*. It is the maximum percentage of the loan that you could pay each year and still receive the desired percentage on your cash investment.

*Operating expenses are cash charges such as property taxes, wages of management and maintenance personnel, insurance premiums, maintenance operations, etc.
   Operating expenses do not include non-cash charges, such as depreciation and investment tax credits.

2. Now calculate your monthly and annual mortgage payments.
   A. Select mortgage term .... 30 years
   B. Select mortgage interest rate 13%
   C. Consult interest table below. Find intersection of year
       and % 11.07
   D. Divide your intended mortgage amount   ($200,000 ÷ $1,000)
       by $1,000 200
   E. Multiply C by D. This is the total   (11.07 × 200)
       monthly payment covering principal and interest $2,214
   F. Multiply E by 12 for total annual payment covering   ($2,214 × 12)
       principal and interest $26,568
   G. You calculated that you had $28,400 available for debt service on your $200,000 mortgage. Your mortgage calculation shows that you have to pay only $26,568 each year to cover principal and interest. This means that you could realize a greater return than the 12% you desired. The difference provides you with a cushion for possible increases in operating expenses and rental delinquencies and vacancies.

CHART 26 (*continued*)

Interest Rate	Mortgage Term			
	15 Years	20 Years	25 Years	30 Years
10%	10.75	9.66	9.09	8.77
11%	11.36	10.32	9.81	9.52
12%	12.00	11.02	10.54	10.29
13%	12.65	11.72	11.28	11.07
14%	13.32	12.44	12.04	11.85
15%	14.00	13.18	12.81	12.65
16%	14.69	13.91	13.58	13.45
17%	15.39	14.67	14.39	14.26
18%	16.10	15.43	15.17	15.08

other investments. You must fully research not only the property you're considering, but also the area where you hope to invest.

Is it growing? If so, what sort of development is taking place? Is it the kind of development that is likely to increase the value of your purchase?

What is the local legal situation? Are there very tight, restrictive zoning restrictions that on one hand might preserve the locale surrounding your purchase? Do those laws box you in insofar as utilizing the property is concerned? Are there rent control laws there? How might these affect you?

If the area is growing, which it should be, what changes could halt or even reverse the expansion? How would this affect the value of your property?

Assuming that you have researched these questions and have weighed the answers, there is more you need to know. The environmental and safety issues cited above are a small but important part. There are other considerations:

- Is the building in an area that is, for instance, flooded from time to time? Does the building currently on the site comply with all local laws? What is the building's condition?

- Are you affected by easements that effectively reduce the amount of property available for your use?

- Why is the property being sold?
- What, beyond the purchase price, will it cost you to own the property? Perhaps taxes are high, or the existing building is expensive to heat or cool. Perhaps it is occupied by a tenant who has an unbreakable, low-rent lease.
- What can you reasonably hope to realize from the purchase, and how long must you wait before profits appear?
- Are your plans for the property so good that you can feel fairly sure that you will succeed?

A good place to start is the county courthouse or office building—wherever the recorder of deeds or county clerk is located. Spend some time among the files. You can learn what the real estate market has been like in the area in recent years. It can be useful to follow a property back through several sales, to determine its fortunes throughout the years. Don't be fooled by deceptively low prices, because money was worth much more in real terms only a few years ago.

Real estate courses are frequently offered by adult education programs, community colleges, or local real estate associations. They can be a big help to the would-be real estate investor.

RENTAL PROPERTIES. Buying either residential or commercial properties, then renting or leasing them to occupants can be a fine way to make big money in real estate; but, again, it isn't a sure thing.

Your success or failure at such a venture hinges largely on the amount and quality of research you do ahead of time. If you are considering residential properties, ask yourself:

- What is the housing market like in the area?
- Is the rental occupancy rate high? Is this because of demand or because of other factors, such as rent control?
- Unlike other investments, rental units require maintenance, public relations, and other activities (some, like eviction, rent collection, and repair of a trashed apartment, quite unpleasant). Are you prepared to do these things yourself? If not, do you have any idea what it will cost to have your building managed for you?
- What are the market prospects? Is the area declining economically, or growing? Is the occupancy of the building chiefly students from a nearby college (enrollments in general are going down, and students

tend to be hard on the walls and carpets on weekends); young couples just starting out; or perhaps a quiet, sedentary, older group?

- What is the rental history of the building? Has it consistently made money?

- What are the costs of owning the building? Beyond the price, there are costs such as utilities, maintenance, and the like.

- What is the turnover rate? You make no money on empty apartments, and a high turnover rate increases your work and costs substantially.

- What kind of shape is the building in? Will you have to begin replacing fixtures and appliances soon?

You will face many of the same questions when considering a commercial structure. Here, location is of greater importance. The history of the building and the prospects of the area's economy are critical, too.

Increasingly, if the building you are considering contains retail space, you must assess the impact of nearby shopping centers and malls, which have made virtual ghost towns out of once-busy retail areas in many towns.

Unless you are experienced in ownership of rental buildings, you may find it more attractive to invest in some kind of limited partnership, run by people who have a good track record in the field. They are familiar with all the headaches and know how to treat them.

Rental real estate's prospects for the 1990s reflect the prospects for the nation's regional economies: The population and business shifts underway are expected to continue. Some regions will boom, while others will decline. Fortunes will be made by those whose estimates of the future prove correct. Money will be lost by those who buy what seems like a bargain in a place where such bargains become increasingly common because there is no one to rent them.

LIMITED PARTNERSHIPS. The third basic way of investing in real estate is to buy land or buildings, improve them, and then either sell or rent them. One way of doing this is through what is called a limited partnership. All these require of you is money, though you would be wise to invest some careful study before you ante up.

They work like this: A developer or management company seeks to acquire property on which homes or other structures are to be built, or property with existing buildings that the company plans to turn into a cash producer.

In order to make the purchase or construct the buildings, the company—

instead of borrowing money—sells parts of the project to individuals or other companies, who become limited partners. Their say in how the project proceeds is limited. It is very much like buying shares in the development.

If the development is a huge success, the partners make a handsome profit. If it fails, the partners lose.

As is true with almost all real estate ventures, one problem the investor faces is liquidity. With real estate, there's generally no way to turn your investment into cash quickly without incurring a substantial loss. The same holds for limited partnerships. While it is possible to sell your stake in a development, it is not as quick or easy as selling other kinds of securities.

The original reason for limited partnerships was to provide a passive tax loss to offset active profits. But the 1986 tax reform law made short work of that, and now those losses may be used only to offset passive income. This greatly enhances the notion that the purpose of the enterprise is to make money.

If you are offered a limited partnership, one of the first things you should consider is the track record of the managing partner. If the person sponsoring the project has a long string of successes, great.

Even then, you should look closely at the project itself. The most successful developers have been known to go out on a limb, only to have that limb sawed off by an economic downturn or some other factor.

As a rule of thumb, the safest of these investments involve the purchase of existing, occupied buildings. This is because the income potential of the buildings is already established. They are less of an unknown. It then becomes a matter of weighing the investment against the likelihood and size of the return.

It is much riskier to invest in a new development, because these are more likely to fail. On the other hand, if a new development is successful, it is likely to produce far more profits than a limited partnership in an existing structure would.

Limited partnerships, then, relieve you of the responsibility of physically taking care of the property in which you're investing. But they require that you do as much research on the property as you would if you were buying it alone, and they require additionally that you research those who are offering the partnership to you.

BUYING MORTGAGES. Another way to invest in real estate is through the purchase of discounted mortgages.

Here's how it works: The holder of a mortgage at below-market interest seeks to raise cash. Because the mortgage yields less than an investor could find elsewhere, the mortgage holder has to reduce, or "discount" the price of the mortgage—sell it for less than the principal outstanding—in order to increase the effective yield.

There are several ways you can buy discounted mortgages, but more and more it is through a private sale, not unlike some sales of property itself. This is especially true when high interest rates force home owners to become lenders of last resort—that is, they provide the mortgage themselves. They then sell the mortgages. This adds a second level to their sale, but ends up providing them with the cash they were seeking to begin with.

You can also arrange to invest in mortgages through a mortgage broker. Or you may purchase mortgage-backed, government-guaranteed securities, or shares in a mutual fund that specializes in such investments, about which there is more in Chapter 10.

Before you buy a discounted mortgage, make sure that your lawyer carefully scrutinizes the terms of the mortgage and of any other mortgages or liens on the property. These items have everything to do with the amount of risk involved in the investment.

Because mortgage interest is taxable income, you want to consider the after-tax yield to determine if the investment is a good one for you.

OTHER WAYS TO PROFIT FROM REAL ESTATE. If, after careful research, you have decided that a real estate investment makes sense for you, but you do not wish to take on the responsibility of managing such an investment (or you simply can't find a property you wish to buy), there are ways of realizing profit from the real estate market.

One of them, as mentioned above, is through mortgage-backed securities. These are issued by the federal government and by various commercial companies, and often have peculiar-sounding names, like Freddie Macs and Fannie Maes. They are worth discussing with your broker in any case, even if you are not especially interested in buying real estate. They offer high liquidity, a good yield, and, generally, quite good safety.

You may wish to invest in a real estate company or a peripheral industry. This is much like investing in shares of an investment house when the stock market is volatile and busy. Brokers make money on commissions based on volume more than on price of shares. The same holds true, to some extent, in real estate. The activity in the field is what makes money for a broker, with price a secondary consideration (because real estate commissions are a percentage of the selling price).

If you anticipate a building boom, then shares of a construction company or a supplier or manufacturer of building materials may be in order.

Alternatively, you might want to buy shares in a company that has extensive real estate holdings. A number of retail companies, for example, own property the value of which exceeds the book value of the stock itself. If you anticipate an upturn in the value of retail sites in the areas in which the company does business, such an investment might be right for you.

You may also buy shares in a real estate investment trust. These are trusts that invest solely in real estate through the offering of shares. And, of course, there are real estate-based mutual funds.

BEWARE OF SCAMS—THEY'RE SMOOTHER THAN YOU THINK. The old joke about swampland in Florida for sale isn't just a joke. The real estate scam is as lively as it's ever been; it has just gotten more sophisticated.

As the 1980s wound to a close, one of the biggest real estate swindles in history was unfolding in Florida. It involved a fly-by-night outfit based in Orlando. The Florida Comptroller's Office said that instead of selling warranty deeds to homes and property, the company dealt in something called "contracts for deed."

The outcome was that hundreds of buyers, who believed they were coming to own their homes, in fact merely owned liens against those homes and were in line behind lienholders of higher priority, with the total value of the liens far in excess of the value of the properties. Hundreds of buyers found they had bought nothing, and hundreds of sellers found they had essentially given away their properties. In some cases, dozens of people purchased "contracts for deed" for the same property.

Instead—

- When buying or selling property, check the credentials of the agent with whom you're dealing. A state license provides a degree of safety, because you have recourse to the licensing agency in the event of suspected fraud.

- Get a good real estate lawyer to watch out for your interests, whether buying or selling. They know what to look for in ferreting out scams. They can also translate complicated contracts for you. Additionally, a lawyer specializing in real estate will likely know the reputation of the company you're dealing with, and will be in a position to warn you if it has been known to dance on the fringes of the law. Though lawyers are expensive, they're far cheaper to use before the fact, in formulating a safe contract, than they are afterwards in court, suing to recover your losses.

- Do not accept anything other than the property itself as collateral, if you're the seller, and avoid anything other than a warranty deed to the property if you're the buyer. While these two items do not necessarily indicate fraud, they should set off alarm bells in your mind.

- Title searches and title insurance are absolutely essential, whether you are the buyer or the seller. Banks require this before they will lend money to purchase real estate. If yours is a face-to-face, cash transaction, not involving a bank, you should insist on the same protection.

- Demand that the transaction be recorded. Any insistence that this not be done is virtually a sure sign of foul play.

Sad though it is, real estate fraud is still a very profitable business in many parts of the country. It is possible to remain within the law—just barely—and get away with it. It is also possible for dirty dealings to remain below the surface until after the crooks have blown town. You can't always count on regulatory agencies to bring the culprits to justice, and you can seldom count on them to recover your money. You certainly can't afford to undertake the investigation yourself.

You have to protect yourself, and that requires the greatest of care in either buying or selling property. Purchase of a home is likely to be the biggest investment you'll ever make. It surprises me always how easily the hucksters are able to sweet-talk buyers and sellers into making such an important decision without taking even the simplest of precautions.

FINANCING, REFINANCING, AND HOME EQUITY OPTIONS

CONVERTIBLE ARMs—A POPULAR MORTGAGE OPTION. Convertible adjustable-rate mortgages give you, the borrower, the option to trade in your adjustable-rate loan for a fixed-rate loan. And as you focus on market volatility and interest rate swings, you appreciate knowing that you have the option to lock into a favorable interest rate at some future time.

Convertible adjustable-rate mortgages are becoming an increasingly popular type of adjustable-rate mortgage. They are especially advantageous to the home buyer who can't qualify for a fixed-rate mortgage, but would very much like to have one.

Additionally, many borrowers are justifiably uncomfortable with the traditional ARM since they don't know what next year or the year after will bring as far as interest rates go.

In general, initially lower interest rates tend to attract more home buyers to ARMs than to fixed-rate mortgages. But with a convertible ARM, you enjoy the best of both worlds: You still can take advantage of the lower ARM starter rates, but the difference is that you can convert your ARM into a fixed-rate mortgage when interest rates fall.

If you are thinking of opting for a convertible ARM, the pluses include:

- If you feel uneasy about an adjustable-rate mortgage, a conversion option gives you an out. In the meantime—this is a critical point— you get the benefits of an ARM. Initially lower rates of ARMs mean lower monthly payments for you, for at least as long as those rates last. What's more, it is usually easier to qualify for an ARM than for a fixed-rate loan.

- The fee you pay for a conversion option, to be employed if interest rates drop, is typically much less than it would cost you to refinance your loan. Refinancing can cost as much as 5 to 6 percent of the total amount you are borrowing. If that amount is $100,000, you will pay from $5,000 to $6,000 to refinance.

- Details vary from lender to lender, but all charge some fee to convert. While some lenders charge up-front fees for the option to convert, others charge a premium only if you exercise the option. Shop around for price as well as conversion terms. These charges and other factors vary greatly. Fannie Mae, for example, originally charged a 1 percent conversion fee, plus a processing fee of up to $250 to convert. Later, the association dropped the 1 percent charge.

And remember: Convertible ARMs typically lose their assumability once you convert from ARM to fixed rate. This can have a significant effect on your ability to sell the property, which means it raises the issue of liquidity. Fortunately, few people look upon their real estate investments as liquid holdings (save, perhaps, for those taken in by the old swampland scams).

HOME EQUITY CREDIT—THE GOOD AND THE BAD.
Many of you are discovering there's no place like home—particularly if you own one and are looking for quick cash. Home equity lines (HELs) allow you to use the equity in your home to secure a line of credit you can tap when its needed.

With a traditional second mortgage, you get the loan in one lump sum; with an HEL, a homeowner is given a revolving credit line that may be drawn upon by simply writing a check, or in some instances, by using a credit card.

This flexibility is both tempting and dangerous. If you get in too deep, you risk losing your home. It's that simple.

This is why some critics charge that home equity lines of credit symbolize how we as individuals (not to mention as a nation) have been falling deeper and deeper into the quicksand of debt. It should come as no surprise, they argue, that HELs are so popular—enabling someone to turn a three-bedroom ranch or split-level into a giant credit card. Caution is clearly in order, especially among those who tend to be undisciplined spenders, which means almost everyone in the country.

If, despite the warnings and the dangers, you decide that you want an HEL, consider:

- What is the cap on your HEL? And is there a floor (or limit on how low your interest rate can drop)? There must be a cap on the interest rates you may be charged over the life of the credit line. Make sure you pay attention to this figure, because it lets you know just how high your interest payments can go during the life of your loan, making you better equipped to judge if you can meet your payments in a "worst-case scenario."

- What are the additional fees and extra up-front costs? Few lenders charge points, but closing costs can be hefty and can vary tremendously. Closing costs can include appraisals, legal fees, title searches, and recording costs. Some lenders waive certain fees. Investigate.

- Are there annual fees?

- What is the repayment schedule? Most are extremely lenient, which may sound great, but constitute a potential financial nightmare as your interest compounds. Are you only paying off interest and not principal? (This is common.) Will you end up with a huge balloon payment in a few years?

- Are you reading the fine print? There may not even be any fine print. Don't go by advertisements; many can be misleading.

- The biggest and by far most important question to ask yourself: Are you about to erode the equity in your home for unnecessary spending?

REFINANCING. At some time or other you'll probably consider refinancing your home, either to raise cash or to take advantage of a lower interest rate, or both. It's happening all around you. Should you join the stampede? What basic rules should guide you in this vital decision?

If the refinancing is limited to the existing amount of your mortgage debt, the answer is relatively easy: How quickly will you begin saving money?

But if the refinancing involves increasing your mortgage, it isn't all that simple. Taking on additional debt in order to reduce the amount you pay requires much more profound deliberation. It may help for you to ask yourself these questions and answer them as honestly as you can:

- Will you live in the house long enough to earn back the refinancing costs? If the residence is a pure investment, do you plan to hold it long enough for refinancing to make sense?

- Are you comfortable taking action that will result in a larger lien on your family's home?

- Would this new obligation change your lifestyle or restrict your disposable funds?

- Why do you want to refinance? Is it to merely take advantage of much lower interest rates? Or is it to raise money? If it's the latter, how is the additional money to be used?

- Will the return on the new money equal or exceed the cost of borrowing? How much of the interest—if not all of it—is tax deductible?

If the answers to the above questions are positive, it's time to tackle the second batch of considerations when you are thinking about refinancing—the hidden costs. Here are the major things you should think about:

1. A second closing. When you refinance, you once again must go through closing, which inevitably means additional legal fees—not only yours but those of your lenders.

2. Appraisal. This charge covers the cost of making sure your house is worth enough to justify the amount you want to borrow.

3. Title insurance. To determine if there are liens against the property, a new search may be required. Even if you use the same lender, there will be new title insurance and the cost of paying for a new search.

4. Document preparation. Notary services and recording taxes may also apply.

Additional costs might include mortgage filing fees, new survey or update charges, and mortgage taxes, as well as possible escrow for school and real estate taxes. For guidance on other costs, your best source is your mortgage representative. Your lender for the new loan will tell you how many points you will have to pay. Each point equals 1 percent of the loan amount.

Once you have calculated the expense of refinancing, it's time to ask yourself the essential question: How soon will the savings in monthly mortgage payments equal the extra cost of refinancing?

A rule of thumb: If the drop in interest rates equals the points you have to pay your lender, refinancing will pay off in about a year. During the second year, or maybe the third, the other costs will be recovered. After that, the savings will start to add up. Generally, it doesn't pay to refinance if you'll be moving within two years or if your mortgage is nearly paid off.

If a prepayment penalty is involved, it will take longer to see any savings. But even then, refinancing usually becomes a plus in five years or less.

In summary, the time and energy spent on refinancing a mortgage can be considerable, but the rewards and benefits can be meaningful, especially if the home will be a long-term holding.

ENVIRONMENTAL HAZARDS

In the last few years, it has been discovered that some buildings can be hazardous to your health. Valuable structures suddenly not only lose their value, but become terrible liabilities—in some cases having to be stripped down to the frame or even destroyed.

The worst offender is a mineral called asbestos. It is naturally occurring, but when run through various processes it has been transformed into everything from sound-deadening insulation to fire-proofing material (it doesn't burn) to exterior shingles.

In short, it was one of the most versatile, most popular building materials in existence. Truly wonderful stuff. Material that builders could be proud to use, and that owners could be proud to have in their buildings.

Then tragedy struck. It was discovered that asbestos can be a hazardous material. If inhaled, it can result in cancer.

There erupted a panic, called for or not, to remove asbestos wherever it may be found. This led, in turn, to stringent disposal requirements for the asbestos that had been removed. The whole process became very expensive.

This was followed, quite naturally, by lenders who became very wary about lending money for buildings that contained asbestos.

Today, an asbestos inspection is a necessity before you purchase any sort of building. It's unlikely you will get financing without it. Beyond that, it's very likely that you will face an expensive clean-up process or you will be unable to sell the building. In short, asbestos has grown to become a very serious concern.

After the jury came in on asbestos, building owners scarcely had time to breathe before there was a new worry: radon. Radon is a radioactive gas that results from the decay of other radioactive elements that commonly occur in subterranean rock and even in the soil itself. It percolates up to the surface, where it blows away. Or, at least, it's supposed to blow away.

When builders loaded up on insulation during the 1970s and 1980s to make structures energy efficient, they sealed up structures as tight as drums. The radon that bubbled up beneath homes and other buildings then had no place to go. It collected in the homes.

Breathed over time, radon causes lung cancer. Unlike asbestos, radon is a substance the effects of which seem to be in little doubt: As many as 50,000 cancer cases, according to some estimates, can be attributed to it annually, among people who breathe it without even knowing they are doing so.

It turns out that radon occurs in greater concentrations in some places than it does in others. There is a vein of rock in soil crossing part of New York, New Jersey, and Pennsylvania, for example, that produces truly enormous quantities of the deadly gas.

Fortunately, it is fairly easy to test for the presence of radon. Even more fortunately, it is fairly easy to solve a problem if one is found. It is not even particularly expensive.

The most commonly used solution is to install a ventilation system in the basement or sub-basement of a building that has been shown to carry a high concentration of radon. This blows the radon outside, where it can be blown away, before it has a chance to move to the rest of the building.

So. Asbestos and radon. That about wraps up this kind of problem, right?

Absolutely not!

Environmental concerns are likely to play a far greater role in determining the value of buildings in coming years than they have in the past—and their role in the past has not been inconsiderable.

Think of the Love Canal area of upstate New York. Or Times Beach, Missouri. Both are communities that had virtually to be abandoned. (One might also think of Centralia, Pennsylvania, a town that for years had to deal with a huge fire in an underground coal vein. One by one, homes and other structures became uninhabitable.)

Think, too, of the times that property or buildings have been found, years later, to have been contaminated by previous tenants, to the point that the buildings had to be destroyed or the property bulldozed, with the top soil scraped away and taken—expensively—to a toxic waste disposal facility. It takes little checking of local newspapers to learn of such an incident near you.

There is an important lesson here. It is no longer possible to just slap down a building any old place, nor can one safely purchase a structure simply because it seems to fit the bill.

Now you must carefully research previous uses of the site, to make sure that the land itself is not contaminated. You must find out previous uses of the building, to make sure there are no traces of some deadly substance waiting to cost you money, or worse.

You must carefully search any outbuildings, if your purchase is to be of industrial or business property, to make sure there is no storage there of materials that would be costly to dispose of. It has become a far more hazardous investment.

You must, of course, survey for asbestos and radon.

If you are investing in property through pooled ownership, a joint venture, or a limited partnership, you are no less obligated to see that these things have been done.

It looks as though an important trend in this regard in coming years will be the issue of indoor air pollution. We've touched on this with the radon discussion, but indoor air pollution goes far beyond that. It involves things as simple as ventilation and as complicated as the location of the building in question. In some regions, raw materials used in preparing mortar and cinder blocks are more highly radioactive than they are elsewhere, creating a radon-like situation in some buildings.

It's worth keeping an eye on. The whole ecological movement, which is of critical concern to everyone, or should be, is finally coming into its own. This means that costs will be incurred by owners of property that has operated at cross purposes with environmental concerns. It is in your interest that you do not end up paying, undeservedly, for the offenses of others.

13
━━━ COMMODITIES ━━━

The commodities world is, indeed, a fast-paced, dangerous place.

In fact, the commodities exchanges are nothing more or less than real-world, high-stakes gambling casinos. In their simplest form, they are where providers of commodities—grain, meat, metals, and other raw materials—agree to provide a certain quantity of their respective commodities for a certain price on a certain date.

If the price of that commodity plunges in the interim, the provider makes out like a bandit. If it soars, the buyer does. When the provider signs a delivery contract, the risks and potential gains are transferred to the buyer.

But it's more complicated than that, because those contracts to deliver materials are themselves securities, to be bought and sold as the fortunes of whatever material you've bought rise and fall. Droughts, mining setbacks, legislation, and general political conditions can cause wild price swings. As a result, the value of the contracts varies.

Making the situation more dangerous still is the low margin requirements for commodities investing. It is possible to buy contracts by putting down only 10 percent. The professionals count on earning a huge return on their investment. But it is always possible, and not uncommon, to lose your entire initial investment and more.

Here's an example: With a $10,000 investment, you buy control of $100,000 worth of, let's say, wheat. A few days later, word comes in that the growing season has been especially good, and a bumper crop of wheat is expected. The price of wheat falls. Your $100,000 is now worth $70,000. You owe $20,000—the $10,000 you invested is gone, and you must come up with twice again that much.

Then word comes that price supports are likely to be reduced. The price drops still further. You owe even more.

Then—this might as well be a real horror story—some country that buys a lot of wheat from the U.S. does something to anger the American government, and we decide to stop selling them wheat. This lowers the price even more.

You may have seen the handwriting on the wall early on and tried to sell, but no buyer could be found because the commodities exchanges place limits on the amount prices can rise or fall on a given day. This can make it impossible to cut your losses.

Of course, you could also buy your wheat at the low end of the scale, after all this has happened. Then we make friends with the foreign government again, Congress decides to keep the price supports, and wheat skyrockets. You've made a tidy fortune on a small investment.

All this is why the big brokerage houses insist that new commodities clients have a specified amount of money—usually $10,000 to $20,000—that they're ready to lose, and several times that amount that they are willing to have at risk.

Take that advice very carefully if you are thinking of a commodities investment, because it is more than a safety net: It is a safety net that you're likely to use. Studies have shown that more than three-fourths of the individual investors who buy into commodities lose their money. The odds are better everywhere else except the lottery.

In one unfortunate case, one couple—who had become sophisticated investors—lost their $700,000 portfolio, fell into debt for over $1 million more, and had to declare bankruptcy because of losses they suffered trading options in *one day*.

Why do these exchanges thrive, then, if everyone loses money? Everyone doesn't. Remember: For every fortune lost, there is a fortune won. But the winners are the big commodities companies, who have staffs of analysts, and the big end users, who come to buy the materials they need to manufacture their products. You don't stand a chance against them.

The issue of insider trading on the commodities exchanges is an unhappy one, but it does not tip the balance away from commodities speculation by individuals. That scale was lopsided long ago. Nor does the scale tip in your favor in times of high inflation. The commodities exchanges are pools of sharks, and it's easy to meet a bloody end there. While it is true that certain commodities do well during inflationary periods, just as others do well during times of great uncertainty, these factors do not raise the likelihood that you will make money to an acceptable level. If you are determined to invest in commodities, you will need far more knowledge than this or any other book can impart.

Enter the "public funds." These are, in essence, commodities-backed mutual funds. The differences are that they invest in futures and their liquidity comes at the end of the month, rather than daily. Some have performed quite well.

They're not for everyone, but for many people, they make sense from a standpoint of diversification. Some investors are uncomfortable with the volatility. It needs to be discussed with a good advisor and you must give it careful thought before you make a decision.

A reason to put some money in them? October of '87 is the best one—that's when diversification became more than just a word.

If you already have a wide-ranging portfolio, you may want to put as much as 3 to 6 percent of your investment dollar into a well-managed public fund.

As in all fund investments, it's critical that you learn everything you can about the fund before you invest. Learn the philosophy of the fund's management. Some are extremely aggressive, while others are more sedate, looking for long-term growth. The latter are, of course, safer.

AGRICULTURAL FUTURES

One way to invest in commodities is through agricultural futures. These are the "pork bellies" (a fancy name for bacon) you sometimes hear of—as well as cocoa beans, orange juice, corn, wheat, sugar, hogs, cattle, and soybeans.

Under a futures contract, the producer agrees to sell a set quantity of a set commodity at a given price to be delivered at a set future date. Futures contracts originally arose to enable producers to shift some of their business risk to speculators. With futures contracts, producers (such as farmers)—unwilling to risk low prices when their crop comes to market—know what their sale price will be, and can plan accordingly.

Ironically, the futures markets have so evolved that agricultural commodities now play a secondary role to other futures, such as precious metals and stock and stock index options. And less than 2 percent of all futures contracts are settled by delivery. Instead, a seller of a contract will simply buy a contract due on the same date to "offset" his obligation.

Agricultural futures contracts are sold on exchanges around the world. The largest are the Chicago Board of Trade, the Chicago Mercantile Exchange, the New York Cotton Exchange, and the Coffee, Sugar & Cocoa Exchange.

Investing in commodities was generally profitable in the late '70s and early '80s, when the country was plagued with high inflation. They have been in a prolonged sharp slump for several years now; some commodities have declined in value as much as 75 percent.

Even when conditions are relatively favorable, however, the lion's share of profits are made by the insiders and experts. For example, one team of investors made a fortune in cocoa bean futures in the late 1970s. How? Instead of relying on often unreliable government projections concerning the condition of the crop, they journeyed to Africa and inspected the crop first hand. This information advantage enabled them to invest in cocoa far more intelligently than their rivals.

PRECIOUS METALS

It's pretty, it's shiny, but as many unhappy investors have learned, gold is just another commodity, subject to the same nerve-wracking fluctuations as any other.

Gold's value usually remains relatively constant, even when the value of money falls. Usually, but not always. As late as 1970, it was possible to buy gold overseas for less than $40 an ounce. It peaked a decade later at $875. But no one who bought gold at $875 is happy about it, though. The inflation and the general world of uncertainty that led to panic resulting in the buying of the metal eased off. The following year the value of gold had dropped by well over one-third.

Insofar as the economy is concerned, gold scarcely fuels the engines of industry. It is what economists call a "store of wealth." It doesn't actually do anything. It becomes dead money, an item in stock rather than a flowing part of the economy, usually holding its value well while currencies rise and fall. This is its strength in bad times and its weakness when times are good.

Silver is even worse. Those who bought silver at $50 per ounce in 1980 watched themselves lose four-fifths of their investment—80 percent—in months. The chief effect of the silver panic of 1980 was to force industrial users to find less expensive silver substitutes or ways of doing the same job with less silver. This means that the need for silver in industry has gone down, reducing the metal's intrinsic value.

That doesn't mean, though, that these metals, plus platinum, have no place in your portfolio. Think of it as a little something extra, like caviar, to be purchased only after the other, wiser purchases are made. Your savings account should be able to sustain your family for three months or more; your insurance, mutual fund, and blue-chip stock investments should be sizeable and in order; and you should have a little bit of money that you are willing to lose before you buy gold, platinum, or, especially, silver.

Gold, and to a lesser extent other precious metals such as silver and the current glamour metal, platinum, appeal to the highly emotional, and herein lies the rub. Precious metals, if one is to make money on them, must be dealt with dispassionately.

There are four ways one commonly invests in precious metals:

- Coins and bars. The U.S. and a number of other countries produce .999 fine (pure) gold coins in a variety of sizes. These are to be distinguished from coins sought by collectors which have value beyond their intrinsic metal content. It is also possible to buy bars, in sizes ranging from a tenth of an ounce to hundreds of ounces. The physical possession of impressive-looking ingots is a major driving force for many who purchase the metal for all the wrong reasons, such as their belief that it will see them through some sort of impending apocalypse. It is, for the rest of us, a problem. Beyond the commissions that are paid when gold is bought and sold, there are storage costs which can cut substantially into whatever profits you hope to make, unless you want to bring your purchase home, which you probably do not want to do.

- Futures contracts. These are like other commodity contracts, and simply specify that you will buy or sell a specific amount of metal at a set price on a certain date. Speculative and risky, these are a quick way to lose a lot of money in a hurry, and are best left to the pros.

- Mining stocks. Obviously, mines do best when the price of the metal they produce is high. This is for two reasons: First, they make more money on what they produce. But second, the price specifically determines how much they produce. That's because some mining operations that are not cost-effective when prices are low become profitable when prices rise.

- Metals mutual funds. These are usually a combination of all of the above, with professionally managed investments in all three categories. Because of the professional management, and because they eliminate much of the bother of actually possessing gold, they can be a wise choice. But a particular fund should be studied very carefully before you actually hand over any money.

Because metal is an investment with heavy emotional overtones, it is particularly subject to fraudulent dealings—everything from selling gold-plated brass bars as being pure gold to selling stocks in a worthless mine. So-called "boiler-room" operations, where phone solicitors offering gold-based get-rich-quick schemes fleece you of your money, have become especially popular in recent years. You must beware of such schemes. It makes more sense to deal with a reputable dealer or broker than it does to do business with someone who phones you out of the clear blue. (See Chapter 15.)

If the precious metals are so dangerous, who then would ever want to buy them? Professional speculators do, as do industries that actually use the metals.

Investors should consider them only as part of a widely diversified portfolio, and then only if they can afford to lose much of their investment or, at least, afford to have it sit idle, producing no income.

14

COLLECTABLES AND
—OTHER TANGIBLES—

You have no doubt heard stories about the New Englander who, while going through old boxes, finds a rare edition of Hawthorne or Melville that turns out to be worth hundreds of thousands of dollars.

And you've seen the ads that suggest there are untold riches to be found in the rare coins among your pocket change.

There's a good chance that you've even allowed yourself to daydream that there's a thing or two in the attic that could put you on easy street.

Those daydreams, while enticing, aren't very practical. Just happening on a rare book or a rare coin is not something you plan to do. Every year a few people enjoy that kind of good fortune. Even more win the lottery—and the lottery is certainly not something to count on.

Which isn't to say that tangible objects can't be good investments. You may find good bargains from time to time, and your purchases may appreciate.

But investing in collectables, art objects, precious metals and gemstones, and other similar items is a risky business. Values in some fields are dictated almost entirely by the fashion of the day. There are risks and costs that you do not find in other investments.

One of the great attractions, in fact, and one of the great costs in collecting is that it becomes a way of life. It is not like other investments, where you can phone your broker and order a certain quantity of this or that. Instead, the serious collector combs flea markets, thrift shops, pawn shops, garage and estate sales, and the like. The serious collector gets in touch with others who have a similar interest, either informally or at collectors' meets.

For this reason, collecting can seldom be thought of exclusively as investing (despite what collectors say). When you consider the time involved, you could almost always make more money doing something else. To get a sense of what serious collecting entails, see Chart 27.

Most collectors have gotten into collecting because of their love of the objects themselves. If they like something, they buy it. They are therefore hard-pressed to think of their collections in financial terms.

Collecting is not a field to enter solely to make money. Unless you are genuinely interested in what you're collecting, it will not be a rewarding pastime.

Unless you have an interest beyond the financial one, you are unlikely to do the homework necessary to do well. Often, minor variations differentiate common items from very rare ones. Unless you have done your homework, you won't know the difference, and may on one hand pass up a real collector's prize or on the other hand, pay a premium price for a pedestrian item.

THE COLLECTING STRATEGY

The difficult thing about collecting is that, like many investments, it requires you to anticipate what will happen.

The current trend of collecting elegant, classic fountain pens from the 1920s and 30s has manifested itself in many ways, to the extent that there are businesses in many major cities that do nothing but buy, sell, and restore old writing instruments. And certain wrist watches—some of them a mere 30 years old—are selling for many times their original prices.

The trick to making a collecting hobby become profitable or at least pay its own way is the anticipation of what will become popular.

The collectable value of an item is governed largely by the fashion of the day. Groups of people seem to start loving the same things at the same times. By then, it's too late to start buying for investment.

As an example, the popularity of certain kinds of classic wrist watches made other types of watches good investment bargains.

The square, art deco designs have developed quite a following. This means that the prices on other styles fell by comparison. Wrist watches are popular now, so pocket watches can be had at good value. A decade ago, pocket watches were in demand. Collectables are like neckties—they fall into and out of fashion relatively quickly, but if you hang onto them, they'll become stylish once more.

An eye for quality is essential. Items that have intrinsic value will keep it long after faddish collections have faded.

CHART 27

A Guide For You To Evaluate Collectibles

Make a photocopy of this form for each significant collectible that you should evaluate carefully before you buy.

DESCRIPTION OF COLLECTIBLE: _____

_____

_____

FROM WHOM AVAILABLE: _____

_____

COST: _____

Date: _____

Evaluation Factors*	Your Evaluation.
Date produced	
Condition/grading	
Unconditional written guarantee of grade?	
Rarity/scarcity	
Is it a fad-type collectible? Might it fall out of vogue?	
Could future events have an impact on its supply, demand, and value?	

Prior ownership (additional value having been owned by someone prominent?)

Does it have aesthetic appeal as well as investment appeal?

Listed in standard reference sources?

Liquidity for resale (ready markets and pricing)?

In demand? (Amount of investor interest)

Irrefutable evidence of authenticity (unconditional written guarantee)?

Have you had it appraised, or is there a recent written appraisal by a reputable independent source?

Is it perishable (such as rare currency being subject to creases, folds, pinholes, rounded corners, faded seals and colors, and the like)?

Has it had or will it need any restoration? If so, can this be done satisfactorily? How costly will this be?

Registration or certificate of title required?

Will it require provision for special delivery handling to you?

Will it require special insurance coverage?

Will it require special safeguarding (protective storage on your premises or elsewhere)?

CHART 27 *(continued)*

Will anything be required to maintain it in optimum condition?	
Are the price and any other costs (such as commissions) fair?	
Can you really afford it?	
Would you be investing too much in this one collectible rather than diversifying the same amount over more less-costly objects?	
If the seller is a dealer, is there a buyback policy? If so, at what pricing formula? Is the dealer well established, so as likely to be able to honor a buyback agreement?	
Other factors:	

*All evaluation factors may not be applicable to all types of collectibles.

There are organizations and publications serving almost all areas where collections are possible. One place to start is to pick up a copy of Collectors News & The Antique Reporter (Box 156, Grundy Center, Iowa 50683).

How do you get started collecting? Chances are you already know. If you have sufficient interest in a particular field to begin collecting its memorabilia, then you probably have already met people knowledgeable in the field.

Get into it slowly; don't buy beyond your knowledge. Attend swap meets and visit other places where the objects of your affections are likely to be found. Some of the best prices, and some of the most inflated ones, can be found at flea markets and tag sales. Old railroad switch lamps, for instance, are growing in popularity and in price. But they can still be found in junk shops and second-hand stores at reasonable prices. Railroad devotees probably know the differences among switch lamps, which is good, because some are very rare while others are quite common.

Always know before you buy. And remember, condition is everything. Just because some old watches and fountain pens are valuable, don't think that every old watch and every beat-up pen is worth even the trouble of carrying home.

BOOKS

If you do everything right, you can make money in collecting rare books, but if you do everything right, you can make money in any sort of investment.

As in other fields, some authors or subject areas are at any given time more popular than others. If you buy a particular author or choose an area at its peak of popularity—such as comic books a couple of years ago—you will pay top price. The trick is to anticipate those authors or areas that are ripe for a rise in value, and form your collection before the stampede begins.

The biggest money—and the biggest risk—can be found in two areas: the extremely rare, extremely expensive books usually found only at special auctions, and first editions from notable authors. Some collectors specialize in signed first editions, and there is even a monthly book club that sells these, new, to collectors. Whether the special collectors' volumes will rise in value, though, is yet to be seen.

Rare book prices can drop dramatically. As authors become unfashionable, the value of copies of their works can plummet. This is why for the beginner it's probably safer to pick a subject area than a particular author. Within that field you may specialize further. An acquaintance, for example, collects books dealing with herpetology, the study of reptiles. Within that, he also collects the books of an early herpetologist, Raymond A. Ditmars. One day, while looking for a copy of a Federal Writers Project book on reptiles, he found a set of books written by that depression-era government agency. He began collecting those as well. It turned out that the Federal Writers Project collection soon skyrocketed in value, and he was able to sell that collection—sans the volume on reptiles—for enough to make several expensive and important purchases for his main collection, of books about snakes, turtles, and lizards.

When purchasing a collectable book, pay close attention to its condition. Slight defects can mean big money when it comes time to sell. And don't accept a marred volume because it's offered to you at a low price, unless you simply want it to read. The low price will be more than reflected when and if you seek to sell or trade.

Instead, always go for quality. Better to get a perfect specimen of a less-valuable book than a tattered copy of a collector's dream.

Specialize. A random collection of various volumes is not of the value of a collection dealing with specific topics, such as natural history in the 19th century, aviation in its formative years, or even old cookbooks.

Get to know the subject and get to know your dealer. Let him or her know the books that specifically interest you. Ask for advice and even referrals. Find out the names of dealers who specialize in your area of interest, and contact them. The prices of books vary widely, and an expensive volume in one city—or even at one dealer—may be relatively cheap in another place, where there are fewer collectors specializing in that field.

It is generally not wise to purchase collectables by mail, but with rare books it's sometimes necessary. It is possible to arrange for a dealer in a distant city to ship a book to your dealer for your inspection. This will probably cost a small amount for shipping and insurance, and may drive up the cost somewhat to cover what amount to sales commissions to both dealers. If you go the direct route—that is, have the book shipped to your home or office—make sure that you have a right of return.

Make sure, too, that you have a place to store your books. Extremely valuable ones should be kept in acid-free packages or wrapped in special plastic that prevents deterioration. Sad to say, but it's a risk to read rare books or even keep them on a bookshelf, just as handling a rare coin can reduce its value.

Attend rare book auctions. If you live in a small town, this can be inconvenient, but it's worth it. Perhaps you can join with other collectors in your area to attend together an auction in a nearby city. Or your interest may rise to the point that you will plan a short vacation around attending an auction in a distant city. You needn't go there to buy; just pay attention. Talk to other collectors, especially ones in your area of interest. Forming friendships in your chosen field can result in great benefits. The greater the number of knowledgeable people who know what you're seeking, the greater the chance that you'll find it. Correspond with others who share your interest.

Most important, always know what you're buying. There is a story, probably apocryphal, of a new collector of law-enforcement books who happened upon what he was sure was a collector's prize: An autographed copy of *The Untouchables* by Elliott Ness. He paid an arm and a leg for it, but didn't mind—this would clearly be a wonderful centerpiece for his collection. Only later, when he bragged to other collectors about his prize, did he learn the expensive and embarrassing truth: Ness died before the book was published. The autograph was a fake, and reduced the book's value to below that of a volume with no inscription at all.

ART

Paintings that just a few years ago were within the price range of many galleries are now selling in the multi-millions of dollars. Many of those art treasures, brought to this country by enormously wealthy Americans a generation or two ago, are now being taken to Japan by enormously rich persons and companies there. Now is a good time for investing in the secondary art market—engravings and other prints, especially signed, numbered ones. Some have already skyrocketed, as anyone who has bought a Norman Rockwell print recently will tell you.

If you're interested in investing in art, do your homework. You probably won't become an expert, but you will probably rise above the "I don't know about art, but I know what I like" attitude. Seek the advice of experts. Learn what the price history is in your area of interest. Different kinds of art fall into and out of style, with a resulting effect on price.

Buy what you like and are comfortable living with. This is a kind of aesthetic hedge. Even if your masterpiece doesn't grow in value as much as you'd like, at least you'll have something you're proud to hang on the wall.

(This, though, can work against you. Because some investment costs are tax-deductible, it behooves you to have the Internal Revenue Service think of your art purchases as investments. The IRS is much happier to do so if you can prove that your collection has been kept in storage. Auditors are less likely to allow deductions for pretty pictures you've used to decorate your home.)

Choose your dealer carefully. While not every reputable dealer is a member of the International Fine Print Dealers Association, such membership provides a little extra insurance from the fraud that seems always to be lurking nearby. This is especially important if your art investment is to be in the hottest area of affordable work right now, high-quality prints.

Like most of us mere mortals, you may feel a little nervous stepping into a top-drawer gallery. But those galleries achieved their status through a combination of service and savvy business. Many of the smaller galleries are just fine, but most tend toward the avant-garde, which is the art world's equivalent of high-income stocks and bonds—highly speculative. It's better to wait until you've invested in a few high-quality pieces before diversifying and investing in that extremely promising unknown. And faddish artists can be overnight wonders, their work rising and falling in value like an inverted V.

Get to know your dealer. Establishing a relationship with a gallery can be one of your best investments. Once a reputable dealer knows your tastes, your purpose in purchasing art, and your financial limitations, he or she will be able to steer you toward purchases that will be just what you are looking for.

Many galleries and some dealers offer a buy-back agreement that lets you trade up to better pieces as time goes on. These can be both a good indication of the gallery or dealer having confidence in the product and a hedge that establishes something of a "floor" value for your acquisition.

Think quality. A small piece of obvious quality is a far better investment than a bigger piece that may not be quite as good.

Finally, spend within your budget. No matter how tempting, if you cannot afford a particular piece, don't let its charms convince you that you can.

Counterfeits: Just a few years ago, it was possible to purchase lithographs and prints by such notables as Dali and even Picasso for a few hundred dollars.

They all got sold, but the supply didn't diminish and the prices rose only moderately. Why? Because dishonest though enterprising people—and crooks are certainly enterprising—were counterfeiting them and selling them to uneducated and unsuspecting buyers.

Fortunately, an organization of reputable print dealers, the International Fine Print Dealers Association, is spearheading an effort to keep the art business honest. That group has been a clearinghouse of reports of phony prints, and keeps them catalogued. If there's a question, a dealer can contact the association.

The industry group also runs in its monthly newsletter a list of fakes known to be in circulation, and cooperates both at the organizational level and through its dealer members with law enforcement.

There are various types of art works, such as paintings, sculptures, photographs, collages, and prints. Old masters or at least fairly established artists can be found in standard reference materials and sell with enough frequency to have established ready markets and pricing. As to contemporary art works, no one really can predict which works and artists will make it.

Certain artists, styles, or periods may be in fashion for a while, and then fall out of fashion. Even prices for some of the masters have declined in price from time to time.

Here are some guidelines to collecting art works: Distinguish minor-but-good works by major artists from minor-and-poor works. Be sure a work is authentic; if necessary, consult a museum curator or other specialist before buying. Determine a work's history of ownership (known as "provenance"). How often has it been sold in recent years (a frequently-sold work may be of dubious value)? Is the work in good condition?

Keep abreast of what's going on through the art columns in newspapers; news magazines; and "trade" magazines covering the art scene, gallery openings, auctions, and museum shows. Also, you should visit museums, galleries, and auctions. As to auctions, when researching an artist's auction record, here are some points to check out: Has the artist's work sold at many auctions or just a few? Were the auctions at major houses or small? Did the works sell? Did sale prices exceed pre-auction estimates or fall short? Who purchased the works—a museum, a knowledgeable collector, or the artist's own dealer?

Collecting prints is one of the most affordable ways to begin collecting art. Prints should not be confused with reproductions. Original prints are impressions on paper made from a printing surface created by the artist for the purpose. The number of copies (also called impressions) should be limited; the printing surface (matrix) should be destroyed after the printing. The artist usually signs each impression and numbers it in the margin. Generally, the smaller the edition, the more valuable the individual prints.

Of course, collecting art isn't just a matter of monetary value; it also can be a great source of other enrichment, and may even outweigh dollar value to you.

As is true with other collectables, art works are subject to the fickle whims of fashion. Today's inexpensive purchase could be tomorrow's record seller; but tomorrow's record seller could be the next day's record loss. For this reason, serious involvement is required if you intend to make money buying and selling art. Without a sense not only of the art itself but of people's attitudes as well, you will not be able to predict the whims of fashion. Whether or not you profit then becomes largely a matter of luck.

CAMERAS

Camera collectors who have made their purchases carefully and who have applied their knowledge in picking the right time to sell have made out like bandits in the last few years.

One type of German 35mm camera, the Leica rangefinder series, sold typically for $300 in 1976 and brought four times that much just two years later. That's because in the years immediately following World War II, European refugees found that those cameras were far better stores of wealth than were the often-dubious local currencies.

When there was high inflation in America in the late 1970s and early '80s, many of those same people again put their money in the small, high-quality cameras.

After inflation went down, so did the price of Leicas, although they have never approached their earlier low prices.

Today, a new group of players has come onto the scene, and prices have risen again. These new collector-investors are the Japanese.

After years of exporting high-quality photographic equipment to the United States, the Japanese are now seeking to use some of their plentiful cash by buying some of their cameras back!

As a result, some cameras, real classics, that you could get for a few dollars not long ago are now valued in the hundreds. Others have just disappeared from the market. You can't find them at all.

There are even camera dealers who do nothing but act as agents for Japanese collectors, buying from Americans at almost unheard-of prices.

The market has changed. Camera collectors don't spend as much time in camera shops. Now more deals are made through private sales and at camera shows.

There is almost a "camera underground," a circuit of camera collectors nationwide. Their bible is *Shutterbug* magazine (5211 S. Washington Ave., Titusville, Florida 32781), which has articles and display advertisements. But the hard-core collector spends time poring over the classified advertisements. Bargains can be found here, though the ads are all but undecipherable to those who don't know cameras.

Like any collectable, the value of a camera, even a high-priced classic, is determined by nothing other than how much you can get for it. The range of prices is wide, even within a particular model. There are regional differences; one brand may be hot among collectors in one part of the country, while its price hasn't risen at all elsewhere.

Additionally, there are minor variations among seemingly identical cameras. Factors such as the color of the lettering on the shutter-speed dial can greatly influence the value of a camera, if one variation was manufactured in limited quantity. That's why camera collecting is an area for the truly dedicated. The dilettante will lose money.

What are the factors that affect the value of a particular camera?

- High quality. Cheap, junky cameras are collected by only a few people, and their prices are low. A camera that is recognized as a landmark design, that was expensive when it was sold, is likely to hold its value.

- Rarity. As with all collectables, a limited supply coupled with a substantial demand results in higher prices.

- Condition. Most collectors will reject all but those cameras that are in perfect condition. Even the tiniest of scratches, nicks, and dents will reduce the selling price of a classic camera by sometimes hundreds of dollars.

- Popularity. This is the wild card. Some cameras are extremely popular, while others have never gotten the attention of collectors. Those who have made money collecting cameras have done so by anticipating what is likely to become popular. Those who recognized the renewed Japanese interest, first in purchasing quality German cameras, then in buying back cameras they made themselves, have made a lot of money. Collectors study the market carefully. When they find a particular type of camera that they believe ought to be collectable but that has never taken off, they will start buying them. Then they will wait. Sometimes, they become big winners. Frequently, they are lucky to end up breaking even.

Areas to avoid include old folding cameras. Many people unfamiliar with camera collecting assume these are of high value, but with few exceptions they're not. Old folders are chiefly decorative items, of use as bric-a-brac or handsomely displayed in showcases.

Camera collecting can be a wonderfully rewarding, though expensive, hobby. But it is only when it is undertaken with long study and extreme care that it can be profitable as well.

RARE COINS

One of the most popular hobby-investments is and always has been coin collecting. But, as in other fields where there is a lot of money and there are a few who have more dollars than sense, the sharks have been quick to circle, and it has become easy for the uninitiated to get eaten alive.

The situation has gotten so bad that even the Federal Trade Commission has joined in, in cooperation with coin collectors' groups, in the hope of alerting would-be collectors to ever-increasing fraud.

Don't buy until you know what you're doing, advises the American Numismatic Association. The ANA sets standards for, among other things, determining the condition of coins.

Over-grading a coin—that is, selling it as being in better condition than it really is—is the commonest kind of fraud encountered by coin collectors. Grading coins is a very technical skill, and only a few people are qualified to do it well. The best are certified by the ANA.

Why coin collecting? It's an investment plan that's enjoyable and, undertaken carefully, it can be profitable as well. It has what is known in the trade as the "fondle factor"—investors have something tangible and, often, quite pretty. This can, of course, be a weakness, tending to take investors' minds away from the steely business sense they must apply if their hobby is to be financially rewarding as well as fun.

Investment-grade coins are not the pennies stuck into collectors' folders sold at hobby shops. They're usually high-priced gold or silver issues in pristine condition. They are sold by dealers or at auction. The age and rarity of coins play a part in their value, but their fame and popularity also enter the picture.

A distinction must be made between coin collecting and coin investing. There are now joint ventures being traded on Wall Street that are based on rare U.S. coin investments.

But that is very different from the magazine advertisements that suggest that if you buy this book or that one, you'll soon find a fortune in your pocket change. It doesn't happen anymore, if ever it did.

Almost every youngster in this country at one time or another spent time trying to find a 1909-S VDB penny, the rarest and most desired of the Lincoln head pennies, made famous largely in the advertisements on the backs of comic books.

If you find one now, it's certainly worth something. But if it's uncirculated, it's worth up to 100 times as much. There is very little value in used coins.

Investors who want to maximize the value of their collections frequently specialize—pick a particular type of coin and try to assemble a complete set. Sets are almost always worth more than the sum of their parts, which is what makes collecting worthwhile.

There are costs involved beyond the prices of the coins you buy. Dealers add a mark-up. There are storage costs. And the difference between wholesale and retail prices is high, so a given coin has to rise substantially in value before it can be sold at a profit.

How does one get started in coin collecting? The first thing you do, before you buy a single coin, is study, study, study. Most libraries have substantial sections on coin collecting, and this is a good place to start. There are three pamphlets you should send for as well:

- "What You Should Know Before You Buy Rare Coins for Investment" is published by the Professional Numismatists Guild, Box 430, Van Nuys, California 91408.

- "Consumer Alert: Investing in Rare Coins" is put out by the Federal Trade Commission and the ANA. You can get a copy by writing the FTC, 2806 Federal Building, 915 Second Ave., Seattle, Washington 98174.

- "A Consumer's Guide to Coin Investment" is another federal government publication. It's available by writing to Department 594T, Consumer Information Center, Pueblo, Colorado 81009.

Then, when you're ready to make your purchases, there are some precautions you can regularly take:

- Make sure that whatever dealer you do business with has subscribed to the ANA code of ethics. This means that the dealer has sworn not to over-grade coins and has agreed to a specific mediation process in the event a customer believes there has been wrongdoing.

- Be extremely leery of mail-order coin dealers. Some are honest and reputable, while others are not. A popular practice is to sell "subscriptions" whereby for a fixed amount each month, the subscriber receives coins in the mail. These are generally sold at retail book value and are in the stated condition. But they are often coins that are not particularly popular among collectors, and you are likely to have difficulty selling them at all, never mind at a profit.

- Don't fall for pretty packaging. Even the most worthless coin is very impressive when it's in a beautiful red velvet case.

- Consider buying from the U.S. Mint. The government itself offers commemorative coins to collectors, and these have traditionally gone up in value. Some U.S. commemoratives are worth truly astronomical sums, and complete sets can be enough to retire on. It is usually fairly inexpensive to purchase these as they become available as new issues. Just don't plan on their value rising dramatically overnight.

Over the years, coin prices have more than kept pace with other collectables and in fact with other investments. But for every dollar made, there have been many dollars lost, by those whose "valuable" collections turned out to be worth little more than face value.

In recent years, there has been yet another way for investors to get involved in rare coins as investments. There are now rare-coin-backed mutual funds. While these funds remove all the excitement of coin collecting, they substitute the benefit of professional management. They are worth considering if you are interested in the profit potential of rare coins, but lack the time, knowledge, or money to get heavily involved.

NEW COINS

From time to time, the designs of U.S. coins are changed. This happened in the early 1960s, when the silver content of the coins was removed. It happened again in 1976, for just that year, with the production of bicentennial coins.

You might think that these changes are likely to represent new investment opportunities. But those opportunities won't be found where you expect, according to the experts.

When American coinage changes, there is a rush to sock away a few of the old coins and a few of the new ones. That means that the coins most likely to be saved are the ones least likely to become rare over time. Those who saved rolls of bicentennial coins, for instance, would have done better putting the money practically anywhere else.

(The government loves you to buy coins and keep them. That's because it costs much less than their face value to produce coins, so when they're not used for anything, it's profit. The same holds true for commemorative stamps. They cost little to produce. When they're not used, it's all profit.)

There have been exceptions. If you saved all your silver coins during the changeover from silver to the nickel-copper sandwich now used, you would have made out like a bandit, especially if you sold them during the ridiculous silver craze of the late 1970s. That's because of their silver content, though, not because of their value as rare coins.

If there is a production problem at the mint, imperfect coins are rounded up and destroyed. But sometimes the error isn't caught until some of the coins—no one ever knows exactly how many—are released to circulation.

That happened in 1989 with some coins minted in Philadelphia that weren't fully struck on the obverse—"heads"—leaving the date indistinct and the mint mark absent. Extensive press coverage helped the price of these coins to rise to a high of about $200. They then dropped rapidly to below $50. But their story isn't over yet.

Being a rarity, and a well-publicized one, they are likely to be worth much more in, say, 50 years. Whether they will be worth more than the same amount put into another investment remains to be seen.

The only predictable effect on values that is brought about by a change in coinage is an effect on numismatics as a whole. Whenever coins get a lot of publicity, prices in general go up, because people become interested in investing.

Typically, people think of buying a roll or two of the new coins, to put away in hope the value will rise. This piques their interest. They talk to coin dealers, perhaps read a little about the subject, and make a few purchases, which can either be wisely chosen or silly. If they maintain their enthusiasm, they may develop the skill and gain the knowledge necessary to make money investing in coins. If not, the coins they already have remain, soon forgotten, perhaps to show to their grandchildren.

Here's what a change in coinage means to you: If you have coin investments, their value may rise over the months that follow. If you're interested in coin investments, this is not the best time to buy. Some brokerage houses now deal in rare coins, which can be a source of expert advice.

But by all means don't go out and buy rolls of the new coins, hoping they will come to be of great value. They almost certainly won't.

GEMS

In 1988, an enormous ruby and the world's largest flawless diamond went on the auction block, only to be yanked back when they failed to draw the minimum bid.

Such a thing would have been unheard of only a few years earlier. What happened?

During the late 1970s, inflation was rampant and the gloom-and-doom fringes of society were in full voice. There was a rush to put money in "stores of wealth"—items and commodities that would hold their value when money did not. Even as gold ran up to more than $700 an ounce, high-quality diamonds more than doubled in value virtually overnight.

The diamond market got so frenzied that the giant cartel DeBeers took out ads warning investors that prices had gotten out of hand. Tiffany & Company did much the same thing.

As inflation decreased and the economy began to move forward more rapidly, gemstones lost a little of their sparkle. There were so many places where investments would do more for the investor.

When considering diamonds and colored stones as investments, you must pick your way carefully through a minefield, as it were:

- Gemstones don't provide income. Profits, if any, come solely as capital gains.

- They are a highly emotional investment. Movies and novels about the gem trade in its various facets, so to speak, have been successful over the years. Nobody ever wrote a potboiler about municipal bonds. For this reason, it's difficult to look dispassionately at gemstones as an investment, and this opens the investor to a world of scams.

- The small investor is likely to enter the market with less information than he or she would require before speculating elsewhere. This results in an expensive education. High-pressure seminars, mail-order sales, and buy-back agreements exist to prey on such investors, and are to be avoided.

- Investment gemstones are different from jewelry gemstones. Most stones used in jewelry are of a quality far too low to be thought of as investments.

- The price of gemstones, particularly diamonds, is subject to political considerations far more fragile, and situations far more likely to arise, than those which the gloom-and-doom people seek to avoid. South Africa and Sierra Leone are the chief diamond producers. Enough said.

- The investor can be eaten alive by commissions and markups. Diamonds are often sold at twice their wholesale price. The best deal an investor can negotiate will reduce that by as much as two-thirds, meaning the price will still be a third above wholesale. And when it comes time to sell, the price offered is always below wholesale. This means that the price must go through the roof for the investor to break even—and this is before sales commissions are added. During the late 1970s, when diamonds went wild, investors were disappointed to find that, even when prices doubled, they actually realized 5 percent or less when they sold, which didn't even keep up with inflation.

If, despite the danger, you decide to invest in gemstones, a few precautions can reduce the danger:

- Deal only with reputable companies. Check with the Better Business Bureau, the Federal Trade Commission, and the state attorney general's office before giving your money to a dealer.

- Never buy stones sight unseen. Unlike stocks and bonds, and even gold, gemstones have individual characteristics that determine their value. Make sure that what you buy is what you receive.

- Never buy without getting an independent appraisal. It is best if you make the acquaintance of an appraiser yourself, someone who can explain to you what the appraisal means. The retail value of the stone, so often used in diamond-district appraisals to convince a purchaser that the deal offered is a good one, is useless, because you will not sell the stone at retail. Be certain that the appraiser is certified by the American Gem Society, the organization that works to keep the industry honest.

- Study the market before you invest. The American Gem Society (5901 West Third Street, Los Angeles, California 90036-2898) offers an information kit for would-be gem purchasers. Get it and read it just as you would study the factors involved in other investments. If you lack the interest to study the subject, put your money somewhere else.

- Find a place to store your purchase. Safe-deposit boxes used to store gemstones purchased for investment are tax deductible.

An investment in gemstones should be undertaken only after long, careful consideration. It has certain limited value as a hedge, but its dangers usually outweigh its advantages. Only the most careful of investors will do well in the gemstone market. Buyer beware.

WINE

There's a relatively new investment that's becoming more and more popular. It's not quite like commodities trading, because there's less risk, and it's not like trading in gems or precious metals, even though it involves a degree of glamour.

It's investing in high-quality wines.

The mention of wine investment probably causes you to think of people who purchase a case or two of wine, take it home, save it for years, and hope to sell it at a profit but probably end up consuming it instead.

Obviously, that couldn't be called an investment at all.

Investing in wines works like this: For an agreed amount of capital, you purchase a specified number of bottles or cases of a promising wine. It is stored for you in the conditions of temperature, darkness, and so on that allow it to mature to its best potential.

After several years—usually four or more—you sell the wine, either through a wine brokerage or at auction.

Indeed, the profits have become such that some of the best California vintners are keeping substantial quantities of their own best years off the market, hoping to realize the gain themselves several years down the line.

Wine investing has long been popular in England, and a few Americans have done it in the United States for several decades.

Like any investment, it is not a sure thing. But with care you can do very well, and with care plus a degree of luck, you can realize truly impressive profits.

A well-known New York wine authority points to his daughter's college education as an example. "My daughter went through college on 100 cases of Port," he says. "When she was born in 1964, I bought 100 cases of Port for less than $3,000. When she was ready to go to college, it was worth $90,000."

"It didn't work out that way for my son: he was born in a bad year."

A number of different wine investment plans are available. Several specialize in the best California wines, while others concentrate on the top-drawer French chateaux. There is even talk of a wine-based mutual fund forming in the near future.

How does one go about investing in wine?

- Don't do it unless you're interested in wine. While the returns on wine investments have ranged from good to astronomical, this is largely because the investors have been very knowledgeable, and have backed the right vintages. Lately, the opinion of the wine writers has been very important. But by the time the news is published, it's too late to get really low prices. Fortunately, the potential of a given year is known in the industry before it hits the papers. But you won't be in on that knowledge unless you are paying close attention. And in any case, so to speak, the enjoyment of investing in wine is lost if you look at it as just another investment.

- Make sure the investment package includes storage and insurance, and that you figure out the costs ahead of time. Wine bottles can break, and storage can be very expensive.

- There are exceptions, but wine is usually an investment you want to stay in for a minimum of four years. You can get out before that, but usually it's then hardly worth the bother.

- Consider your tax picture. Wine investments can offer substantial advantages, because its appreciation is untaxed until the wine is sold.

- Stick with the best years and the best chateaux. There are only about 50 wine investment properties in the entire world. Those are where the most dramatic appreciation takes place. The secondary chateaux offer wine that involves less of an initial investment, but the increase in value will be less, also.

- Buy case lots if possible, because they're easier to sell and because the per-bottle price is generally lower.

The romance of investing in wines stored in a French cave or a California cellar is a big part of the allure of wine investing. It is possible to visit one's investment, to actually look at it, even to bring home a bottle for a special occasion. More than just a commodity, it is a tangible item that improves with age.

And coming back from France with a bottle of wine is a far more romantic notion of commodity trading than the trader in pork bellies who brings home the bacon.

A FINAL NOTE

The joys of collecting often go beyond (and sadly, sometimes replace) financial gains. But if you intend to make money collecting anything, be it art or books or coins or wine, you should do your collecting in a businesslike way. Keep track of the date and place of purchase and prices of each item in your collection. Keep an inventory of your holdings, such as is found in Chart 28. Pay attention to the market in those things you have purchased, for just as with securities, this is the only way to determine when to buy and when to sell.

CHART 28

Registry of Collectibles You Own

Adapt this form to your particular needs, such as for a collection (of stamps or coins, for example) rather than an individual item. Make copies to record your various collectibles.

ITEM(S)

Description: _____

Condition/Grading: _____
Rarity/Scarcity: _____
Evidence of Authenticity and Grade: _____

Registration/Certificate of Title: _____

Appraiser (Name, Address, Phone No., Date of Appraisal): _____

PURPOSE

Primarily: ☐ For investment   ☐ For hobby   ☐ For personal aesthetic appeal
        ☐ Other: _____

For a Combination of Above: _____

ACQUISITION

Date Acquired: _____

From: Name: _____ Phone No.: ( ) _____

Address: _____

City: _____ State: _____ Zip: _____

□ Dealer □ Retailer □ Auctioneer □ Collector □ Other: _____

COST

Purchase Price .... $ _____

Commissions to: _____ .... _____

Taxes: _____ .... _____

Cost of Any Special Information/Counsel: _____ _____

Any Appraisal Cost: _____ .... _____

Any Travel Cost (to View, to Buy): _____ .... _____

Any Delivery Cost: _____ .... _____

Any Repair/Restoration Cost: _____ .... _____

Any Other Cost: _____ .... _____

Total Cost $ _____

CHART 28 *(continued)*

RECORDS

In Whose Name(s) You Own Item(s): _____

_____

Where Item(s) Kept: _____

Where Your Records Are Kept: _____

INSURANCE

Description of Coverage: _____

_____

Name(s): Of Insured: _____

Of Policy Owner(s): _____

Insurance Company (Name, Address, Phone No.): _____

_____

Insurance Agent (Name, Address, Phone No.): _____

_____

Policy No.: _____ Effective Dates: From: _____ To: _____

Premium: Amount: _____ Payments Due: _____

15

HOW TO THROW
— YOUR MONEY AWAY —

For some reason, Americans have always had a soft spot in their hearts for swindlers. From Mark Twain's story about the California frog loaded with shot to the lovable grifters seen in George Roy Hill's motion pictures, we find confidence artists to be lovable rogues.

Of course, that isn't the true picture at all. Everywhere there is a dollar to be made, there is a crook in the running for it. Far from endearing, these people cheat and steal from everyone they can. Those who are the easiest targets are often those who can least afford the loss.

The con game has become much more sophisticated over time. It is much more difficult to tell the good guys from the bad guys. This means that you need to check out the credentials of everyone with whom you plan to leave much money at all.

More difficult to sort out are those who would give you financial advice or warnings. Sometimes they are governed by the best motives in the world. Sometimes not. But the ones on the far reaches of the spectrum are almost always wrong. Give them a wide berth.

It used to be—maybe it still is—that you could turn to the back of almost any magazine and see advertisements claiming that for a specified amount of money (generally sent to a post office box) you could receive information on how to make thousands and thousands of dollars through the mails.

If you sent off the money, you would often as not receive a mimeographed letter in return. It would tell you that the way to make thousands of dollars through the mails is to take out an ad just like the one to which you responded and, when the money started rolling in, send out letters just like this one.

There was talk at one point that the postal authorities were finding a way to crack down on this sort of behavior, but were having difficulty in that it didn't seem to be illegal. Last I heard, they were pursuing it under the same statute that forbids chain letters; because they are a pyramid scheme, and if everyone followed the advertiser's advice, pretty soon the supply of suckers would be exhausted.

Whatever happened, it did not grow to be an enormous national problem. But it serves to illustrate a point.

The world is full of would-be Pied Pipers and of people looking for someone to listen to. The world is also full of people who want very desperately to believe that there are shortcuts and easy answers to life in our terribly complicated world.

Of course, there are no real shortcuts and few easy answers. A little careful study can prevent you from wandering the wastelands in confusion. But no one is going to show you the path to miracles.

GLOOM AND DOOM

There is a portion of the population that is certain that apocalypse lurks just around the corner. This group also seems to favor stockpiling gold. If the apocalypse comes, it's doubtful gold will be of much use. But it is, I suppose, a logical extension of the belief that gold tends to hold its value in times when other stores of wealth, and securities, have pretty much lost theirs.

The danger comes when the idea that we should stockpile, for example, gold, or the idea that disaster is about to strike, becomes more mainstream.

This was certainly evident in the early 1980s, when people fearful of raging inflation in the United States (which, nevertheless, was far below what it is in some other countries that have failed to collapse), ran the price of gold to $800 per ounce and beyond. By golly, they were going to be safe!

That same $800, invested in shares corresponding to the Dow Jones Industrial Average, would have more than tripled in price during the 1980s—never mind the dividends. That ounce of gold is now worth about half of what was paid for it by panicked citizens who thought they were purchasing safety.

The herd mentality is a popular and powerful force, and it is one that is to be resisted. Keep your own counsel. Those who are dishing out advice and suggesting that you do this wacky thing or that are not willing to bear the responsibility should their advice fail and cost you money. You're the one who has to do that.

Along about that time, a few financial "experts" gained some notoriety by advising people to buy silver. Their advice received some currency in the popular and even the financial press. Silver, they said, was going to be the savior of all those smart enough to heed its call.

During the 1980s, silver lost an astounding 85 percent of its value.

There are those as well who publish books on how to survive this thing or that, some financial setback that the author is predicting. Some authors describe the best way to make it through the approaching cataclysm of a specified year. When the year comes and goes, but the disaster has not, some have even changed the schedule and gotten another edition by bumping the scheduled disaster back a year or two. If it goes on for very long, though, this sort of thing can get embarrassing. One can only hope that they invested all their profits in gold or, even better, silver.

There are no space ships readying to beam financial disaster rays at us or anything of the kind. While there are very real dangers both in and to the world, and while the world situation is changing rapidly, there is no cause for panic, or even for much more concern than you would normally have over your personal finances.

Have you seen those shows on late-night television in which the host's explains how they know the one and only true and foolproof way to enormous wealth? Virtually always, these plans require no investment on your part (except for the hundreds of dollars you are asked to send to the program's sponsor) and no brains whatsoever.

Fact is, their little plans don't work. They simply prey on the hopes, fears, and dreams of people who can scarcely afford to be taken in. By any standard of moral justice, these guys should be filling striped suits and making big rocks into little rocks in the hot summer sun. But they get away with it. And people fall for their pitches.

Of course, if these characters knew how to round up these millions and millions of dollars, they would be out doing it, instead of thumping the tub on television.

It is not my intention to ascribe motives to any of these people. Some of them—maybe all of them—truly believe in what they're saying and doing.

It *is* my intention to tell you that you follow them at your peril.

Let's see if we can establish a guideline here.

It's probably a good idea to completely avoid making any financial decisions based on the suggestions or advice of the outermost 25 percent of popular financial thought. Think of this as being like the Olympic Games, where for some events the highest and lowest scores are disregarded.

If someone is being surprisingly gloomy—or surprisingly cheerful—in issuing financial advice, forget about it.

The fact is, there is nothing that will serve you as well as ordinary common sense with a little sound financial planning and attention to what you're doing. If you employ those things, you won't need to be warned ahead of time about the disaster that may be coming, because you'll be in position to deal with it when and if it arrives.

THE LOTTERY

One of the most unconscionable swindles ever is being perpetrated by the very people who used to arrest those who perpetrated exactly the same swindle: It is the various lotteries that have become all the rage in the U.S.

Every so often, the television screens are full of laughing, hopeful people whose smiles and optimism result from their having just purchased lottery tickets. Television makes much of new "record" lottery prizes.

What is never shown, though, is all those long faces the day after the lottery drawing, the day after they've lost, when the certain hope of immense riches has disappeared without trace like a soap bubble, leaving a once-hopeful throng to face a day just like any other—poorer, but frequently no wiser.

Psychologists say that lotteries allow our wishes to take command. We suspend good sense, because we're allowing those wishes to be a little closer to reality, if only for a day or two. The problem comes when those wishes don't let us go back to our workaday world once the drawing has come and we have lost, as we almost inevitably will.

The sad fact is, those who put money on the various state lotteries most frequently are those who can least afford it. A national survey done not long ago found that people at the poverty level spend, on average, 2.1 percent of their income buying lottery tickets. The lottery is, to some, the chief investment vehicle.

As a tax, it is the most regressive ever invented, because the poor actually pay more than the rich, both as a percentage of their income and in actual dollars. The lotteries have come to play on the prayers of the poor that through some miracle they will be able to rise from their condition.

Nor have lotteries proved to be the big money-makers states had hoped they would become.

Lotteries in 26 states in 1988 generated $13 billion. Some of that went to paying off winners. A great deal of it went to paying for administration of the lottery itself—commissions to dealers, purchase of those fancy computer terminals, and salaries of lottery employees. Only $5 billion made its way into state coffers.

During one Pennsylvania lottery frenzy, television featured excited interviews with people who had spent $1,000 to $5,000 buying chances.

"I'd better win because this is the mortgage money!" gushed one. Lionizing such behavior is a poor idea. There is little sense in making fiscal irresponsibility an heroic act.

"It's really very sad," says a New York lottery vendor. "I have people come in here and spend $25, $50 buying lottery tickets and playing the numbers. The people who do this aren't well-to-do. They're poor; they can't afford it. Some are on public assistance. You'll get the occasional guy in a business suit, but he buys one ticket. The ones who buy dozens are the ones who are really desperate."

Should you play the lottery? There is certainly no sensible financial reason to do so. State lotteries do what those same states consider illegal when done by anyone else, the justification being that the end—money for the state—justifies the means. And besides, it is reasoned, people would gamble anyway.

The Emperor is wearing no clothes. A lottery ticket is in no way an investment. Your chances of winning are infinitesimal, almost nonexistent. It is true that someone wins—just as it is true that a rock, thrown blindly, must land somewhere. The likelihood of it coming down in a predictable place, though, is slight.

You may buy a ticket once in a while, as a lark. But this is entertainment, not investment. The tragedy of state lotteries comes when those who can ill afford it stake their all on what amounts to a pipe dream.

An acquaintance, who fears flying, puts it differently: "Whenever I have to fly on a business trip, I buy a lottery ticket ahead of time. That's because your chances of winning the lottery are about the same as being killed in a plane crash. I figure that if I win the lottery, I won't take the flight."

AVOIDING THE CON ARTISTS

The tired old saw, "Opportunity knocks but once," has been used to promulgate more ill-advised, half-baked, and totally crooked investment schemes than the rest of the pitchman's bag of tricks combined. Hundreds of thousands have learned too late that the opportunity that knocks but once is usually the one best left unanswered.

Opportunity—real opportunity—knocks, then waits patiently while you check its credentials.

Real investment opportunity isn't usually a fleeting thing. More often, it bangs relentlessly and, too often, goes unheeded. Witness the huge majority of Americans who refuse to make regular savings, to stop during the year to appraise their tax situation while there's still time to do something about it, or do any of the many simple, common-sense things that mark the real path to safety and security.

Opportunity, they've been told, knocks but once.

That is the story con artists hope you will believe. They are experts in the field of opportunity. They are quick to recognize a way to make a dishonest buck. Many of their scams indicate intelligence and talent that shows they would have succeeded in any line of work.

Their reasons for choosing to pursue ill-gotten gains are best left to the sociologists. But it's important to recognize that today's generation of con artist is extremely clever and sophisticated. FBI and state attorneys general offices have racks of files involving people who were unaware they'd been had a year or more after they parted with their money.

This is a boom time for swindlers in America. That is in part because individual investors have lost confidence in many of the traditional places to put money—the stock market and savings and loan institutions, for instance.

Investors figure that the game is fixed, no matter how reputable it is supposed to be. As a result, there is a lot of money available for the taking.

Such a cynical view is an invitation to trouble. It's true that the reputations of many institutions have been tarnished in recent years. Con artists have learned to play on that cynicism and use it to cheat worried investors out of their money.

There are new and clever confidence artists playing new and more elaborate con games every day. While it's impossible to keep track of them all, trends can be identified.

What follow are some of the more popular scams, the ones you are most likely to encounter. This isn't to say that the older, more widely publicized swindles aren't still lining the pockets of a world of slick talkers. These instead illustrate how sharpers manage to operate just outside, and in some cases just inside, the law.

TELESCAMS—A GROWTH INDUSTRY

Today's confidence schemes more often than not are perpetrated by telephone. There are several reasons for this.

The first is that the telephone gives a sense of intimacy while preserving nearly absolute anonymity.

The second is that phone con artists can work out of "boiler rooms," which are offices with banks of phones and operators who have little training. Those operators work from carefully rehearsed scripts. The scripts are flexible enough that there is a ready answer to any reply you might make. You can be pressured into making an "investment."

The third reason is a legal issue. The U.S. Postal Service's postal inspectors have amassed an impressive record of catching those who engage in mail fraud. Lacking a comprehensive national telecommunications fraud law, swindlers quite rightly believe the telephone is safer.

(Local and state regulatory agencies, often working with the telephone companies, have geared up their enforcement efforts, and a number of states have statutes criminalizing telephone fraud. In addition, because swindlers frequently work from nearby states in the hope of avoiding capture, groups of state securities regulators have formed to protect their common interest.)

Your first line of defense is simple enough: Use your common sense. A total stranger phones you and spins a fanciful tale wherein you give the stranger, sight unseen, hundreds or thousands of dollars. At some point the stranger will send you your handsome rewards. Does that make any sense? If you're parted with your money that easily, it's surprising you have any to fork over.

Tragically, the elderly are frequent victims. Boiler room swindlers seem particularly adept at talking older Americans out of their retirement nest eggs.

Investment industry and federal and state regulatory agencies have identified some of the things that should raise a red flag in your mind.

- Beware of salespersons, usually on the phone, who ask a string of questions that require "yes" for an answer. For example: "Would you like to make a lot of money on a small investment with little risk?" Later, your answers will be twisted to make you feel foolish if you don't go along with the scam.

- Never agree to anything without asking some important questions: What are the commissions and hidden costs? Get specific answers. What are the risks? Remember, if it were such a sure thing, the guy on the phone wouldn't need to have a job phoning people about it.

- Ask for a copy of the "firm's" risk-disclosure documents. In fact, insist upon it. Insist, too, on copies of the prospectus and other literature. Real offerings have them (as do some phony ones). If the salesperson says this deal requires you to act quickly, say that you're not interested, period. You will probably be told that opportunity knocks but once. In this case, that's probably true: If you make it clear that you're not falling for it, you'll never hear from those particular swindlers again.

- Ask what regulatory agencies govern the "firm" in question. Demand specific answers. The salesperson, if a swindler, will either try to give you a fuzzy answer or else give you an official-sounding agency name. It's figured that you won't check, anyway. Call their bluff. Check with the agency.

- Explain that you certainly aren't interested in conducting business over the telephone and would like to know where the firm's offices are.

- Find out how to liquidate your investment, should you decide to sell. On what exchanges are these securities traded? Verify the response, to make sure you're being told the truth.

- Insist that the entire proposal be mailed to you, using the U.S. Postal Service. This is a big turn-off for con artists, who do not want to run afoul of the postal inspector.

- Ask how the salesperson got your name. Swindlers sell their lists of prospective marks to each other. They also buy mailing lists.

- Ask if the salesperson would be willing to explain the proposal to your lawyer, accountant, or banker. If the answer is anything but "yes," say you're not interested and hang up.

- Ask for a listing of the firm's principals and officers. You may get an answer, but in any case, you'll be making a swindler very uncomfortable.

- Insist upon references—not individuals, but a reputable bank or brokerage firm.

- Ask for a phone number where you may phone the salesperson back.

By now, you'll have a good idea whether you're dealing with a legitimate outfit or not. Check the references you've been given. Study any prospectus or literature sent to you. Chances are that literature won't come if the offering is a swindle; however, in some cases, elaborate literature has been provided by thinner-than-air "investment firms."

It should be noted that some perfectly legitimate companies do employ telemarketing techniques in hopes of gaining new customers. But those companies will be ready and willing to provide satisfactory answers to your questions.

A salesperson who can't or won't answer all your queries satisfactorily is certainly not someone with whom you want to trust your money. And by the simple act of asking all those bothersome questions, you'll certainly give the seller of phony investments a very real headache.

THE BOOM IN PENNY STOCK SWINDLES

"Penny stocks" is the name given to many company shares selling for five dollars or less. These are highly speculative issues, to say the least. There are those who have made fortunes in penny stock speculation—just as there are those who have won the lottery.

The fact is, penny stocks might make an interesting hobby, but they're no place for you to risk your future.

But the con artists, being con artists, have a different tale to tell. Posing as reputable brokers, they will cite impressive—though fictitious—statistics that illustrate how you, too, can become fabulously rich in penny stocks.

Again, the pitch is usually over the phone.

The situation got so bad that finally, in 1989, the Securities and Exchange Commission adopted new rules to protect you from this kind of treatment.

The "cold-call" rules apply to unsolicited sales pitches made by brokerages involving unlisted "pink sheet" stocks. The rules are aimed at stocks selling for $5 or less, offered by companies with $2 million or less in tangible assets.

About 70 percent of such stocks are so-called "blind pool" offerings, meaning that the company was organized solely to raise money. You are never told what is to be done with the money. Instead, you're told that the company has a great management team with an unparalleled string of successes. Perhaps the name of a company or two will be tossed out.

If these managers have repeatedly succeeded at anything, it's been at bilking would-be investors out of their money, offering worthless paper in exchange. In the vast majority of cases, they take the money, jump into a pre-arranged merger, and cash out, leaving investors empty-handed.

The SEC's "cold call" rules require an exchange of documents between the brokerage house and the customer. The broker must inquire, for instance, about the customer's income, net worth, and investment goals, and must use this information as part of a "brokerage suitability check." If the broker fudges on this and is caught, he or she can be prosecuted. The SEC reasons that this will protect the honest brokerages, while giving the crooked ones enough rope to hang themselves.

Exchange of information through the mails, as now required, provides a cooling-off period, making it less likely that the customer can succumb to the pressure of a single phone call. No new orders can be taken over the telephone; they now require the customer's written approval.

The SEC reasons that this will help in two ways: First, a customer with time to think it over will be a more difficult target for con artists. Second, such a rule is easier and cheaper to enforce than are difficult-to-prove fraud statutes.

While these new regulations may help reduce the epidemic of penny stock swindles, you must be your own first line of defense. The simplest and best means of defense is to ignore stock pitches made to you over the telephone by unknown brokers.

While penny stocks are far from the safest investments even in the best of circumstances, the new rules are not aimed at honest brokers dealing in these highly speculative issues. Instead, they're designed to weed out those brokers who make a chancy investment a sure failure.

If you want to buy a stock, fine. Study the company. If you conclude that it's an investment you want to make, talk to an established broker. But *you* make the call. Know who is on the other end of the line. Doing business with someone who phones out of the clear blue, whose reputation you cannot possibly know, is flirting with disaster.

THAR'S GOLD IN THEM THAR SUCKERS!

Con artists have struck gold with mining swindles that bilk Americans out of billions of dollars each. These have reached crisis proportions.

While so-called "dirt pile" operations have received a lot of publicity, they are but one of many sophisticated confidence schemes that have taken trusting—too trusting—individuals for $5,000, $10,000, and in one case $120,000.

The mining scams remind one of the movie "The Sting," but there's an important difference: These are not kind-hearted scalawags plying a fairly harmless but illegal trade. They are big-time crooks, specializing in sun-belt schemes designed in large part to rob older Americans of their retirement savings.

Phony mining scams took on new life in the late 1980s, when there was a lot of publicity about the resurgence of gold and silver mining in Nevada, according to the FBI. People wanted to cash in on the legitimate mining successes there.

So did the swindlers. They were quick to dig in the pockets of the unsuspecting.

The phony mining investments are very sophisticated. A prospective "mark" is contacted by telephone. An impressive prospectus is sent out.

The documents are impressive. They contain all sorts of information— the mines the company is working, or land the company owns. There are also very enthusiastic geologists' reports.

In one popular swindle, the mines and the land may exist, but the company doesn't own them and doesn't have the mineral rights. The geologists either don't exist or are in it for part of the take.

Sometimes the company claims to have come up with a wonderful new process that makes it economical to refine gold that was previously unrecoverable. This is the tactic employed in "dirt pile" schemes. The processes don't exist, but the thought of them causes many people to suspend their common sense and buy into what amounts to a latter-day philosopher's stone.

The FBI reports that some investors want to come out west and actually see the mines. When they arrive, they're shown nice offices in a modern corporate building, then taken to the mine.

Sometimes it's a hole that goes 50 feet into the ground, then turns right and stops. The people aren't actually taken inside. They just see equipment and busy-looking workers, and they are happy.

According to the FBI, there have actually been cases where the real owners of a real mine were there, and they wondered who these people who showed up were, but didn't think anything of it—figured they were from the bureau of mines or someplace.

So the investor, taken in by this brazen approach, forks over money and is told that it will be a while before there's a return on the investment. After a year or so, he or she starts to get upset and takes action—writes a letter or two, makes a phone call, threatens to go to the authorities.

The smart operators soon send a check for a hundred dollars or so. This calms down the investor. Then, a month or so later, comes what the FBI calls a "lulling letter." Designed to calm an upset sucker, the letter says there has been a problem with weather or equipment or a rock slide, but not to worry because things will be on track again soon.

As a result, it can take 18 months or more before the investor knows he's been scammed. By that time, the crooks are long gone.

How can you avoid being taken in?

- Be wary of mining investments that offer you a guarantee. In most cases the swindlers guarantee you a minimum return of 150 to 300 percent on your investment. Legitimate mining operations know they can't make any such guarantees.

- Unless you're very well acquainted with the mining industry, avoid exotic mining investments—things like buying gold still in the ground or entering into limited mining partnerships. If you're interested in mining investments, buy shares in a mutual fund or in mining companies that have registered with their state's appropriate regulatory agency.

- Remember that even legitimate mining companies can make no promises. The science of mining has come a long way, but there is no guarantee that a given company will strike the mother lode. Still, your chances with a legitimate company are real, while the con artists will promise you everything and give you nothing.

LAND SWINDLES

The joke about swampland in Florida may be as old as the hills, but there's still some truth in it. Real estate swindles are still being perpetrated, although perhaps with more finesse than they were in the past.

One of the biggest ones in history (one that, coincidentally, happened in Florida) will probably not be sorted out by the turn of the century. It involved a corporation that relieved owners of their homes, securing millions of dollars in loans with one piece of valueless property, and failed to provide the owners promised new homes.

Land scams in various forms have become more sophisticated but no less common. Some involve sales of the same piece of property, usually undeveloped, to many different buyers. Others offer lots in proposed new communities, with guarantees of streets and other services by a certain date. By that time, the company has folded, the principals have divided the money, and the buyer either owns worthless land or a worthless piece of paper that is title to nothing.

Fortunately, it's not difficult to protect yourself:

- When buying or selling property, check the credentials of the agent with whom you're dealing. A state license provides a degree of safety, because you have recourse with the licensing agency in the event of suspected fraud.

- Get a reputable real estate lawyer to watch out for your interests, whether you are buying or selling. They know what to look for in ferreting out scams. They can also translate complicated contracts for you. Additionally, a lawyer specializing in real estate will likely know the reputation of the company you're dealing with, and will be in a position to warn you if it has been known to dance on the fringes of the law. Though lawyers are expensive, they're far cheaper to use before the fact, in formulating a safe contract, than they are afterwards in court, suing to recover your losses. That is, if you can find someone to sue.

- Find out if the development company or real estate company you're dealing with has a good reputation. Check with the Better Business

Bureau. A trip to the local courthouse is worthwhile, so you can find out if there are any lawsuits past or present against the company, and what they involve. This can be difficult, because companies that deal chiefly in real estate fraud frequently go out of business, reopening later under a new name, often in a different location.

- Do not accept anything other than the property itself as collateral, if you're the seller, and avoid anything other than a warranty deed to the property if you're the buyer.

- Title searches and title insurance are absolutely essential, whether you are the buyer or the seller. Banks require this before they will lend money to purchase real estate. If yours is a face-to-face transaction, not involving a bank, you should insist on the same protection.

- Demand that the transaction be recorded. Any insistence that this not be done is virtually a sure sign of foul play.

Sad though it is, real estate fraud is still a very profitable business in many parts of the country. It is possible to remain within the law—just barely—and get away with it. You can't always count on regulatory agencies to bring the culprits to justice, and you can seldom count on them to recover your money.

You have to protect yourself, and that requires the greatest of care in either buying or selling property. Purchase of a home is likely to be the biggest investment you'll ever make. It surprises me always the ease with which the hucksters are able to sweet-talk buyers and sellers into making such an important decision without taking even the simplest of precautions.

PARTING WITH YOUR SURPLUS MONEY

Some of the trickiest swindles are those that just barely stay inside the bounds of legality. These often deliver—technically—what they promise. But what they promise is usually something you could get for free, or at little cost, all by yourself.

There's no greater example than the growing number of companies that promise to help you get unbelievable bargains at government sales of surplus, seized, and recovered property.

Advertisements for these companies frequently appear on the backs of magazines, but they are being heard more and more on radio and television. They generally say that you can get boats, airplanes, and shiny red sports cars for pennies on the dollar.

Frequently, the ads contain an example of someone who has realized enormous savings. A popular one is a man who purchased a fishing boat worth thousands of dollars for only $10! (The boat sale actually took place, but it was a mistake, and those responsible took a lot of heat for it.)

What these companies are doing is not illegal, because they do provide a service, though a questionable one, says the General Services Administration in Washington, D.C., which oversees many auctions of property seized by the federal government. The advertised claims about costs are suspect, says the GSA, and you are not given any information that you can't get on your own for free.

In return for an amount of money ranging from a few dollars to hundreds of dollars for subscriptions, the companies provide lists of government-sponsored auctions and sealed-bid sales.

They don't tell you about all the caveats involved in buying from federal, state, or local governments:

- In every case, the agency involved is interested in getting a fair market price for the merchandise offered. If there is property that is worth a great deal, the sale will be highly publicized.

- In many cases, the items for sale have been used extensively. They come with no guarantees. You must pay cash, and once you've paid, you're stuck with your purchase.

- In the case of automobiles, airplanes, and boats, there is seldom the necessary paperwork available. What you receive for your money is a receipt and the item. You're on your own to come up with a title, registration, and so on.

The advertisements often make much of the fast sports cars popularized on action television series. You are led to believe that every drug bust nets the feds several of these, and that the government will do almost anything to get rid of them. That's simply not true.

Instead, there are basically three kinds of government sales. The first involves surplus government property, and is conducted by the General Services Administration. This includes everything from used office equipment to real estate next to a federal prison.

The GSA conducts its sales through auctions or sealed bids, depending on what is being sold. Every item has a reserve price. If it fails to bring a bid as high as the reserve figure, it is withdrawn.

Information on upcoming sales is available from the GSA office located in each major city. You can also get full information there on the procedures for bidding. In some GSA regional offices, there is even a recorded phone message listing the dates, times, and locations of upcoming sales.

The second is military surplus. The Department of Defense no longer sells any weapons or airplanes to the public. In fact, the military no longer even parts with its used jeeps except as scrap after they've been crushed or cut into unrestorable pieces. (This is because military jeeps have been deemed unworthy general transportation vehicles, and the government is not interested in defending itself against anticipated lawsuits.) What military surplus that reaches the public does so only after it's been offered to other branches of the federal government and to state and local governments.

But what about all the great army surplus bargains you've read about for years? Today, equipment and even clothing has gone through most of its useful life before it's offered. There are occasional exceptions, but the field is scarcely ripe for picking. The surplus property division of the Defense Reutilization and Marketing Office does sell items from time to time, through either sealed bids, auctions, or, occasionally, through retail warehouse sales at military bases.

To get more information, call the DRMO at the nearest military base. They'll put you on the mailing list for sales in your area, and will provide listings of items to be sold. To find out about other military surplus, send a letter to Department of Defense Surplus Sales, P.O. Box 1370, Battle Creek, Michigan 49016.

The third kind of sale is of seized, recovered, or unclaimed property. These sales are usually conducted by the federal marshal's office or by state and local police forces.

Fast cars, fast boats, and airplanes seized during drug investigations are impounded and held by the Marshal's office until the trial is completed. If the defendant is found not guilty, then the property is returned. If the verdict is guilty, then it is forfeited to the government.

But the government is not going to pop a quarter of a million dollars to buy a Ferrari or Lamborghini to use to make undercover drug buys. So when agents need a vehicle like that, they get it from seized property. The government gets first pick, and what's left over is what's sold.

What's more, when items of great value—such as expensive sports cars or art objects—are to be sold, the sale is frequently handled through a private auction house. Sales of valuable real estate are no longer done at auction; now they're handled through real-estate agents.

There can be bargains here, but no miracles. Items seized by the federal government are sold at U.S. Marshal's sales. To find out about them, contact the marshal's office at the nearest federal courthouse. Remember: The professionals are aware of these sales, too. Expensive items are likely to draw their attention—and the marshal publicizes these sales well in advance, especially when high-ticket items are involved. Local police conduct occasional sales of cars, bicycles, and other property that has gone unclaimed. For information about such sales, call your local police department.

What service is offered, then, by the companies that claim to give you the inside track on government sales? They make the calls and send you lists of lists the government agencies have sent them. They also lead you to believe that you'll be in for incredible bargains, so they sell you unrealistic dreams, too.

But the idea of semi-secret government sales, known only to the privileged few who are willing to pay for the information? Nonsense.

It's to the government's advantage to have as many people participate as possible, because that ensures that the items will go for the highest prices, which is the government's objective. If this were such a money-maker, the people selling the information would be getting rich buying and reselling the stuff, instead of peddling information.

The companies selling free government information have been investigated repeatedly, but it's been concluded that what they are doing is, technically, legal. That's because to gather information on sales by different agencies, you would have to make several phone calls.

This way, you only have to make one phone call, at a cost that is not a bargain in anyone's book.

16
YOUR CHILDREN'S
─── EDUCATION ───

College costs now commonly run in excess of $10,000 per year. Tuition has steadily increased, as have costs of room and board, books, and other materials. There is no reason to believe the trend will change.

Part of the problem is due to that old bugaboo, the aging of the baby boomers. When they were of college age, new facilities were built to accommodate them. But because the generation that followed is so much smaller, many of those facilities are going unused or under-used.

The costs of operating colleges and universities do not depend to any large degree on the number of students enrolled. The marginal costs of one student more or less are slight. This means that fewer students are footing a bill that is proportionally much higher per student, because the fixed costs are divided among a smaller number of them.

It also means that you must begin preparing for your children's college education from the time they are born—or earlier.

By now there should be no question in your mind that a college education is one of the best investments you can make. The Census Bureau reports that a college graduate will typically earn twice as much, over the course of a career, than his or her high-school-only contemporaries.

(You should note, too, that computer literacy is fast becoming as essential as the ability to read and write was just a few years ago. This means that you should do everything you can to see that your youngsters grow up comfortable with computers. While it is too early for there to be reliable statistics on the income effects of computer literacy, there is no doubt that it will make a big difference.)

Fortunately, as the cost of education has grown, so has the range of options available to pay for it.

Because of the increase in tuition and other costs associated with education, because of the trend toward innovation in investments and finances, and because of continuing changes in the tax and regulatory structures, it's best to formulate your education investment plan with the aid of a qualified investment advisor. The picture changes almost daily.

CHOOSING A SCHOOL

One of the toughest realizations most parents have to make is that their children may not be potential Ivy Leaguers. There is a range of talents and aptitudes that a child may display, which is why there are so many choices of higher education available, from trade schools to graduate schools. It's important to find a comfortable fit. For help in doing this, see Chart 29.

That means finding a school that meets your child's needs, as well as being affordable. Very often, the choice will be made in part by the financial aid that's available.

INNOVATIONS IN FINANCING EDUCATION

For the most part, saving for college is like that for any other long-term financial goal. But recently, there have been exciting new ways for parents to save especially for their children's education.

U.S. SAVINGS BONDS. Among the most secure investments you can make, savings bonds now offer competitive yields as well, based on the interest paid on long-term government bonds.

More important, it is extremely easy to build a college fund with savings bonds. In most cases, you simply arrange with your employer's payroll department for a bond to be purchased for you each week. You can spend as little as $25, which will buy you a bond with a $50 face value—its redemption value at maturity. You never see the money you're using to buy the bonds, so you can't spend it.

Interest from savings bonds is tax-deferred; that is, you pay it only when you cash the bond.

Until the tax reform act, it was important that bonds purchased to finance a child's education be purchased in the child's name, with the parent as a beneficiary, not as co-owner. This was because otherwise the interest would be taxed at the parents' rate, which was higher.

But because of tax reform, that tax advantage no longer exists. And because of changes in savings bonds, it usually wouldn't apply to bonds ear-

CHART 29

Evaluating a College or University

Qualities to Advance Your Career

- Curriculum
- Faculty
- Accreditations
- Degrees or certificates
- Guidance counseling
- Regard by future prospective employers
- Help in finding jobs
- Library
- Other:

Personal Factors to Consider

- Chances of getting in
- Costs
- Financial aid from the school
- Refund policy if a student leaves
- Student body
- Housing
- Campus
- Medical, religious, athletic, and extracurricular activities
- Social life
- Location
- Other:

marked for education. That's because the interest from savings bonds purchased to cover education costs is now tax free if the family income is less than $60,000 per year. This makes savings bonds an even more attractive option—one you should certainly discuss with your financial planner.

EDUCATION BONDS. These state bond issues are becoming increasingly popular. Begun in the 1980s in a handful of states, these are typically general obligation bond issues to finance the state's general fund. They offer advantages to parents or grandparents who buy them to finance a child's education. These advantages may be in the form of reduced or eliminated taxes or even a reduction in tuition if the student attends college in the sponsoring state.

The disadvantage, of course, is that the student may well end up attending college in another state, making some of the reasons for purchasing the bonds disappear.

The education bonds that have been issued so far have sold well, and many states that don't currently offer them are considering plans that range from special education issues (in which the bonds finance colleges and universities while at the same time allow more students to attend them), to an education provision on most of the state's general obligation bonds (which offers advantages to purchasers of any state bonds, so long as the purchaser intends to use the proceeds to finance a student's education).

The field is changing rapidly, so it's a good idea to consult your financial planner or broker to find out what's available at any given time. Make sure you find out whether you can convert the bonds you purchase into other kinds of investments for education should it one day become prudent to do so.

TUITION PRE-PAYMENT. Hailed just a few years ago as the wave of the future, tuition pre-payment became more of a ripple. Though the plans differ somewhat, they essentially require you to pay now for your child's education sometime in the future. Because you pay at the current tuition rates, you can save a great deal on an education that will be delivered later, presumably at a time of higher tuition.

The problem is, if the child doesn't achieve the school's academic standards—or simply decides not to attend college—the amount refunded is the amount paid. There is no interest added, which means the parent suffers not only a loss of income from the money had it been otherwise invested, but a real loss due to inflation.

What's more, if the student enrolls but then flunks out, there is no refund.

THE OLD STANDBYS

In addition to the newer ways of saving for education, there are a lot of more traditional methods that may suit you. Most of these are discussed in greater detail elsewhere, but here are how they stack up when the goal is financing education. (To get an idea of the amounts of money involved, see Chart 30.)

SAVINGS ACCOUNTS. There's no soft way to put it: These are a poor choice when saving for a college education. Compared to almost any other interest-paying investment, savings accounts rate a poor second place. What's more, it's easy to succumb to the urge to dip into the till whenever financial need arises. It's far better to put your education savings into an investment that pays you more—and is a little more difficult to get at.

The exception is when savings accounts become an educational tool themselves, for teaching a youngster the importance of saving. By all means, help your children open individual savings accounts at a nearby bank or savings and loan. Help them learn to make regular deposits from allowances or the earnings from part-time jobs.

Teach them, too, the importance of establishing financial goals and saving to reach them. For instance, after the savings account has grown a bit, the youngster might want to take some of the money and purchase a savings bond (for long-term savings), while leaving part of the money in the account to pay for a special purchase, provide spending money on vacation, or the like.

EMPLOYEE STOCK AND SAVINGS PLANS. If you are an employee, especially of a large company, there is a good chance that your employer can help you save for your children's education.

The most basic programs are standard employee stock ownership plans or 401(k) plans, which are discussed in detail elsewhere. They allow you to invest a portion of your income, which may be matched by employer contributions. The employer contributions make this one of the highest paying investments you can have.

But many companies also have special programs for the children of employees. These can range from special investment plans designed to finance education to company scholarships, which may be awarded based on a student's grades and which pay part of his or her tuition based on how well the student is doing.

(Many companies also offer tuition reimbursement to employees who themselves sign up for courses that will help them to do their jobs better. If

CHART 30

**A Check List of College and
University Costs**

- Tuition
- Books
- Supplies
- Equipment
- Laboratory charges
- Fees (such as for library, school newspaper, and athletic and other student activities)
- Living expenses (such as for room and board) other than would be incurred living at home (such as for food, clothing, recreation, etc.)

---

you're eligible, it's a golden opportunity to add to your own education and value on the job.)

You would be foolish not to check with your company's benefits advisor about what plans are offered and, if your family qualifies, to enroll.

If you are a member of a labor union, find out whether your union offers scholarships, tuition aid, or other education financing.

MUTUAL FUNDS. These are among the best of the standard investment vehicles when it comes to financing for educational goals. The funds you invest in should be picked carefully and should have a long track record of safety, prudent investment philosophy, and growth. There are, of course, mutual funds offering investments in just about every financial area. You want to pick the ones that concentrate on long-term growth.

You also want to have your dividends and capital gains distributions automatically reinvested. That way, the money your investment makes will itself make money.

STOCKS. Shares, if purchased carefully, can be an important part of the education portfolio. The important thing to do is choose stocks based on their potential for long-term growth and then keep them unless there is a compelling reason to sell. The chances are that part of your education investment will be in stocks, whether you purchase shares directly or not. That's because almost all employee and 401(k) plans are stock investments, as are many mutual funds.

It is unwise to put all of your savings for education into stocks, because there have been, and can continue to be, stock market setbacks and out-and-out disasters. Individual companies can and do fall on hard times. Diversification is essential, not only among stocks but among investment types—stocks, mutual funds, government and commercial bonds—for safety as well as growth.

BONDS. Under the new Treasury Direct program, it is possible for you to open what amounts to your own account at your nearest Federal Reserve Bank. This means you can buy federal bonds without having to pay a broker and without paying for storage. This can make these investments very attractive indeed, and there is certainly no safer a place to put your money. If you want to park a chunk of cash and forget about it, here's the place to do it.

There are also state, municipal, and corporate bond issues of varying safety, terms, and yield, as well as bond funds. For education, it's best to invest only in very highly rated bonds. When looking at local government issues, make sure to find out what tax advantages may be yours, for they increase the effective yield. You are interested in zero-coupon issues, because you want the yield to be paid at maturity, rather than as income.

BOND-LIKE INVESTMENTS. Unit trusts behave a little like mutual funds and a little like bonds. Unlike mutual funds, unit trusts are a fixed portfolio. Like bonds, the yield is fixed. Among the best for financing an education are those made up of government mortgage-backed securities and/or high quality utility issues.

Zero-coupon certificates of deposit, issued by the Federal Deposit Insurance Corporation in values up to $100,000, are another good choice. They offer high yield and extreme safety.

OTHER OPTIONS. In the past, some parents have purchased a condo or co-operative apartment near campus, and rented it to their matriculating offspring. They then benefited from the tax advantages of owning the second home, and often appreciation in the value of the apartment or townhouse more than covered the costs of the child's education.

But that's not as easily done anymore. The tax advantages have largely disappeared, and the certainty of home appreciation has, too.

Still, a good financial advisor is likely to have several innovative options in mind, one of which might be right for you.

FINANCIAL AID

Financial aid comes in four forms: loans, grants, scholarships, and work-study employment. Every prospective student should inquire about financial aid, no matter what kind of school he or she will attend. This is done at the same time the student gets other information about the school, and the aid application is submitted when the student applies for admittance.

LOANS. There is no better purpose for borrowing than for education. Still, borrowing should be the student's last resort; only if he or she has not accumulated enough over the years in savings and investments, and scholarships and grants are not available.

If you, as the student, have to borrow, don't borrow more than you can reasonably expect to repay; the same advice holds true with all forms of loans and credit. If you can't work the numbers out, refigure on the basis of attending a less expensive institution—not only for reasons of tuition, but also so that you can live at home. Also re-explore possibilities for financial aid that you will not have to repay, as well as part-time off-hours job opportunities during the school terms, and weekends and vacations full-time. Of course, you have to be careful you don't undertake such a heavy employment schedule as to impair your educational advancement.

When as a student you calculate repaying educational borrowing, be realistic. Don't expect that upon graduation you are assured of obtaining the kinds of high-paying jobs you read about, because they're the exception rather than the rule. Through the school's appropriate advisory office, you may be able to get in touch with some graduates to find out just how it's working out in practice repaying their educational borrowing.

Bear in mind that your investment in your education probably offers greater potential return than any other investment in your lifetime.

General Loans: This is when you simply borrow money from a bank or other financial institution. They may or may not require collateral. They are generally the financing method of last resort.

Guaranteed Student Loans: Because repayment is guaranteed by the federal government, these loans are available at interest rates much lower than those otherwise available. Students then begin repayment after graduation. Because so many students have "skipped out" on repayment, the government has established tough new enforcement tools. These loans can be a lifesaver, but don't think you can get away without repayment.

Supplementary loans are available to cover educational costs beyond tuition and fees.

In some cases, credit toward repayment is given for community service work after graduation. The terms vary, but it's worth investigating.

These loans are provided by conventional lending institutions. Application should be made when the student is accepted by the college or university.

Direct Student Loans: Administered by the school's financial aid office, these need-based loans work in much the same way as guaranteed student loans, except that application is generally made when the student applies for admission.

GRANTS. Tuition grants differ from loans in that they are generally lump-sum payments that do not in most cases have to be repaid. The recipient may be required to pursue a given course of study or be involved in a particular field or project.

They may also be awarded to deserving students of a particular ethnic or social set, or they may be awarded to the children of members of a particular organization or employees of a particular firm.

SCHOLARSHIPS. These do not require repayment and are usually awarded on the basis of academic achievement, although many schools, seeking to attract students from differing ethnic and economic backgrounds, have set aside special scholarships for deserving young people from those groups.

If your child has a special interest in science or engineering, and has done well on SAT tests and has generally good grades, military scholarships may be attractive. ROTC scholarships pay for college expenses and provide a small stipend. For excellent students, appointment to one of the military academies is possible. Some students may want to enter the military soon after high school, in which case they may accumulate up to $10,000 toward college once they have left the service.

WORK-STUDY. Many colleges offer work-study programs, in which all or part of a student's tuition or other expenses is waived in exchange for the student holding a job at the college. This can include anything from working in a dormitory dining hall to work in the school library. When possible, most schools try to match jobs to students. For instance, a job might include work in studies being conducted by the graduate department of the student's major subject.

GETTING INFORMATION. The best place to start is with the student's high school guidance office. Counselors there are able to realistically assess the student's potential and provide information both as to schools worthy of consideration and as to the financial help that is available. The middle of the sophomore year is not too early to begin making inquiries.

Before deciding on a school, you and your child should plan to visit it. This should be done on a typical day during the school year. This gives the student a chance to get a feel for the place and to take a look at the facilities and programs that are offered.

GETTING A HEAD START

Students who have done well in high school, or who have experience outside of school that applies to academic subjects—even students who are self-starters and quick at independent study—can often "quiz out" of classes. That is, they can receive course credit (without paying tuition) for passing tests on those subjects.

The chief ways of doing this are through Advance Placement tests and through what is called "CLEP," for the College-Level Examination Program. Both of these result in students being allowed to waive certain course requirements. Not all schools recognize all credits gained through these tests, however, so you should check with the college beforehand.

Additional information on these testing programs can be obtained from your child's high school guidance office.

TEACH YOUR CHILDREN WELL

Not only can you provide for your children's education (or that of your grandchildren, nieces, nephews—whatever), but you can yourself teach them the single best lesson they could possibly learn: financial responsibility.

There are many ways of doing this, of course. The most valuable may be one that teaches a youngster the importance of savings and investment, as opposed to something that simply grows, sight unseen.

Several strategies provide this valuable lesson, all for as little or great a price as you care to spend.

First on my list is U.S. Savings Bonds. They can be purchased for as little as $25, with a face value of $50. Savings bonds are unsurpassed in safety. Their yield is respectable. Beyond that, they provide something tangible to give a child (the bond itself) and an enforced lesson in savings (the bond can't be cashed at all for six months, and must be held for the long term to reach full face value). A child thinking of cashing in a bond a year from now will instantly see the cost of dipping into savings—the difference between the cash and face values.

What's more, the young person might decide to set aside part of his or her allowance or earnings from a part-time job in order to build a "collection" of savings bonds.

There are other financial gifts that are educationally rewarding, too.

The traditional one is a savings account. While this is not the highest yielding investment in the world, it is unsurpassed in helping a youngster learn to save a portion of his or her money. Opening such an account is not as simple as once it was, because there are now minimums required to open an account at many savings institutions. It is important to shop around to find a bank that is flexible in balance and deposit requirements. It should also be accessible to the child—a bank across town isn't a good idea unless the child's parents are willing to provide transportation.

Should it be a passbook account, or one that provides monthly or quarterly statements? The statement account has its definite advantages. The child receives mail with graphic proof that his or her money is growing. Basic record-keeping skills can be learned in this way. And it imparts a feeling of importance to have to tend to "business." While the stock market is shark-infested at the moment, this doesn't mean that a share or two of a company won't provide a good investment as an educational gift. Perhaps you might want to give a few shares in the company where you work, or in a company involved in an area of special interest to the child.

Whether the stock performs particularly well is not really the prime consideration in this case. Instead, it will lead the youngster to follow the company on a day-to-day basis, learning the things that change the value of its shares. The child will receive the company's annual report which, with a little help from an adult, can provide a real education in the way corporations work.

Following the company in the newspaper can impart important habits and skills and, should the child become really interested, he or she can learn other research skills as well.

None of these financial gifts is complete without a little talk about the joy and excitement of saving and investing. Psychologists tell us our savings habits are often formed at an early age. A good way to help form sound ones is to convince the child that savings can be just as exciting as dropping quarters into a computer game. A big part of any of these gifts, then, is following up on them and helping the child take an interest in his or her investments.

There is another kind of gift, one that the child is less likely to fully appreciate now. That involves a larger investment for the child's future, which obviously is not handled by—or handed over to—the child. Zero-coupon bonds are a good choice. A trust fund is another.

Another possibility is the purchase of U.S. Treasury securities through a Treasury Direct account at your regional Federal Reserve Bank. Treasury Direct eliminates much of the overhead in buying and holding government securities, and the investments are perfectly safe.

Whatever your gift, it becomes even greater if you explain it to the child. When a youngster becomes aware that money put away now will turn into something wonderful in the future, he or she learns that there is a connection between savings now and goals later, and might even show enough interest to follow how those investments progress.

It's the best gift money can buy.

17

PREPARING NOW
—FOR RETIREMENT—

Lf you are to retire in the manner you would like to, it is up to you to make it happen.

In fact, if you are to retire on more than bare essentials, you must establish a multi-barreled approach to it at once. That's because the population is aging. Services that you have come to count upon, or plan to come to count upon, will become much more expensive.

Meanwhile, your assets may prove to be worth less than you think and are counting upon. The baby boomers have their homes already. The generation that followed them is much smaller. They've already led to the closing of schools and financial crises at colleges. They will lead to a diminished demand for homes, and an increase in prices in areas where labor, now in short supply, is a big part of the service or product.

The organized retirement systems, both public and private, in this country were established, however, with a retirement age that was very close to what then was the typical life expectancy. Now, with more and more Americans living longer and longer, the demographers see a crisis looming. At the least, it will severely tax our retirement system, placing a heavy burden on those who are still working, because they are the ones who have to support those who are retired. At worst, it will result in an enormous generational battle, with the economic fate of the country at stake.

This potential for conflict will surely make retirement and pension systems one of the leading issues of the 1990s.

Retirement systems, you see, are not merely huge bank accounts where you make deposits now for withdrawal in the future. In most cases, those deposits are made and invested, but distributions are made from the current pool of funds. In other words, money paid by today's workers can be sent to today's retirees.

This isn't a problem so long as there is more money going in than there is coming out. But because of an unprecedented demographic feature of the last half of this century, that will not be the case for very long.

WILL YOU BE READY FOR RETIREMENT?

You should always have a good idea of your current net worth, your current financial picture, and your short-term and long-term financial goals. If you float like driftwood, you will be swept out to sea.

If you haven't already done so, you should figure out your assets (home, securities, other property, cash) and your liabilities (mortgage and taxes owed, other debts), and subtract the latter from the former to get an idea of your net worth. Do not over-estimate the value of your possessions.

Try to estimate the same things for your projected age of retirement.

Now you're in a position to begin setting your retirement goals. Figure your income and your cost of living. Project how much you'll be able to save and invest. It is a good idea to get planning help from an outsider, but it's best to avoid those who have something to sell. This is not to criticize such advisers. It's simply best to get advice from a paid advisor whose only product is helping you plan your financial future.

BUILDING ON A PLAN. If you have no financial plan in place, you need to formulate one.

Begin planning for your retirement by looking at your current financial goals. Have all your resources been spoken for, through purchases, saving for your children's education, and the like? Are all your investments income producers, or have you invested in securities that offer long-term growth?

If you're just starting out, you probably believe you have many years to prepare for retirement, so you can put it off. Not so! Young, unattached people should sock away as much as possible for the future. This is because you have fewer things demanding your money than you will later. It's also because money invested today begins making money today. It builds wealth for you without you having to do anything but keep an eye on it, to make sure you shouldn't shift it from one investment to another. A little bit of attention and investment now will save an enormous amount of worry and heartache later on.

(There's another reason to start planning for retirement today: Life expectancies are growing and, as you will see elsewhere, medical costs are, too.

Though there is no crystal ball that provides vision with absolute clarity, it's probably safe to say that there's no such thing as too much money put away for retirement.)

If you are single, or have no children and plan none for a few years, you can be a little more aggressive than you'll be able to be later on. Look for rapid appreciation: Investments that not only grow, but grow quickly. That way, you'll have a bigger bundle to put into more conservative investments once your responsibilities have grown.

Many young couples—and even individuals—invest in homes early on. This is a good thing, though it must be done more cautiously now than in past decades, because a home is not the sure investment it once was. To get a better sense of your situation, see Chart 31.

Once you've gotten established and your family is growing, you need to reappraise things a little. You should do many of the things described above, but you can't be as aggressive in choosing your investments. Why? Because you have less time to recover in the event of a major economic downturn. Look at tax-sheltered plans, such as IRAs, employee stock ownership and 401(k) plans.

Make sure, too, that your affairs are in order should something happen to you. You do not want to imagine your family having to suffer because your assets are tied up. Many books the size of this one could be written merely listing the horror stories of well-to-do families thrown into turmoil because the breadwinner (or, more and more, breadwinners) didn't face the unhappy prospect that they were mortal. (See the section in this chapter on Estate Planning.)

As you grow older still, your situation will change still further. Your children, now grown and away from home, will be less of a responsibility. You may want to set aside some money for the education of your grand-children, but you probably won't feel the pressure in this regard that you did for educating your own youngsters. Your home is paid off, or at least your equity in it is substantial.

Now, with you in your 50s, is the time to begin thinking about what you want to do when you retire. While living a life of leisure may sound appealing from time to time, it is probably not what you want to do.

A LOOMING PENSION CRISIS (IF THINGS WEREN'T BAD ENOUGH)

Private pension funds in the United States carry balances totaling $1.7 trillion. As the 1990s began, there were only about 250 regulators keeping

CHART 31

Use this matrix to keep track of financial factors that need adjustment because of your life experiences changing from about age 45. Check relevant boxes below and then adjust relevant factors.

Check Experience, then Financial Factors	Life Experiences that trigger financial moves	Planning		Career			Money Management				Insurance					Home	Investments by Objectives					Estate	
		Budgeting	Taxes	Inflation	Development	Earnings	Employment Benefits	Checking and Savings	Credit and Borrowing	Government Programs	Medical	Disability Income	Long-Term Care	Life	Property and Liability	Home	Capital Preservation	Income	Growth	Appreciation	Tax Advantages	Planning	Will
	YOUR LAST CHILD LEAVES HOME																						
	YOUR EMPLOYMENT OR BUSINESS PROGRESSES																						
	A NEW CAREER IN MIDLIFE																						
	SPOUSE RETURNS TO WORK																						
	YOU UPGRADE YOUR LIFESTYLE																						

CHART 31 *(continued)*

Check Experience, then Financial Factors	Life Experiences that trigger financial moves	Planning			Career			Money Management			Insurance						Home	Investments by Objectives					Estate	
		Budgeting	Taxes	Inflation	Development	Earnings	Employment Benefits	Checking and Savings	Credit and Borrowing	Government Programs	Medical	Disability Income	Long-Term Care	Life	Property and Liability	Home	Capital Preservation	Income	Growth	Appreciation	Tax Advantages	Planning	Will
	CARING FOR AN AGING PARENT																						
	DIVORCE OR SEPARATION																						
	YOU REMARRY, BLENDED FAMILY																						
	ADVERSITIES (HEALTH, CAREER, INVESTMENTS)																						
	INTO YOUR RETIREMENT																						
	DEATH IN THE FAMILY																						

an eye on the money in the till. As the inspector general of the Department of Labor has warned, that's a recipe for disaster.

The temptation to misuse the enormous pension pool can be, and in some cases has been, too great. This on top of a pension system that will certainly creak under the strain when, in a few years, distributions begin to exceed collections. Only money that has been invested very wisely will provide a return sufficient to meet the demand placed on it—even then, it's by no means certain it will be enough.

The situation is made worse by the aging of the baby boomers. They will retire within a few years of each other, so mismanaged pension funds will quickly collapse. Crooked trustees, of course, hope to be long out of town by then. They still have several years to work their dishonest ways on pension funds before they are likely to be found out.

To top it all off, one-third of the pension funds lack government insurance—even though a general pension bust would throw the government itself into a bone-chilling crisis.

It is a terrifying prospect. But how bad is it?

The first thing you must remember is that most pension funds are very well managed. That having been said, the Labor Department is able to look at fewer than 1 percent of the 870,000 pension plans, and they have found an astonishing number of abuses.

These abuses have included using pension money to finance questionable businesses owned by relatives of pension trustees, use of pension money to finance expensive vacations for trustees, and even use of the pension fund to finance a hostile corporate takeover. Money has been lent, unsecured, to friends and relatives of trustees. In some cases, the trustees have provided themselves with cars and other perquisites—all at the fund's expense.

This doesn't just apply to company pension funds. Some of the most blatant, enormous, and illegal abuses have involved union pension funds, though much has been done to correct these abuses. Sadly, the money lost is seldom recovered.

As a rule, any use of pension money that deviates from the goal of providing a secure retirement for covered employees is an abuse. The problem is uncovering those abuses.

You must act as the watchdog over your own pension holdings. It's up to you to pay attention and to track down such abuses as may be taking place.

The best thing to do when you believe you have found questionable use of pension funds is to take your questions to the nearest regional office of the Labor Department. That failing, employees have the right to bring civil action against the pension fund trustee.

If you believe you've uncovered embezzlement or kickbacks, rather than simple incompetence, you have recourse to the FBI, which can launch a criminal investigation.

How do you begin to look into your pension fund?

- If the fund covers 100 or more employees, it must file an annual report. You will receive a summary of this, but you may obtain a copy of the full report (though there may be a small copying charge). Smaller plans must file once every three years, but the rest is the same.
- Look first at the bottom line. Has the fund lost money? If so, why?
- Look at the administrative expenses. If they are obviously excessive, a closer look is warranted.
- Ask for a copy of financial statement form 5500, which lists the investments the pension fund has made. Apply the common sense test to them: Are the investments obviously being mismanaged?
- Check the investments of pension money. Are there big losses from investments in unknown companies? Are friends and relatives of the trustee or trustees being hired at high rates?

Again, most pension funds are administered honestly and skillfully. Some aren't. You won't know which applies to your retirement nest egg unless you look.

Otherwise, you could be in for a terrible shock, come retirement day.

EARLY RETIREMENT

As you reach your 60s, retirement will probably seem a reality to you for the first time. One of the things you may consider is early retirement.

How much will it cost you in Social Security benefits if you retire early, before you reach age 65? Currently, you can retire at age 62 and receive 80 percent of the monthly benefit you would have received had you waited until you reached 65.

To reach an informed judgement on when to retire, anyone who will be wholly or partly dependent on Social Security must find the answers to several questions:

- Are you fully insured? Don't automatically assume that you are, especially if you entered the work force late.
- How much credit has accumulated in your account?
- What does Social Security figure your primary insurance amount will be at age 65? This is the amount of the basic Social Security payment

that you would receive at age 65, based on the history of your earnings so far.

To find out, call your regional Social Security office and request SSA Form 7004. When you receive the form, answer the questions it asks and return it. The answers to your questions will be sent to you in about six weeks.

Unless you intend to survive solely on Social Security and savings, your decision whether to take early retirement probably should be made after noting how much you are allowed to earn following retirement. This amount changes fairly frequently, so you should check with Social Security to find the latest amounts. Suffice it for now to say that the amount is the least for retirees under age 65; higher for those between 65 and 70; and, at this writing, unlimited for those above 70; after which time you can work full time, make as much money as you can, and still receive full monthly Social Security benefits.

At age 65, a non-working spouse is also entitled to a benefit equal to 50 percent of a living, retired husband or wife's primary insurance amount. A working spouse whose earned benefit is larger than the 50 percent will receive the larger amount. Non-working spouses can, like their working husbands or wives, begin receiving "early retirement" benefits at age 62.

Don't overlook any of the benefits to which you might be entitled. Chart 32 provides a handy checklist.

All this is according to the law as it is at this writing. There is little question that benefits and rules will change, though the direction in which they will change is unknown.

You should also find about your company or union pension plan's attitude toward early retirement. If you have been with your company for some time, or if you are an executive, there's a good likelihood that the company will not only allow you to take early retirement, but will pay you to leave before age 65. (This has been especially true in recent years, as corporate reshufflings have led to reduced work forces through attrition. Frequently, this attrition has come in the form of very attractive early retirement plans.)

Still, do not be dazzled by what seem to be huge lump sum payments for taking early retirement. This is not money you'll want to spend. It's money you'll want to invest, with the income from it contributing to your support. Even in the best of investments, the yield from such a lump sum is likely to be disappointingly small.

You may be in a position to negotiate, though. For instance, if you are participating in your company's employee stock ownership or 401(k) plan, as you should be, you may be able to put part of that lump sum into investments that are matched by the company. It may be possible to retain a kind of semi-employee status that allows you to continue to take advantage of such a program, even though you have left the company. You'll certainly never know unless you ask.

In any case, a few years before you retire you should sit down and coldly appraise your retirement plan. What income would you have? Is it enough? What changes in your way of living do you expect retirement to bring? Are these realistic? Do they allow you happiness and freedom from fear? Do they make sufficient allowances for those unexpected occurrences that, unexpected though they be, become increasingly likely with advancing years? Do they consider how inflation can shrink your retirement funds? Chart 33 shows the truly alarming erosion inflation inflicts on savings and fixed incomes.

Now is the time to answer these questions, while there's still time to alter the answers.

RETIREMENT INCOME

Pensions are one of the two kinds of income you can look forward to upon retirement, the other being the results of your investments.

Because needs and companies are different (and, it sometimes seems, because nothing is simple anymore), there are several different kinds of pensions, though they can be broken down into three categories. See Chart 34 for an explanation of how proceeds are distributed.

The first is what's called a capital accumulation plan. You or your employer or both have contributed to the plan during your working years, and when you retire you receive your distribution as a lump sum.

The second, called a defined benefit, is what you probably think of when you think of a pension. You receive a check each month, the amount being based on how much you earned each year and the number of years you worked. The formulae involved in figuring this can be extremely complicated, because your income varied from year to year and the amount of weight given to each year can vary.

The third is an integrated plan. You are guaranteed a certain amount of income each month. Part of this comes from Social Security. The company pension fund makes up the difference.

There is another kind of pension, called Social Security. This isn't entirely fixed-income, because payments (usually) rise with inflation. To qualify, you must have worked and contributed to Social Security for a specified amount of time. Non-working spouses can collect Social Security at one-half the working spouse's rate.

CHART 32

Guide to Employment, Pension, and Other Retirement Plans
(Participants may have more than one type of plan)

Integrated Plans	
Various Plans	Some of the plans below may take into account the participant's Social Security retirement benefits.

Qualified Defined-Benefits Plans Tax-exempt by the Internal Revenue Code	
Flat-Amount Plans	All participants receive the same benefits if they meet the minimum years-of-service requirements, regardless of how much they earned.
Fixed-Benefit Plans	Participants receive predetermined benefits of a stated amount or of a stated percentage of compensation during entire employment or during a specified number of years prior to retirement.
Unit-Benefit Plans	Participants' benefits are based upon a predetermined formula combining both the level of preretirement income and number of years of service.

Qualified Defined-Contributions Plans (also known as Capital Accumulation Plans) Tax-exempt by the Internal Revenue Code	
Thrift or Savings Plans	As an incentive for employees to save, employers contribute amounts equal to all or part of each participant's contributions.
Money-Purchase Plans	Contributions by employers are based upon fixed formulas. Benefits to participants are based upon investment performance of the plans (accumulated principal, growth in value, and reinvested interest, dividends and other income).
Targeted-Benefit Plans	These are hybrid plans, primarily money-purchase plans, but also combining targeted defined benefits. Methods for determining employers' contributions are different from those in straight money-purchase plans.
Profit-Sharing Plans	Employers contribute specified percentages of profits, which may be a flat percentage on all profits or percentages on a sliding scale of profit levels. Employees may be permitted voluntarily to contribute additionally to their accounts.

CHART 32 *(continued)*

Employee Stock Ownership Plans (ESOPs)	These may be bonuses in company stock contributed by employers or they may be employee stock-purchase plans subsidized in part or entirely by employers. One form of the latter are PAYSOPs (Payroll Stock Ownership Plans).
401(k) Salary-Deferral Plans	A portion of an employee's compensation is contributed to the plan and the income tax on this amount, and on any matching contribution by the employer, and any earnings on the plan are deferred until distribution.
403(b) Salary-Deferral Plans	These are similar to 401(k) plans, above, except they are for employees of non-profit, tax-exempt employers, such as educational, charitable foundation, and religious organizations. They evolved from Tax-Sheltered Annuities (TSAs) for teachers.
SEP Plans	In Simplified Employee Pension (SEP) Plans, employers make contributions directly to employees' own Individual Retirement Accounts (IRAs).
Deductible Employee Contributions (DEC) Plans	DEC plans are a variation on SEPs, above. Employees make their IRA contributions to their employers' established retirement plans, rather than into IRAs separately maintained by these employees.
Individual Retirement Accounts (IRAs)	Employees establish and maintain IRAs for themselves and their spouses. Income taxes on some contributions and on growth in value and reinvested earnings in these accounts are deferred until withdrawals in accordance with tax regulations.
Keogh Plans	Self-employed individuals establish and maintain these plans, which are similar to IRAs.
Non-Qualified Plans Not tax-exempt by the Internal Revenue Code	
Various Plans	These plans may be structured in many ways. They are established and maintained by employers to provide incentives for employees and to single out accomplishments and provide additional benefits for selected employees. Employers are not required to report to the government on coverage and operation of these plans.

Note: The trend in recent years has been more to defined-contributions plans and less to traditional defined-benefits plans. With defined-contributions plans, employers are not obligated to provide guaranteed benefits as they are with defined-benefits plans. Such plans adversely affect employers if investment performance falls short of this commitment.

CHART 33

How Inflation Shrinks Your Dollar

The dollar you put into your retirement portfolio today is not the dollar you will take out for active retirement living. The following chart will assist you in making long-term estimates of actual money's worth.

Figures rounded to the nearest cent							
Years	4%	5%	6%	7%	8%	9%	10%
1	96¢	95¢	94¢	94¢	93¢	92¢	91¢
2	93¢	91¢	89¢	87¢	86¢	84¢	83¢
3	89¢	86¢	84¢	82¢	79¢	77¢	75¢
4	86¢	82¢	79¢	76¢	74¢	71¢	68¢
5	82¢	78¢	75¢	71¢	68¢	65¢	62¢
6	79¢	75¢	71¢	67¢	63¢	60¢	56¢
7	76¢	71¢	67¢	62¢	58¢	55¢	51¢
8	73¢	68¢	63¢	58¢	54¢	50¢	47¢
9	70¢	65¢	59¢	54¢	50¢	46¢	42¢
10	68¢	61¢	56¢	51¢	46¢	42¢	39¢
15	56¢	48¢	42¢	36¢	32¢	28¢	24¢
20	46¢	38¢	31¢	26¢	22¢	18¢	15¢

% = annual inflation rate

There are also several kinds of investments that are either designed specifically to provide retirement income, or else that are especially attractive when formulating a retirement plan.

Insurance annuities are especially attractive because the interest they make is tax free until they are mature. Retirement annuities, which is to say those that mature when you plan to retire, offer the advantage that you are taxed in your new, presumably lower bracket.

You make regular payments to the annuity during the course of your career, just as you would pay toward a life-insurance policy. Upon maturity, you are paid either in a lump sum (which can negate the tax advantages) or periodically. Your principal (the amount you paid) is not taxed, because you have already been taxed on it, when you earned it to begin with. The interest, though, is taxable.

Annuities are a good way to prepare for retirement, especially if you

CHART 34

Methods for Distribution of Funds in Pension Plans			
Lump Sum Payments in Cash or Securities (such as company stock)	*Periodic Payments in Cash or Securities*	*Withdrawals Because of Hardship Conditions (Typically, definition of hardship is liberal)*	*Loans Against Funds in Plan (Such loans carry a reasonable rate of interest)*
Upon permanent disability	Lifetime annuity (for as long as employee lives)	Such as:	Requirements usually include:
Upon termination of employment	Lifetime/term-certain annuity (for as long as employee lives, but for not less than a fixed number of years). Upon death of recipient, any remaining balance is paid to estate	Medical bills	Limited to amounts specified in plan
Upon reaching tenure or specified age		Down payment on a home	Must be repaid within predetermined period (generally five years)
Upon retirement		College tuition	
Upon death		Financing an auto	
			Must adhere to a specified repayment schedule
	Joint and survivor annuity (for as long as employee and spouse or the survivor lives)		
	Term-certain annuity (for a fixed number of years, but not longer than recipients' life)		

don't care to be attentive to an investment portfolio or if you have difficulty developing the discipline necessary to save. Because of their near-absolute safety, they may also be a part of a diversified retirement investment portfolio.

Because they do not offer maximum growth, though, annuities are not quite as advantageous as careful investing in stocks, bonds, and mutual funds.

Savings accounts are at or near the bottom of the list of income-producing investments. Because their yield is near—and sometimes below—the inflation rate, you get your money back in real terms, but little more. Though they are very safe, they offer no other advantages. Interest is taxable when it is credited to the account, so there is no concern about lump-sum distributions.

IRAs, Keoghs, and 401(k) plans are good for a variety of reasons. In the case of 401(k) plans, your contribution is often matched in full or part by your employer, making it one of the best investments you can make. In addition, all these plans offer special tax advantages, which allows a larger part of your dollar to work for you.

Though stocks, bonds, mutual funds, and other similar investments offer a greater degree of risk, they also yield more than many other kinds of straight—which is to say, not favored by the tax laws—investments. Except in the event of apocalyptic happenings, they can be quite safe enough for retirement, if they are chosen and managed carefully.

Depending on when you purchased it, and the market conditions at that time, your home equity can be a great retirement resource. Home prices rose beyond all imagination (and, perhaps, beyond all reason) in the 1980s. If you purchased your home before then, there's a good chance it has appreciated substantially. What's more, if you have lived in your home for three of the last five years and you are more than 55 years old, up to $125,000 profit on the sale of your home is tax free, though you may not enjoy this tax-free status on the sale of subsequent homes.

If you are a veteran, or if you were in government service, you may be eligible for federal retirement benefits beyond social security. Certain others may be eligible as well. Your financial planner should be able to help you determine if you qualify.

Have you planned well enough? Will your investments, pensions, and so on see you comfortably through retirement? Following the instructions in Chart 35 will tell you.

INFLATION: THE ENEMY OF RETIREMENT INCOME.
During the 1980s, inflation totaled a little more than 60 percent. What this

means is that each dollar lost nearly two-thirds of its value during that turbulent decade. Someone who retired on the first day of 1980, and who was living comfortably on a fixed income then, is anything but comfortable today.

This means that what seems like more than enough money to live on now may be pitifully poor in a decade or two, when you'll need it.

PLANNING YOUR ESTATE

The whole purpose of estate planning is to make sure that your passing will not create hardships for your family beyond that unhappy event, which will be quite enough hardship itself. It is not a gift to your family, it is an obligation you have to them. It is also a very meaningful final way to tell your family that you love them.

Nor is it something you can justifiably postpone. The tragedy of a young life ended through accident or sudden illness is all too common. It is compounded when that person, looking forward to a full and fruitful life, has failed to make the proper preparations.

Your estate and all the issues connected with it will certainly be discussed one day. Because you are the only one who has virtually absolute power over it, it's best if this discussion takes place while you are in a position to do something about it.

This means that from time to time you need to hold a family meeting. If you have no children, or if they are very young, this may simply be with your spouse. Make it light-hearted: Say that you want to make sure they are able to devote full attention to grieving over you, so you want to get the humdrum stuff out of the way now.

What it amounts to, in many respects, is seeing that family financial goals will continue to be met should you disappear from the picture. This is not as simple as it seems, because on top of everything else, you will no longer be a source of income. That's why estate planning is more than simply dividing up your possessions. A family estate planning meeting isn't a "who wants what" session.

You need to discuss the changes that have occurred in your family's life since the last time you had such a discussion. For example, as your earnings grow, you might want to increase your life insurance. Your financial plan will have changed to reflect this additional income. And remember, your estate plan should be designed to keep your financial plan on track even after you are gone. (There are ways you can defer income so as to minimize your tax exposure as well. Your financial advisor can help you formulate a strategy for this.)

CHART 35

Will Your Retirement Income be Enough?

(1) Annual retirement income you will need (expenses) or desire (expenses plus)— in *today's dollars* .... $ _____

(2) Adjustment for inflation:

  (A) About when will your retirement start? (Enter 5, 10, 15, or 20 years.) .... _____ years

  (B) Your estimate of average annual rate of inflation between now and your retirement (enter 4%, 6%, 8%, or 10%) .... _____ %

  (C) Refer to "Calculating" table below. Enter number from table where years (from #2A above) and inflation % (#2B) intersect .... _____

  (D) Multiply projected retirement income (#1 above) by number in #2C. This is your retirement income adjusted for inflation .... $ _____ (#1 × #2C =)

(3) Your estimated retirement income from current sources:

  (A) Annual income you now project from Social Security, retirement plans, savings, investments, etc.—*in today's dollars* .... $ _____

  (B) Your estimate of average annual rate of growth or cost-of-living adjustment (COLA) for amount in #3A (enter 4%, 6%, 8%, or 10%) .... _____ %

  (C) Refer to "Calculating" table below. Enter number from table where years (#2A) and % of growth/COLA (#3B) intersect .... _____

  (D) To calculate the increased value of your projected annual income when you will need it for retirement, multiply #3A by number in #3C .... $ _____ (#3A × #3C =)

(4) Will your retirement income be enough?
(A) Which is larger: the amount on line #2D or on line #3D? ....
(B) How much larger is it? .... $ _____
(C) *If the amount on line #2D is larger, you will need more retirement income. If the amount on line #3D is larger, you will have enough retirement income.*

Table: Calculating Annual Rates of Inflation and of Growth/COLA

Years	4%	6%	8%	10%
5	1.22	1.34	1.47	1.61
10	1.48	1.79	2.16	2.59
15	1.80	2.40	3.17	4.18
20	2.19	3.21	4.67	6.73

Don't forget older relatives who might one day call on you for support. The difference between a comfortable retirement and the worst kind of loneliness and poverty might well be the actions you take in planning for them in your estate.

Do your children look forward to college, have they graduated, or are they pursuing some other course of study? The answers will affect and, as they come to pass, change your estate planning picture.

Have you divorced? If so, there's every likelihood that you are less likely to favor your ex-spouse in your estate plans than you were before.

Once you've realized that there are changes to be made in your estate plan, you must act on them. Good intentions aren't good enough. You must discuss these changes with your financial adviser and your lawyer, who will make the appropriate moves for you or advise you as to the things you must do to bring them about.

The rule of thumb is this: Every occasion of great celebration or great sadness in your life or that of your family will likely involve a change in your estate plans.

DRAWING UP A WILL. If you don't already have a will, you should have one drawn up immediately.

If you have a will, but your situation has changed substantially since it was drawn up, you should get a new one. For example, your children may have finished college and married, but now there are grandchildren. The contents of your will are likely to change, because the goals you wish it to reach have changed.

Simple advice, but advice that's ignored by millions. While it's true that there are pleasanter tasks than one that forces us to recognize our mortality, it's a minor discomfort compared to the disaster that can take place in the absence of a will.

For years, will-making kits have been offered to the public. They purport to allow you to draw up your own legally binding will yourself. Now, computer programs that perform much the same function are offered.

In both cases, the cost is less than that of a professionally drawn will. But it may be a poor economy measure.

The American Bar Association points out that these kits may work for those who have extremely uncomplicated financial situations. But they're not for those whose arrangements are or must be more complex. While the American Bar Association certainly has an interest in drawing business to lawyers, a will is so important that it would rather naturally seem to be one of the last places to try to save a few dollars.

The Foundation for Financial Planning agrees. If everyone had the same needs, there would be no point in the huge array of estate planning options, the group points out. Unless your will is unusually simple, it should be formulated in consultation with both a lawyer and a financial planner. Together, they can determine the best strategies for building the legacies you wish to leave.

There are certain advantages, for instance, to establishing a "living trust," which is a property distribution method that avoids probate and that is gaining in popularity. This is not something for an amateur to set up, however.

Conversely, there are non-property issues that should be included in a will.

Before talking with your lawyer and financial planner, though, it's wise to make a list of the things you want to have happen to your estate. This can be a short list of goals. It paves the way for your advisors to put your plans into action.

Once your will has been drawn up, several copies should be made. One can be kept at home with important papers. You may wish to leave the original with your lawyer. If you have named an executor other than your lawyer, he or she should receive a copy.

It may be unwise—even disastrous—to put the original of your will in your safe deposit box. That's because in some states safe deposit boxes are locked immediately upon the lessee's death, which could make the will inaccessible for months while a bereaved family struggles to make ends meet.

It's also unwise, pointed out Gregory Scialdone, to disassemble a will once it has been drawn. If a page is replaced or altered by you and your lawyer, an entire new original should be typed, and copies should be made to replace those at your home and elsewhere. The reason is simple: Evidence that a will has been unstapled and restapled can be used to challenge it—and you won't be available to attest to its genuineness.

Married women should have wills drawn up also, even if their husbands have wills and the wives have no discrete property. This makes provision for distribution of assets and, most important, custody of minor children, should the wife's death precede that of the husband, or they both die at the same time.

You may wish to ask your lawyer (and, perhaps, your spiritual advisor) about "living wills" in your state. In most states, you may specify in advance that you reject (or insist upon) heroic measures to prolong your life even if the prognosis is poor. Be sure to explore the insurance and other legal implications of your decision.

TAXES AND TRUSTS. The law allows you to leave an unlimited amount to your spouse estate-tax free, but the amount you can leave to others is limited, after which the tax can take a hefty bite. Even if you intend to leave the bulk of your assets to your spouse, this is simply postponing the issue. Unless your estate is quite small (and you would be surprised how your net worth can be decreased through inflation and such things as life insurance that, for instance, pays off your mortgage), you should develop a tax strategy to see your family through. One of the best ways of doing this is through a trust plan.

This is something that you probably want to arrange with your lawyer, but it is not necessary that you do so. The trust departments of banks, for instance, can help you formulate a trust.

A trust is a legal arrangement in which someone is appointed to manage some or all of your property. This person is called a trustee. Depending on the way it is set up, it can avoid probate court, thereby transferring the estate quickly. It can also result in lessened estate taxes.

There are many types of trusts, and many variations within the types. It's up to you to decide on the task you wish to do, and, with the aid of your lawyer and financial planner, develop a trust to accomplish it.

Before entering into a trust, you absolutely must make certain that you are aware of all administrative costs and of any ways in which its provisions could escape accomplishing those things you wish the trust to do. One of the chief reasons for establishing a trust of any sort is to provide peace of mind and security not only for your family but for you yourself. This can be achieved only if you are certain that it will do what you want it to do.

One of the advantages of a trust is that it allows you to make sure that distribution of your assets, or the income from them, is accomplished in an orderly way. In this way, your family will not face a confusion of financial decisions following your death. This is of special importance because disreputable operators exist who make their living off of swindling the aggrieved. It allows critical decisions to be made with calm deliberation and as you want them to be.

It can also provide for specific goals, such as your children's education. You would not want to turn the full amount for support and education over to a young child, obviously. A trust can see that expenses are met before, during, and after your children's college education.

It can also ensure that your estate (the "corpus" is the legal term) continues to function as a unit, allowing for your children to realize their legacies as they grow older and have children of their own. This is what one thinks of when one hears of the family trusts set up by the very wealthy. But they are not just for the very wealthy.

There are, basically, two major kinds of trusts—testamentary and Inter Vivos, or "living trusts." The former is created by your will upon your death. All or part of your estate would be handled by a trustee, who has right to buy, sell, mortgage, or administer the estate as he or she sees fit, distributing the proceeds in accordance with your wishes. The distributions are not part of the estate vulnerable to estate taxes.

The second, the "living trust," is executed, and the assets involved distributed, while you are still alive. In their simplest form, these allow for transfer of control of your assets immediately upon your death. They avoid the probate process, which can be lengthy and leave your family having to scrape to make ends meet until it is completed.

A living trust can provide for management of your holdings, to assure continued, smooth operation of your portfolio and other holdings. As with other trusts, a living trust can be tailored to fit your family's situation precisely and to account for any foreseeable changes. This requires consultation with your financial advisor and your lawyer, who can help you bring your wishes to fruition.

The term of the trust is something you must consider, also. How do you want your assets distributed?

Do you have a crippled child? Then you might want to put assets in a Craven trust. This provides for income for the child from those assets for as long as the child lives. It lasts as long as it does because the principal is untouched. Upon the child's death, the principal is returned to your estate.

A short-term trust can provide income to an aging parent. Again, upon the beneficiary's death the remainder of the trust again becomes part of your estate. Taxes on the income are paid by the beneficiary who, presumably, is in a lower tax bracket.

As with other aspects of trusts, you can arrange for distribution over an unlimited amount of time, with an infinite number of variations.

Perhaps you wish to make sure your spouse is supported for the rest of his or her life. An open-ended trust will accomplish this, providing income from assets managed professionally through a trustee you select.

Or you may have young children. You wish to see that they are supported until and through their college years, with money set aside to pay for college. After that, once they've gotten their feet on the ground and have settled enough that you can feel sure they would use it wisely, the trust can be ended, with its assets distributed among them. This is a targeted long-term trust.

If the support and education of your children is otherwise provided for, you might want to establish a trust whereby your assets will grow without distribution, the income reinvested, until a certain time at which the beneficiary receives the income that has accumulated. This offers tax advantages, because it is tax deferred until it is distributed. Trusts such as these are known, not surprisingly, as accumulation trusts.

One once-popular trust that has been legislated into disfavor is the Clifford Trust. This was once a way of sheltering assets by putting them in the name of a child, who was taxed at a lower rate. No more. Due to the 1986 tax reform act, everything above $1,000 that a child under 14 years old receives is taxed at the grantor's higher rate. So much for Clifford Trusts.

It is possible to arrange a trust wherein a beneficiary receives income for a specified period of time—less than 10 years—with the principal then being distributed to the same or another beneficiary. This is called a spousal remainder trust, and while it has some advantages—such as tax benefits, unless it is used to pay alimony or child support—it also has some serious disadvantages. The main one is that the principal beneficiary is fixed once the trust is in effect. It is not subject to change. This means you could choose your spouse and then, some years later, divorce. Too bad. Your ex-spouse gets the money, and there's not much of anything you can do about it.

If you have no close relatives, but do have a cause or institution to which you are devoted, you can arrange a charitable trust that can see that your contributions to that cause or institution continue long after you are gone. A straight charitable trust is like a an open-ended trust, except that the charity is the beneficiary. This provides income and would be useful to, for instance, establish a seat in your name at an institution of higher learning. Nor is it something that you might wish to invoke only upon your death, for there are definite tax advantages to it that you can realize while you are still living. Variations on charitable trusts allow payments to be made to the institution for a period of time, with the principal then going to the institution or some other beneficiary. Alternatively, you may arrange to have income payments made to your family or other beneficiary with the principal, in due course, going to the charity or other institution of your choice.

The descriptions above paint the whole field of trusts with a broad brush, but it would take many hundreds of pages, filled with obscure and very specific language and updated constantly, to cover the subject in full. Still, this should give you an idea of the kinds of trusts that are available.

Perhaps the best approach is to sit down and figure out, with the aid of your family, the goals you wish to achieve through a trust, either beginning now or taking effect after you are gone. Once you have in mind what you want to do, it's simple to discuss with your lawyer and financial planner the best way of establishing a trust to bring it about.

DEATH BENEFITS. While life insurance has important investment aspects while you are still living (cash value, for instance, which can be used to secure loans), its primary function is to see that your family does not go without as a result of your death. For this function, it is unsurpassed. It is also relatively inexpensive, provides a great deal of protection from the outset (unlike an investment portfolio, which must be built over time), and is easy to obtain.

How much life insurance do you need? Simply put, you need enough to replace the income that you would be providing were you still living. Something that is frequently overlooked is that both spouses should have life insurance coverage. A spouse who remains in the home may not directly contribute to the amount of cash flowing into the family, but instead makes contributions that are surprisingly expensive, if outside help is required to do them.

There are two main types of life insurance. One, called term insurance, is what its name implies: It covers you for a specified period. To collect, you must die during that period. Term insurance premiums start low but increase as you grow older.

The other is called whole life or straight life. It covers you for your entire lifetime, which is to say that it will one day surely be collected. Whole life premiums are constant. There are additional whole life insurance advantages. A whole life policy develops cash value. You can borrow against it. Should you drop the policy, you would receive a cash payment. What's more, the policy generally pays dividends that can be applied to the premiums to increase your coverage or decrease or eliminate the premiums. After a certain amount of time, when the dividends equal the premiums, the policy is said to be paid up.

The amount of life insurance you need varies as your situation varies. Early in life, it may be thought of as an investment. Even single people just starting out may want to carry life insurance in their portfolios.

As your responsibilities grow, and your income does, too, you will want to increase your coverage. This enables you to be sure your family will be supported and your income preserved following your death. More information on life insurance strategies can be found in Chapter 5. It is important for you to remember, though, that as your life progresses, you must from time to time reassess not only your life insurance needs, but the beneficiaries you name. These are likely to change.

Some health insurance policies pay what is called an accidental death or dismemberment provision. If yours does, you should make note of it, lest your death be accidental—as opposed to the result of illness. You should also explore with your insurance agent the best way to make sure your family's medical coverage continues—or begins, if your family's coverage is through your job—following your death.

If you are an employee, you should check with your company's benefits department to determine what, if any, death benefits are provided. These could be in the form of life insurance (especially if your death is job related) or pension.

Your individual retirement account should be taken into consideration as well, as should any deferred compensation, employee stock ownership, or 401(k) plan, or your Keogh account if you are self-employed.

FUNERAL PLANNING. Many people wisely decide that it's best to make the necessary arrangements long before the fact. This means that grieving relatives won't have to make important and expensive decisions at a time when they are under intense emotional pressure. The fact that you have helped make the arrangements will be an additional comfort to your family and friends.

- Set aside money to cover the costs. This can be something as simple as an account or CD in a relative's name, or as elaborate as a formal trust agreement. A life insurance policy with death benefits assigned to cover funeral expenses may be the answer.

- Do not make your funeral arrangements a part of your will. This can tie up the money you've set aside to pay expenses.

The American Association of Retired Persons, which has done extensive study on the subject, advises everyone to make funeral plans, but cautions them to avoid pre-paying.

There are several reasons to be wary of the pre-payment plans. The first one is financial.

A typical pre-payment plan calls for you to pay for the funeral at today's prices, which average $3,000 plus an additional $2,000 for in-ground burial. The plan then guarantees that the services you have chosen will be delivered, no matter whether the price has risen.

But funeral costs have risen only 4 to 6 percent per year over the 1970s and 1980s, with no particular reason to believe much of an increase beyond that rate is likely to take place in the foreseeable future. That means that you would be better off putting the money in a CD or other investment, earmarking it to cover funeral expenses.

There is another problem with the pre-payment plans: The pre-payment plans often are good at only one funeral home. If a family moves and wishes to take their pre-paid plan with them, they may have to pay a substantial penalty.

The money you would pay into such a plan is invested by the plan itself. It is no longer under your control. But in 1987, the IRS ruled that the interest received is taxable income. You are liable for it. This quickly turned into an administrative nightmare; funeral homes, after all, are not set up to mail tax statements.

The Federal Trade Commission reports there has been abuse of pre-paid funeral plans, as well. A funeral director in Iowa pleaded guilty to embezzling $250,000 in pre-payment funds. Another plan was being sued by the Ohio attorney general. A plan in Los Angeles was under investigation for misuse of interest paid on pre-payment funds.

Because of the potential for abuses, every state except Vermont and Alabama requires that part or all of the pre-payments be put into surety bonds. This has proven unpopular with the funeral industry, which has come to favor plans that are insurance-backed.

If you choose pre-payment, make sure it contains a guarantee that the services will be delivered no matter how much costs have risen. Find out whether you can take the plan with you if you move. Find out, too, whether you can cancel the agreement and get your money back.

The AARP has prepared several pamphlets that discuss funeral payment plans. They are available free of cost whether you're a member of AARP or not. To obtain them, write the AARP Fulfillment Center, 1909 K Street NW, Washington, D.C. 20049.

WHO OWNS IT?

When you own a home, business, real estate, or much of anything else in combination with someone else, your death can throw things into a complete muddle.

What's more, the arrangements that can make things easiest for the co-owners of your home or other property may not be the ones that provide the best tax advantages. The best you can hope to do is to find a balance of advantages and disadvantages that works best for you.

Joint ownership is the method you are most likely to employ if you are married and most of your assets are to be left to your spouse. Under joint ownership, the surviving owner assumes full ownership, and that's that. The problem is that joint ownership has ramifications that can cause you a world of trouble while you're still alive.

As a result, there is a range of ownership possibilities that can have these assets go entirely to your estate, entirely to another owner, or very nearly anything in between.

This is a situation that requires careful discussion with your financial planner and your lawyer before a decision is made.

18

TAX POLICY IN
——— THE 1990s ———

B elieve it or not, there was good tax news during the '80s:

- Tax shelters were outlawed. These economically foolish schemes served no purpose other than to cut the taxes of their investors, enrich their promoters, and raise the taxes the rest of us had to pay.

- The Taxpayer Bill of Rights was passed. Although it doesn't go far enough, it helps give ordinary taxpayers a fighting chance when the IRS comes calling.

During the 1980s, too, we watched the federal government stride forth with the idea that it could collect less money but spend more.

There were a couple of philosophies behind this, beyond the idea that one can get elected by promising to do magic—which was itself a fairly successful campaign strategy during that loopy decade.

The first was that the fewer the layers of government, and the closer the responsible agency to the problem being addressed, the more efficiently the money would be spent. Mostly, it hasn't turned out that way.

The second was that if we were to spend foreign powers that did not wish us well, notably the Soviet Union, into oblivion, we would end up having to spend less on our nation's biggest ticket item, national defense. This seems to have worked to some extent, but the returns are preliminary and only the 1990s will tell.

Whether the Income Tax Reform Act of 1986 actually represented a reform, too, remains to be determined. Certainly, from the moment it was approved almost everyone began to shout for changes in it. It seems to have pleased no one, but this may be because the promises that were made for it were inflated beyond any reasonable expectation.

What this all means is that today's tax law is not likely to resemble tomorrow's very closely. The tax law is like a giant, squirming hydra—as soon as one head is cut off, two more replace it. (In fairness, the long-suffering employees of the Internal Revenue Service probably think of taxpayers in much the same way.) It would be wonderful to hear the announcement that, inasmuch as the tax law has not changed one iota, the government has decided to save a little money and just use last year's forms and instructions this year. But that is not, of course, the way it works.

So you must constantly adjust your tax position so you will pay as little tax as possible. This is not unpatriotic. This is something to which you are entitled as surely as those who are entitled to payments from the government should receive them. If you feel guilty and believe you should be paying more, give of your money and of yourself to worthwhile charities. Just remember to get a receipt, and to deduct it.

Developing tax strategies has come to be a lot like driving down a road that is wriggling around, but it can be done. True, it does contain a degree of uncertainty that rivals some of the securities markets. So approach it with that spirit: It is another place of rising and falling values, only this is one where you wish to keep your investments to a minimum.

TAXES IN THE '90s

The great imponderable in personal financial planning is: How much will I pay in taxes? No one can answer that question. David T. Wright, Vice Chairman for Tax Services of Coopers & Lybrand, one of the world's largest and most prestigious firms of certified public accountants, shared these thoughts on the driving forces that will govern tax policy in the next decade.

At first blush, any attempt to divine the future of tax policy in the 1990s would appear to be a quixotic exercise. After all, tax laws are not written in a vacuum, but rather are shaped by political considerations, economic performance, and the global environment. However, using the events of the past ten years as a guide, it is possible to outline a vision of where tax policy may be headed in the next decade.

The 1980s were a turbulent decade for the economy of the United States. By far, the rapid expansion of the federal budget deficit had the greatest influence on tax policy. Mergers, acquisitions, and leveraged buyouts also dominated the financial headlines. Regional economies from New England to Silicon Valley to the oil patch experienced booms and busts. The sobering legacy of the decade may be the ongoing bailout of the banking industry in general and the savings and loan industry in particular.

The 1980s were also a turbulent decade for our tax system. Major tax laws were enacted virtually every year. Indeed, the Internal Revenue Code, the compilation of our tax laws, was completely rewritten for the first time in more than 30 years. Tax rates were cut dramatically and the tax burden shifted from individuals to business.

As the national debt continued to skyrocket during the 1980s, Congress became a more active participant in the budget process. The enactment of the so-called Gramm-Rudman-Hollings balanced budget law dictated annual deficit reduction targets while restricting the policy options available to Congress. Meeting deficit targets has required an annual round of government spending cuts and tax increases, which frequently took the form of closing tax "loopholes" or broadening the tax base.

Looking into the 1990s, the scenario is unlikely to change. A continued need to deal with the deficit will make the tax code an ongoing target for change. This incessant tinkering with the tax system will leave businesses and individuals hard-pressed to develop long-range tax planning programs and strategies. As witnessed by the fate of investments in real estate limited partnerships, this year's tax benefits could become next year's tax burden.

The budget deficit and the annual quest for revenue have made it increasingly difficult to enact any new tax incentives or reduce tax burdens on any specific groups. Now, tax changes that increase the deficit must be offset by changes that raise an equal or greater amount of revenue. This, in turn, has pitted tax constituencies against one another in the quest for scarce dollars. This battle will continue to rage well into the 1990s.

Policymakers, too, will be forced to struggle with a series of issues having broad tax implications. The aging of the American work force, the decline in the nation's savings and investment rate, and the questionable status of U.S. economic competitiveness are among the most pressing.

Many families saw their federal income tax bills fall during the past decade. Yet much of the decrease was offset by a corresponding increase in payroll taxes to insure that the Social Security system will be fiscally sound until the 21st century.

At the beginning of the 1980s, Social Security teetered on the edge of bankruptcy, a crisis that still affects public faith in the system. But following overhaul, the reserves of the Social Security Trust Funds have grown, and continue to grow, by tens of billions of dollars a year. Early in the new century, they are expected to rise to some $12 trillion.

There is growing sentiment that the resulting surplus is being used to reduce the overall budget deficit rather than providing for the retirement needs of the current work force. Because the tax most adversely impacts low- and middle-income workers, many groups will continue to press for a reduction of this tax burden. Additionally, attention will need to be paid to the benefit side of the system to assure that future retirees will receive adequate benefit payments.

The debate is likely to continue over the balance of today's burdens with tomorrow's needs as well as the progressiveness of the system. How will it come out? Resolution is far in the future. It is more likely to continue as a balancing act.

Policymakers frequently have used the tax code as an instrument for social and economic policy. Due to the decline in national savings during the 1980s, programs to spur savings are likely candidates for support in this coming decade. Individual retirement accounts and savings accounts to encourage such activities as higher education or home ownership are examples of programs that may be instituted. But once again, the type and scale of these incentives will be tempered by the budget deficit. For the longer term, the aging population will shift from being a consuming society to one more interested in saving . . . current studies already point to that difference.

Likewise, there will likely be some relief ahead for long-term capital gains. Many observers claim that investment in productive assets has fallen in the absence of tax incentives for risk-taking. To remedy this, they argue that the tax system should provide investors with favorable tax treatment for gains derived from productive or income-generating assets. It is not likely, however, that tax shelters will come back, at least not in the format understood in the '70s and '80s.

For many years, economists have argued that our tax laws discourage corporate equity because income from corporate equity is taxed twice, first as corporate profits and then as dividend income in the hands of the stockholders. When contrasted with the deductibility of interest payments, this double tax makes it more attractive for corporations to borrow than to issue stock. In addition, U.S. companies are disadvantaged vis-a-vis our trading partners, as most other major industrial countries provide relief from double taxation.

Expect the Treasury Department soon to offer alternatives designed to end this double tax and remove the bias toward debt. The wave of leveraged buyouts and debt-financed takeovers in the 1980s, which have left many companies highly leveraged and some tottering on the brink of bankruptcy, may cause business leaders and policymakers to settle their differences and reach agreement on reducing the double tax and the bias toward debt.

Corporate taxes could also be changed to enable U.S. business to compete more effectively. Taxes are a major element in world-wide business competition. Some tax changes enacted in the 1980s, such as the limitation on the foreign tax credit, have disadvantaged our companies as they look for new markets abroad.

These changes could include a different tax system, a simplified foreign tax credit, and other incentives so that U.S. business can compete more effectively with new rivals as well as traditional counterparts. (For their part, our trading partners can be expected to continue to respond to changes in the U.S. tax and economic environment, much as they have done in the past several years. For example, expect to see a continued lowering of tax rates throughout the world to compete with those in the U.S. See accompanying International Corporate Tax Rate Chart.)

INTERNATIONAL CORPORATE TAX RATES

Country	Rate	Country	Rate
Australia	39	Netherlands	40
Canada	38	Spain	35
France	42	Sweden	52
Germany	56	United Kingdom	35
Japan	37.5	United States	34

One difficulty that proponents of corporate tax breaks will face is their political unpopularity. Many people feel corporations pay too little tax. One feature of the 1986 Tax Reform Act was its intended increase in the share of taxes corporations pay. (So far, thanks to the corporations' tax lawyers, it hasn't yet materialized.) With new tax laws having to be "revenue neutral" (that is, not make the deficit worse), it will be difficult to decrease corporate taxes if it means hiking individual rates. One way to get around this dilemma would be to offset the tax cut with new corporate taxes, so that the overall corporate tax burden stays the same.

Perhaps the most elusive byproduct of the political changes in Europe and Asia may be the so-called "peace dividend." Calls for glasnost and perestroika and cries for freedom in the Eastern bloc may allow the U.S. to reduce military spending, which currently consumes over one-quarter of our annual government expenditures.

If significant cuts in the military budget occur, should the diverted money be spent on direct government expenditures, such as education or the infrastructure? Should it be used for tax incentives to promote private sector investment, such as research and development? Should it be used to reduce the deficit directly, which would increase the nation's savings rate? Or should it be used to retire a portion of the national debt, which could lead to lower interest rates and a stronger economy?

All of these alternatives offer attractive benefits. One benefit could be greater stability in the tax system. As we pointed out earlier in this chapter, the budget deficit and resulting quest for more revenue have necessitated an annual roller-coaster type of planning. With the relative stability of the moves above, U.S. companies should be able to plan for the future with reasonable confidence that their strategies incorporating the tax outlook would remain viable into the next century.

In any event, the "peace dividend" will not be realized quickly and there will be many claims made on it. If there is no real deficit reduction in the coming years, policymakers may be forced to explore a fundamental change in our tax system—introduction of a consumption-based tax. In other words, a national sales tax.

It cannot be stated strongly or loudly enough that the deficit is getting out of control! Politicians reluctant to cut spending or further raise taxes on a tax-wearied populace fondly eye a national sales tax as an easy way out. But there is broad-based opposition to such a tax from both liberals and conservatives. Liberals say a national sales tax would unfairly hurt poorer people (because the tax would be a flat tax, poorer people would pay a larger proportion of their income in taxes). Conservatives oppose this new tax because they want the deficit to be cut through spending cuts, not new taxes. Throw in the states—who oppose a national sales tax on the grounds that it endangers state and local sales taxes, their exclusive province—and you have an impressive political coalition opposing adoption of a national sales tax.

It does not appear likely that a consumption tax will be enacted in the next several years. Even if the political objections to a consumption tax were overcome, it would take several years to create the bureaucratic structure necessary to administer such a tax. Although a national sales tax would raise enormous sums of revenue, it creates significant administrative burdens and could not be implemented expeditiously.

Because of the nature of a consumption tax, there is little that consumers can do to protect themselves from such a tax, other than give up consuming. This type of tax, however, does encourage savings and as such would be advantageous to those who invest. Consumers would receive some relief if certain types of goods (for example food and medical care) were exempt from this tax.

Nevertheless, debate over this politically sensitive revenue scheme can be expected to continue as long as the budget deficit remains at the top of the national agenda.

19
THE END OF THE
– DISPOSABLE SOCIETY –

Unless we clean up our act right now, we're going to be one of the last few generations of human beings on Earth.

It's become a cliche to speak of the dinosaurs as a synonym for anachronistic, failed creatures. The irony is that the dinosaurs did quite nicely for some 150 million years.

We're working hard at checking out after a scant 2 million years and, unlike the dinosaurs, we're doing our best to take the rest of the world with us.

As the 20th century draws to a close, there is much to be ashamed of. We have done more damage to the earth in this century than we did in the entire history of mankind before. We have undertaken enormous projects with little regard for their effects.

The mountains are being eroded and the trees are being killed by rain that is, in some places, as acidic as vinegar.

The atmosphere has grown so dirty that on some days city dwellers are advised to remain indoors. The canals of Venice stink of garbage and filth and the microscopic plants that feed on such things. The canals of Florida are clogged with non-native plants and fishes, giant toads, and a food chain driven beyond all reason by detergents and effluents from human settlement.

Our burning of fossil fuels is making fossils of us, as it seems already to be forcing climactic changes on the Earth. Some American cities no longer allow construction in areas that are expected to be underwater in a generation or two. Whole countries, among them the world's poorest and most heavily populated, face the threat of permanent, nation-wide flooding.

The peaceful use of nuclear power was one of the things most heavily campaigned for during the first Earth Day over two decades ago. Thanks to thoughtless, uncaring, and poor execution, society has shied away from the technology completely. This may be a case of throwing out the baby with the bath water. But the reality is that there are no apparent arguments in favor of nuclear power that are likely to turn the tide that is running so heavily against it.

And there's some question that at this late date we can do much about it.

This may seem like an odd issue to raise in a book about personal finance, but the fact is that the state of our environment, and how we cope with it, has significant economic ramifications for ourselves as individuals as well as for our nation as a whole. As more and more of us contract disease from our poison-laden environment, we will incur ever more expensive medical bills. As you will see, the environment can affect our personal pocketbooks in other ways. And the costs of cleaning up the environment will have to be paid by someone; who bears the cost will be one of the biggest issues of the '90s.

Apart from its direct economic effect, the environment is important in an economic sense because all investment is designed to produce a brighter future. Our future, for better or worse, is on this Earth. There's little point in building if there's nothing to build toward.

What is needed, the only thing that can possibly help, is the adoption of universal responsibility for the world. That's unlikely, but it's impossible unless we each of us do everything we can to preserve the planet.

ENVIRONMENTAL ECONOMICS

Pollution is expensive. There are at this writing more than $100 billion in lawsuits outstanding against alleged polluters. That figure is likely to grow.

How should you look at the effects of the environment on your investment strategy? Two ways: identify companies that are likely to be hurt by environmental problems and the companies that will profit by dealing with those problems.

Wall Street analysts point to a number of industries that could take a real beating as the environmental issue heats up.

- The chemical and petroleum industries. A single oil spill can result in millions of dollars in liability. Companies can be held liable for unforeseen effects of their products, which can produce truly gigantic settlements and enormously costly clean-up bills.

- The insurance industry. While it is now difficult and expensive to get liability insurance against environmental accidents, companies already hold billions of dollars in such policies.

- Agribusiness. Modern pesticides and fertilizers have maximized farm productivity, but in more and more cases they're found to be harmful when they wash into streams and lakes. Reduced use of these chemicals, though, is likely to reduce crop yields.

- Real estate. The recent announcement that all homes should be tested for radon simply underlines the problem. People who bought homes in Howard Beach, Missouri, in 1970, only to find out that the town was uninhabitably polluted, have learned a terrible lesson, as did homeowners near the Love Canal. Surprising and sudden developments can reduce property value to virtually nothing, almost overnight.

How can you weigh these factors as you consider investments? First, you must consider the potential exposure of a company to catastrophic loss due to environmental liability. Remember: A single accident can cripple a company virtually overnight.

Second, if you are looking to invest in any of the companies formed to deal with environmental problems, do so very carefully. Like many industries that are just starting out, there is likely to be a shake-out phase, where the cream rises and the milk is siphoned off. Investments at this point are risky unless you've studied the companies involved.

Environmental Mutual Funds: "Social conscience" mutual funds (also known as "social responsibility" funds and "ethical" funds) were started in the 1980s to select stocks and bonds whose issuers, in the funds' portfolio managers' view, are morally "clean."

Probably the quintessential ethical sector mutual funds were started in 1989 and 1990, focusing on the stocks of companies involved in environmental fields. One of these is the Fidelity Environmental Services Portfolio, whose prospectus describes its investment possibilities as "companies engaged in the research, development, manufacture, or distribution of products, processes, or services related to waste management or pollution control." Other environmental mutual funds have similar policies. They're one way to participate in the potential rewards—and risks—of investing in environmental securities. (Of course, some diversified mutual funds also invest in environmental securities, but only a small portion of their portfolio holdings are so directed.)

SOLID WASTE

Garbage is big business in America. Every man, woman, and child here produces, on average, a ton of it each year.

American cities, towns, and villages spend more than $5 billion each year to haul solid waste to landfills, some of which are more than 850 miles away from the place the garbage was generated. Some East Coast cities spend $240 per ton—three times the national average—to have their garbage hauled to Kentucky.

With half the nation's landfills scheduled to close by the year 2000 and the cost of the average mass-burn incinerator topping $200 million, solid-waste disposal costs are doubling, tripling, and quadrupling around the country. Those costs are, of course, passed along to the producers of solid waste, which means you and me. Even those solutions are inadequate, with landfills polluting groundwater supplies and incinerators merely changing waste from one form of pollution to another.

These industries are likely to thrive in this environment:

RECYCLING COMPANIES. Aluminum cans have been recycled for some time, as has paper. Paper recycling is especially likely to become more profitable in the coming years, because acid rain pollution has reduced pulpwood crops, driving up the cost of paper. The Environmental Protection Agency and many states and municipalities have instituted programs designed to make recycling more attractive. Growth is expected in the recycling of other metals and even of plastics.

WASTE DISPOSAL COMPANIES. This can be a minefield for the investor, because many such companies have been laced with corruption. New laws being considered on the federal level and by many states are expected to produce a new generation of companies with the technical wherewithal to handle wastes properly. Medical waste disposal, so much in the news of late, is expected to experience a surge of growth.

ENVIRONMENTAL CLEAN-UP COMPANIES. Asbestos removal alone is expected to be a multi-billion-dollar business by 1990. That's because the majority of buildings constructed in the U.S. before 1970 contain the carcinogenic mineral. Removal requires specialized training and equipment; it's not a do-it-yourself project. Companies that handle oil spills and removal of contaminated soil have an all-too-bright outlook as well.

GARBAGE DISPOSAL COMPANIES. The tragicomic plight of the New York garbage barge of 1987 illustrates a leading problem facing the country: We're producing lots of trash and don't know what to do with it. The EPA is funding research in solid-waste disposal. And the Departments of Energy and Defense will step up campaigns to clean up messes they've made around the country. Companies that come up with solutions will fill an almost unlimited demand.

SOLVING THE SOLID WASTE PROBLEM

Proposals to solve the solid-waste problem vary. Some include the requirement that individual consumers separate their garbage by type. Others restrict the use of non-biodegradable products and packaging. Some governments won't buy any paper that isn't recycled. Others have decided to tax heavily packaging materials that are environmentally unsound, which provides an economic incentive to recycle.

Anyone who has purchased a fast-food sandwich, only to find it wrapped in paper, then placed in a colorful plastic box, then put inside a paper bag, has to wonder whether all of this is necessary. The legislators of Suffolk County decided it is not.

In 1988, Suffolk County, New York, passed into law a bill that prohibited retail food outlets—including fast-food establishments and supermarkets—from providing plastic bags and those little plastic foam sandwich and drink containers. Their law promotes the use of biodegradable bags and food packaging. Other communities have followed suit, and still others may be expected to.

What You Can Do: With a little effort, you can help curb escalating solid-waste costs, get involved in protecting future landfill resources, and clear the way for a better environmental future by following a few simple rules.

Ask for plain old paper bags at the grocery store, and forego bags at all when you buy an item or two at the convenience or drug store. Paper bags are recyclable. They're biodegradable. You can use them to carry your old newspapers and paper products to the recycling center.

Much has been made of plastic bags that decompose when exposed to sunlight. While this is a step in the right direction, in most places it makes little difference. The bags and their contents end up buried in landfills, where the sun doesn't shine.

If there is no recycling program in your community, push for one. If you're a member of a civic organization, push your organization to get involved. Some of the most successful recycling efforts in the country are run not by governments but by responsible community groups (who, in many cases, have learned to make recycling pay in cold hard cash).

Find out about local legislation requiring the separation and recycling of solid waste, and legislation that prohibits—or makes economically unfeasible—the use of non-biodegradable, non-recyclable packaging. Many local, county, and state governments are considering such legislation, and the number doing so will certainly grow during this crucial decade. Taking a stand and testifying at public hearings, organizing letter-writing campaigns, and otherwise supporting such legislation will reduce the likelihood that your solid waste bill will rise greatly.

Recycle paper, glass, and aluminum products. It can be profitable for the groups doing the recycling. Old newspapers become new cardboard boxes. Old beverage cans become new ones. It is cheaper to recover these materials than it is to produce new ones, and the processes involved are far more environmentally sound. Any situation where good ecology is instantly good economy is an offer too good to let go to waste, so to speak.

Return glass bottles and aluminum cans. In a growing number of states, bottle laws are in effect, so you're throwing money down the trash chute. You can recover a nickel or more apiece on returns. The return of 10 bottles a week will net you $25 per year.

Patronize fast-food restaurants that don't use those plastic foam containers. Composted paper materials return to the soil in less than a year. Because it so rapidly decomposes, it doesn't use up expensive landfill space. And it actually returns benignly to the environment, unlike plastics that take hundreds of years to break down and produce deadly pollutants when burned.

Help your company take a lead from some of the biggest corporations. Consider a program to recover computer printout paper and other recyclable office wastes. If you have a copy machine or laser printer that uses toner cartridges, have them refilled rather than buying new ones. You'll reduce the amount of waste and save money, too. A local Keep America Beautiful office or environmental group will be eager to work with you to help reduce waste of both money and resources.

Use paper products made from 100 percent recycled paper, especially when purchasing greeting cards and stationery. Patronize stores that do the same, and urge your friends to do so. When stores that offer slick plastic packaging discover that it's costing them customers, they will come around. Perhaps they will even seek to gain customers by improving the quality of the products being packaged.

Don't use spray cans of household products when those products are available in some other form. Learn to live without a few of the environmentally unsound conveniences.

Minimize your use of paper. Although paper is recyclable, saving paper means saving trees. Use handkerchiefs instead of tissues, rags and cloth towels instead of paper towels, and cloth napkins instead of paper ones. You'll save money, and trees, too.

Minimize your use of plastic. Reuse your plastic bags. The bag you reuse means one less bag that can't be recycled.

Use cloth diapers. Disposable diapers are eight times as costly as cloth diapers, and three times as costly as diaper services. Just limiting the use of disposable diapers to when you're away from home will help cut the waste disposal problem these diapers present.

These things are easy, but they do involve a slight amount of inconvenience. In that way, they are like brushing your teeth: It's a bother, but if you don't do it, the alternative is likely to be expensive and painful.

WATER

After air, water is the most crucial ingredient to life. You can live for weeks without food, but you won't last more than a few days without water.

These days, our planet's water supply is in danger. We're running out of drinking water, and we're polluting the water we do have.

Ground water is the source for half of our nation's drinking water. This source is threatened by pesticides, toxic chemicals, hazardous wastes, and solid waste.

Our rivers and lakes are in danger. Although outlawed, residues from DDT and PCBs are so high in some of our rivers and lakes that their fish are unsafe to eat. Urban and agricultural runoff remains unchecked. And medical waste is being dumped in our oceans—a by-product of the solid waste crisis—causing further contamination.

Growth is taxing available water to the limit. For years, southern Californians have relied on water from the Colorado River. But although California is continuing to grow, so are neighboring Nevada and Arizona. The Colorado cannot continue to support this growing population; these days, its running 50 percent below normal.

The water situation has grown so bad, many communities are turning to purchasing agricultural water rights—irrigation water—to meet the demand. California farmers face cuts of up to 50 percent; this could affect fruit and vegetable prices (not to mention the California economy).

What does this mean to you? Examine the water resources available where you live, and especially if you're planning to move. If there's a significant chance of a water shortage due to pollution or demand, you may want to factor this into your decision on where to live. Steps to alleviate water shortages range from conservation limits to expensive public works projects; their cost varies from inconvenience to significantly higher tax levies.

Can't imagine what a water shortage would be like? Think back to the gas crisis. Already, many Americans plan their water use the way we all once planned our gas use.

What You Can Do: Processes to convert sea water into fresh water are under study. Eventually, they'll result in a new source of water. And polluted bodies of waters can be reclaimed. In the short run, though, conservation is the answer. Here are some steps you can take to save water (and cut your water bill):

Cut your toilet's capacity. Forty percent of the water you use daily is flushed down your toilet. By filling a plastic or glass bottle with sand and placing it in your toilet tank, you'll cut the water your toilet uses. Don't use a brick; pieces could break loose and harm your plumbing.

Use aerators in your faucets. They can reduce water usage up to 75 percent.

Don't use fresh water to irrigate your lawn. Collect used water from the laundry, bathroom sink, and shower and use it instead.

Don't let water run while you shave or brush your teeth. Turn the shower on just to soap up and rinse off.

Replace grass lawns with plants or other coverings that conserve water.

Only wash dishes in fully loaded dishwashers.

Use natural household cleaning agents. Chemicals pollute the environment. Biodegradable ingredients, such as baking soda, vinegar, and borax can be combined to produce substitutes for chemical-laden products you now use. For example, baking soda and vinegar can be used to clean a toilet. Two tablespoons of liquid soap and two teaspoons of borax mixed in a spray bottle of warm water make a useful oven cleaner. (Wear rubber gloves and goggles.)

BUILDING CONSERVATION

Since 1986, the reconstruction and renovation of existing buildings has become a bigger industry than new construction.

This is likely to be the wave of the future as well. There are sound economic reasons for it, chiefly the fact that you simply could never afford to build with the same quality as was employed in the construction of some older buildings.

When you think about it, there are few buildings in America that should be torn down at all, by old-world standards. Despite the ravages of time and war after war, it is not difficult to find structures in Europe that were built before Columbus looked for India and found America instead. The American view that everything should be torn down and rebuilt every few years is not a luxury, it is a waste.

Wise building owners have learned that they can fix up an older building and end up with a building much better than they could hope to build from scratch for far less cost. By doing so, of course, they reduce the amount of construction refuse and the drain on resources that takes place when materials need to be manufactured to replace materials that have been torn down and discarded.

This, of course, opens up a whole field of careers and investments. One booming industry of the 1990s is likely to be in construction firms that specialize in renovating and adapting old buildings to modern uses. Companies that are quick to get on this bandwagon will survive and thrive, while others who do not react speedily will suffer from a decline in new construction.

It also introduces a whole new field for architects and engineers. Schooling in these disciplines has focused on new construction, and many graduates are, as a result, unfamiliar with the methods employed in building the structures that they will one day be asked to modify. Again, those who tap the expertise of old construction methods are likely to do well.

ENVIRONMENTAL AUDITS. The trend toward renovation is likely to go hand-in-hand with the requirement for what have come to be called "environmental audits." In the chapter on real estate investments, you will note that some space is devoted to all the invisible hazards that may lurk in a building or piece of property. The concern has become so great that action is mandated in some places and probably will be mandated soon in others.

According to a 1989 survey of real estate professionals, one-third of them believe contaminated land and buildings are the biggest problem facing them today. While not all these people are distressed out of philanthropic concern for their fellow humans or for the fate of the planet, they are concerned. Terrible liability issues are raised which cannot help but get the attention of the most money-grubbing among builders and developers.

There is a list of materials which have come to pollute populated areas. Asbestos, of course, is one. Polychlorinated biphenols, or PCBs, are another; commonly used in electrical equipment ranging from transformers atop electrical transmission poles to components inside old-time radios, they have been found to be powerful cancer-causing agents. The use of PCB-contaminated oil on streets and roads in Times Beach, Missouri, resulted in the town being, literally, closed down.

Lead is another serious concern. From lead-based paints in residential buildings to residual lead contamination at industrial sites, the heavy metal has become a problem demanding ever-increasing attention. Joining it are mercury, which causes terribly crippling and sometimes fatal poisoning, tailings from mines or mills that find or refine radioactive materials, and industrial wastes of every description. The presence of a few rusting drums of an unknown substance at the back of a commercial property has often ended up costing the property owner far more than he or she would have imagined, as specially trained workers in moon suits work for days to cart it away for very expensive disposal.

Enter the environmental auditors. They begin by researching the records and history of the property, which may help them get an idea of what they're seeking. They then go in and take samples of soil and other materials for testing.

The situation has become so active that there are now insurance companies that exist solely to insure environmental clean-ups, and to provide surety against cleaned-up property later being found to be unsafe.

Such an audit is not optional anymore for those who wish to borrow large sums of money to finance the purchase of commercial properties. Lenders require that the audits be done.

As do, increasingly, state and local governments. Illinois requires that land assessment and title search findings be provided to all parties in land transactions, making it easier to fix the blame if the property is found to be contaminated. California, Iowa, Indiana, Connecticut, and Pennsylvania have followed suit. Other states are pondering such measures, or similar ones.

The environment, it is clear, is becoming not just a philosophical and political issue, but an economic issue as well.

DON'T REPLACE, REPAIR

We have fallen into the habit of, when a thing breaks, simply buying a new one and chucking the old. We can't afford to do that anymore.

The first reason we shouldn't do it anymore, which is the one few people pay much attention to, is that it's irresponsible. Our resources are limited and our environment can ill afford to continue to absorb the offal from manufacturing processes. It is more environmentally sound to repair an appliance or other piece of equipment than it is to build a whole new one.

The second reason will come more and more into play as time goes on: New products, before long, are likely to cost much more. After decades of a free environmental ride, companies are going to have to begin paying for the environmental effects of what they do. This cost will of course be passed along to you, the consumer. It has already happened in a few industries. It will happen in more. We can expect a whole round of legislation making it so.

Even if the costs are indirect, we will end up paying them. It is certain that a certain amount of government clean-up of private messes cannot be avoided, because many of those who create the problems then go belly-up, leaving only the government to make such repairs as can be made. This is what happened in Times Beach, Missouri, and in some other places, with the number likely to climb.

It would, of course, be better if the tab for environmental damage caused in manufacturing a thing came along as part of the price, right up front. This would have several effects, all of them desirable:

- It would bring home once and for all how serious the situation is.

- It would encourage people to repair rather than replace.

- It would lead companies to find safer, more efficient ways of producing whatever they produce, because by doing so they could lower prices and become more competitive.

- It would make available a substantial amount of money to start finally to try to undo some of the damage we've done over the years.

There is yet another reason why we should take care of what we have and fix it when it breaks, rather than assume that there's an endless supply of everything available to us at low cost. We are reaching the point when we can't individually afford to be frittering away our money anymore. Go back and read the section on health care in the chapter on insurance. The prices are rising enormously. While some of us may have become accustomed to counting on the government for rising to the occasion and picking up the tab, we're missing the point: The government is us. We'll pick up the tab.

What it comes down to is that we are going to have to take care of ourselves. There is no alternative. The only choice we have is how soon and how responsibly we, individually and as families, begin preparing to do so.

Don't replace it; repair it!

SERVICE CONTRACTS. Would you buy a life insurance policy for the family dishwasher? Sounds ludicrous, but an astonishing number of you are doing just that. And not only on dishwashers, but also on new and used cars, video decks, and other major household appliances and electronic gear.

Enter the service contract. Service contracts are sweeping across the nation under the pitch that with the contracts, you buy "peace of mind." One-half of all new car buyers purchase a service contract, says the Federal Trade Commission (FTC). What's more, a high percentage of families who buy used cars or major appliances invest in some form of service agreement.

A service contract, like a warranty, provides for repair and sometimes even maintenance of a product for a specified period of time. Warranties, however, are included in the price of the product. Service contracts cost extra and are sold separately.

The cost to you for a typical contract ranges from a low of about $30 for a new clothes dryer to $500 or more on a car, depending on the length and the amount of coverage provided. These heavily promoted agreements are almost always a good deal for the seller, but often are not such a good one for you. Before considering a service contract, ask yourself:

- What will this service agreement give me that my warranty won't? Duplicating coverage is not only unnecessary, but also expensive.

- Exactly what is covered by the agreement? Some contracts protect only certain parts of the appliance—often those least vulnerable to breakdown—or only specific repairs. You probably wouldn't want a service contract on your video deck that fails to cover the tape transport mechanism, the part most likely to wear out or break. Most contracts don't cover repairs resulting from any failure on your part to maintain the product properly, or from any misuse by you.

- Who will actually perform repairs? The dealer? Or a specified maintenance firm? Will the appliance by picked up at your home? Bringing a small stereo into the shop is manageable, but what about a refrigerator? If the contract is offered by a local retailer or dealer, you may only be able to get local service. What happens if a problem develops while you are traveling or after you move away from your area?

- Are there additional fees? Service contracts, like insurance policies, often have deductibles. Or you may be charged each time the product is serviced. Also, some expenses are sometimes limited or excluded. For example, auto service contracts may not completely cover towing or rental car expenses.

- Who is responsible for performance under the contract? The FTC often gets letters from consumers who want to know what they can do about a service contract company that has gone out of business. Your best protection is to make sure before you sign a contract that the company is reputable.

A good rule of thumb: Ask the service contract sales representative whether you can buy coverage at a later date. At that point, after you have used the product for a while, you may be better able to determine if you need a contract. At the very least, you may want to wait until your warranty term expires.

Generally speaking, the maintenance history of a product, the amount of use it will get, and the number of its moving parts are usually the three most important factors in determining whether service coverage is cost-effective.

If you have friends or neighbors who have long-term experience with the product, check with them about its maintenance history. (As manufacturers introduce new models every year or even several times each year, this becomes more and more difficult to do. But if you can't get information about a specific model, you still can get information about the reliability of the make.) One or two minor problems over a period of several years may not justify the cost of a service agreement.

Some appliances—say, refrigerators—seldom if ever break down, even when they've been in service for 10 years or more. If your new refrigerator makes it through the warranty period without trouble, you're probably home free.

On the other hand, if you have a big family and know that your new clothes washer is in for heavy duty, a service policy might be advisable after the warranty has expired.

When you buy you should devote more effort than ever before to determining the quality of warranty coverage you are likely to receive. One popular brand of television, for instance, seldom breaks, but when it does, it is next to impossible to get it fixed. Yes, there are authorized repair centers to do warranty work. But the set, once taken there, spends months collecting dust. The reason usually given is that the repair facility is waiting for parts. This claim may even be true. The point is, you are ill-served by a warranty that is only grudgingly honored.

Look into the quality and speed of service (and prices, once the warranty has expired) before you buy. This goes beyond asking the salesperson. Before you make a purchase, consult the consumer magazines and ask around. This is your one chance to avoid being stuck with a product that turns out to be irreparable.

By the time you have settled on a product that you think fits your needs (or, more likely, several such products from which to choose), none of them may be available anymore. If this occurs, find out what improvements have been made, and whether those changes represent tried and true technology, fixing of problems that cropped up earlier, or the loading up of a serviceable model with all sorts of new, untested, and probably unneeded gadgets and features.

KEEPING (OR SELLING) YOUR CAR. Automobiles are perhaps the consumer good with the greatest effect on the environment. Apart from the pollution they cause while being used, automobile manufacturing involves prodigious quantities of steel (made from iron ore, which must be mined) and coal (which must be mined, and then burned to forge the steel). Although steel can be recycled, used automobiles are often abandoned on our streets and highways. And far too often, automobiles are left to rust in lots across America.

Automobiles are a primary candidate for the "repair, don't replace" approach. It's oh-so-tempting to give in to the flashy advertisements on television and in magazines. But simply keeping your old car could be the wiser choice, economically as well as environmentally.

How much has your car cost you in the time you've owned it? Look not only at maintenance and repairs, but also at depreciation. Most cars bought new lose a great deal of value almost immediately. They then depreciate rapidly for the first few years, after which the curve, having no place else to go, flattens out.

Has your car become a maintenance headache? If it requires repairs that approach its value, the question is answered right there. But if you have recently made such repairs, it would be awfully foolish to unload now, with little hope of realizing much of your investment. And, of course, if you've taken good care of it, it should be able to operate almost indefinitely with fairly little maintenance.

Is it a gas guzzler? If you drive relatively little, then the difference between a big-engined behemoth and a fuel-efficient little cutie may amount to only a few dollars per month. But there is movement toward reducing automobile emissions, and that situation is likely to grow more frenzied during the 1990s. Major metropolitan areas are looking at ways to curtail use of automobiles entirely, and it can be assumed that the worst offenders are the ones who will pay the biggest price.

Having these things in mind, look at the price of a new car. What can you expect to receive for the money you will spend? Is it really worth it? Remember, much of your cost will go for depreciation. It will lose value through the passage of time and by the simple fact that you own it.

Suppose you decide that buying a new car is the best choice for you. Before you sign away the family car for a shiny new one, though, you might want to make a few simple calculations. You could end up saving a lot of money by selling your old car yourself.

Automobile dealers accept trade-ins because they know that by so doing, they're selling a car. But if you've ever made a trade, especially at a really big dealership, and driven by the dealer's used car lot a week or two later, you've probably noticed that your old car isn't there.

That is because many dealerships sell all but the most desirable cars they take in trade to wholesalers. This means that there are now two companies seeking a profit on your old jalopy. There is no reason why you shouldn't enjoy this profit yourself.

And if your trade-in isn't worth much at all, a dealer may accept it, but the price of your new car will be higher than if you paid cash, rather than trading.

Let us assume you've decided to sell your car yourself. What do you do?

- Determine its value. You may be surprised, because cars depreciate rapidly, especially in the first few months after they're new. The authorities on this are the Used Car Pricing Book, published by the National Automobile Dealers Association, and *Edmund's Used Car Prices*. Both are available in bookstores and libraries. Be sure to check the tables that list features that increase (or decrease) the value of your particular car. Automatic transmissions are a plus in family sedans; they're a minus in sports cars.

Read the sections that describe the condition of car that's being evaluated. Excessive mileage reduces the value of your car. If you only drove it to church on Sunday, the value is higher. Also, check local ads to determine the going rate for similar vehicles in your area. Convertibles are at a premium in Fort Lauderdale, less so in Nome.

If it's inconvenient to get the NADA *Used Car Pricing Book*, or *Edmund's Used Car Prices*, you can get a good estimate of your car's value by calling the loan department of your bank. They'll tell you your car's wholesale value and loan value.

Figure your own rock-bottom price. This should be at some level above wholesale; a dealer will give you that. Then add 15 or 20 percent to it. This is your negotiating room.

Here's what you can do to get more for your used car:

Completely clean the car. The best bet is to go to a full-service car wash. Have the engine steam-cleaned, the trunk thoroughly vacuumed. Pay attention to details. Remove those old decals from the windows and stickers from the bumper. It would be a shame to lose a sale because the buyer doesn't like your politics. Don't just empty the ashtrays, wash them out so they'll be clean as new.

Make minor repairs. Major repairs, such as a new transmission, are unlikely to recover their cost in increased sale price. If the car needs major work, say so, sell "as-is," and take your lumps in reduced sale price. But minor repairs, such as replacing worn floor mats and cracked tail-light lenses, burned-out dome lights and broken door lock knobs, are well worth the effort. Make sure that all handles are tight, and lubricate such things as door hinges. It it to your benefit to have a mechanic go over the car to tweak it up and make sure it's in the best running condition. This helps you two ways: First, because it will make the sale easier; second, it will help ensure you don't get a surprise return visit from an angry buyer whose new purchase has died just down the road.

Formulate a selling strategy. How to get the best price for your car will depend to some extent on what kind of car it is. An acquaintance bought an old, used station wagon several years ago for $300. Had the seller done even a little research, he would have known that his car was a rare Edsel wagon, worth many thousands of dollars to those who fancy such things. If there's a chance that your car has some enthusiast value, check around. The classified columns in the backs of automobile magazines are a quick and easy guide. You may decide to hang onto your rare gem for the extra time it takes to advertise in enthusiast publications.

If your car is just an ordinary car, as it probably is, you'll want to place an ad in the local newspaper, local "shopper," and possibly in area classified publications dealing only with used cars. Tell the truth. And be realistic about the times when you're available to show the car. Unloading your vehicle should not become a full-time job. You might want to involve the family; many supermarkets and stores have bulletin boards where you can advertise the car. Just make sure to note where your notices have been posted, because you'll want to take them down after the sale, unless you enjoy phone calls from total strangers at 7:30 a.m. on Saturday to discuss a car sold weeks ago.

An important tip: One of the best sales tools you can employ is a good set of records. If you've kept track of maintenance, have all the receipts, and so on, you'll come across as someone who has taken especially good care of the car. This will be very comforting to the buyer. If you haven't kept the records, be sure to start with your new chariot.

The records should be turned over to the new owner. Provide copies and keep the originals, though, of records of payments that have been deducted from your income taxes. You'll still need those in case of an audit.

THERE'LL BE SOME CHANGES MADE

The approaching years call on each of us to make an effort to help the planet survive, and ourselves with it. Each of us can and must play a part. It might involve something as simple as sorting trash and taking what can be recycled away to be recycled.

More than that, it involves changing the way we do things. The point is that we do need to reconsider the ways we do things, from what we do with our trash to whether we build a new home or decide to fix up the old one, to keeping the old car running through careful maintenance rather than trading it in every year or two. We need to think about where and how we get our food.

When the leaves drop in autumn, what do you do with them? Do you rake them, put them into plastic bags, and pile them for clean-up, making them a debit on the environmental balance sheet? Do you then spend money in the spring for mulch to put around the plants in your yard?

Why not compost the leaves, grass clippings, and so on, and let the nutrients they contain enrich your yard and garden?

In an age when one must pay, sometimes, $3 per pound in order to buy tomatoes that actually taste like tomatoes, why not grow your own? Why not put away the excess by canning them, making sauces, and the like? Even a very small vegetable garden can result in enough produce to serve a family well throughout the year. What's more, with a little care you can avoid the chemicals and materials that have led many to suspect that much of what they eat is harmful.

This is just one illustration of how, with a little rethinking and a little labor—labor, by the way, is environmentally sound—we can all live safer, healthier lives on a cleaner Earth, and save money in the process.

20
PUTTING IT ALL
—— TO USE ——

Having read the chapters on the broad range of investments, you probably now have a pretty good idea of the way things work. Armed with this knowledge, you are in a position to make investments, and the markets that trade in them, work for you.

If one piece of advice alone were allowed, it would be this: Never forget the commissions. They are the price you pay for changing your mind. They are the brakes imposed on a tendency to move money from place to place. They are a major reason for discipline in the market, and they are a stern warning against thoughtless investing. They also should cause you to invest for the long term wherever possible.

If another piece of investment advice were allowed, it would be to remind you of the one you already know: Diversify. No company, no industry, no market is immune to unexpected setbacks. During the 1980s, we have seen robust, thriving companies brought to their knees by government action, by changes in the economy, by changes in fickle public tastes, by scandals, by international developments, by the acts of both domestic and international terrorists, and by successful products being diagnosed as hazardous, leaving the company itself liable. We have seen markets shaken on the caprice of computer programs, the caprice of crooks, the caprice of the ill-informed, by changes in interest rates, and so on. The only answer is to own enough of everything that a disaster in any one thing will not take you along with it.

THE GOVERNMENT'S CUT

As we discussed in Chapter 18, the "collect less but spend more money" philosophy of our government that pushed us through the 1980s certainly isn't going to work in the decade of the 1990s. The need for new taxes, as we all know, is now under intense discussion.

Also under scrutiny is the Tax Reform Act of 1986. That calls for reform of the reforms are coming from all quarters sounds as though changes will be forthcoming.

CREDIT

I will repeat. You probably owe too much.

We're not talking here about mortgages on homes, which are the best way that people who are not of enormous wealth can build a stake in the roof over their heads and call the land under their feet their own (though these, too, have come to wriggle uncomfortably in recent years).

Instead, we're talking about money owed to department stores, to oil companies, to credit card companies; money owed on automobiles that were purchased often for no particularly good reason; money owed for education (a wise use of credit, yet the kind of credit that most frequently goes unpaid); money owed by those who, having gotten a little ahead by gaining substantial equity in their homes, immediately climbed down into the hole by taking out a home equity line of credit; and money owed by people whose investments are primarily the property of the brokerage house that loaned them most of the money with which to make those investments.

Money borrowed is money that must be repaid. With interest. Credit is borrowed money, no matter how you explain it away—a useful tool to be used when it is the only aid available. Period.

HEDGES AGAINST THE UNEXPECTED

A friend who was looking over a few early chapters of the manuscript of this book suggested that it be entitled, *Insurance: Your Best Investment.* While that overstates the case, the fact is that in an increasingly dangerous world, insurance plays a bigger part in our lives than ever before.

We cannot always predict the results of our actions, no matter how well intentioned we are. A simple error in traffic, of the sort that we have all of us at one time or another made, could today result in events that lead to a judgement that will haunt you financially for the rest of your life.

A product or a service you perform could do the same thing. Astronomic liability awards are the order of the day. Lawsuits are the rule, not the exception. Even if you win, the expense is more than you can afford.

Earthquakes, floods, and the *et ceteras* of our complicated planet make developing a well thought out insurance package an essential part of your financial planning.

YOUR RETIREMENT RESPONSIBILITIES

Sooner rather than later is the key to successful retirement planning. If you plan to retire on more than basic necessities, a hard-hitting plan should be implemented at once. Bear in mind that what's true today might not be so tomorrow. Today's shortages might be tomorrow's glut . . . influencing prices accordingly. And vice versa.

Another example: The population is aging. Services we have come to count on could become more expensive. And your assets that are worth something in today's economy could, by retirement deadline, be worth a lot less.

Meet with your financial planner. Plan for the worst. If you're pleasantly surprised, enjoy a very happy retirement. The goal is to make sure that the surprise won't be an unpleasant one.

YOUR ESTATE

One of the most selfish human traits, and one of the most noble, is the desire to make a difference—to leave behind some evidence that we once walked the planet, and for that evidence to reflect well upon us.

Nowhere is that trait stronger than it is in this country. Generations of immigrants scraped, suffered, and endured terrible conditions so that their children, their legacy, their footprint on the planet, could have the chance of individual achievement.

It is on this foundation that you must build. You came into this world with nothing, and that is how you will leave. What you leave behind, and what becomes of it, is another matter.

Perhaps, like those long-suffering and noble immigrants, your legacy will take shape in the form of a family. By careful planning, you can see not so much that their days are made easy but that the door of opportunity is always open to them.

Because none of us is guaranteed time beyond this exact instant, it is never too early to see that at least this minimum requirement is met. Too many promising lives that were suddenly and tragically ended have had these misfortunes compounded because those they left behind were thrown into ruin. Don't ever run that risk.

There is another concern that faces you, maybe not now, but at some point between now and the time that the decision is no longer yours. Many is the family that has been driven to bankruptcy by spending its fortune keeping a beloved family member alive for just a few days more. Perhaps you believe that life, at any price, is better than the alternative. That is certainly your decision to make, but it is a decision that should not be made by default, for there is some chance that the decision others make would not coincide with your own. Put it down on paper in consultation with your lawyer, so that you can be sure that it will be followed.

From time to time there are stories of people who die, apparently penniless but in fact possessed of huge amounts of money, and apparently, and in fact, alone. Time affects us in different ways, and none of us can be assured which lot will be ours. If you have no family, be sure that arrangements are made through your lawyer, perhaps with the aid of a friend, to see that, you will get the comfort and care you need should time deal harshly with you. Those stories about people who failed to do so are frequently accompanied by stories of a distant and unknown relative who, out of nowhere, inherits a fortune. They are reported with gaiety, as though the relative had won the lottery. Never is any thought given to the suffering that may well have accompanied the unassigned bequest, or the fact that just a few of those dollars could have eased that suffering substantially.

If you are alone, and by that I mean that you have no relatives for whom you feel some financial responsibility, you may want to leave a lasting mark on the world. Perhaps there has been someone who has gone out of his or her way to make your life easier. Maybe there is a school or college that you would like to remember and, in so doing, create a testimonial to your life. There might be a hospital or a charity that you think highly of.

It is your right to see that the fruits of your labors find a home where you believe they can do the most good. But that will not happen unless you take action now to make it happen.

Do so.

YOUR RESPONSIBILITY TO THE WORLD

It's surprising how many people work hard all their lives to provide a future for their children, but who refuse to do the simplest things to see that there is a habitable world on which their children can live.

This doesn't seem to make much sense at first. But a little thought tells you that the problem lies in the fact that we can't imagine the kinds of changes that are going to take place unless we clean up our act at once.

So clean up your act. Help make it stylish to live a responsible life, not only financially but in terms of the place we all share. It is such a beautiful world. Do what you can to make sure that your children's children's children get to enjoy it. It takes so little effort.

TO PUT IT ANOTHER WAY . . .

At this point you probably are a little downcast, depressed, presuming that my best judgement is that all is lost.

Far from it! I look to the future with confidence and optimism. Opportunities abound, and exciting changes are taking place.

But the world is more complicated. As the opportunities grow, so do the dangers, for surely where there is one, there is the other.

An old piece of advice about investments is still true: Never be the first in, nor the last out. By the same token, try to avoid being the last in or the first out.

Exciting times are ahead. We will take part in things that were the stuff of fantasy within our lifetimes. We already have.

But just as the rewards are higher, so are the stakes. We need to be careful, that's all.

There is no way of being sure what the future will bring. I'm not certain that, were it possible, it would be all that desirable.

The best we can do is do our best.

That means being true to ourselves.

It means casting off the capriciousness of youth and deciding what we want to do with our lives. It means setting goals and setting ways to achieve those goals. It isn't easy, but it wouldn't be nearly so enjoyable if it were. Nor would the sense of satisfaction following a success be nearly so great.

Far from being dismal in outlook, I feel more firmly than ever before that everyone who wants to be successful financially can do so.

It has been the job of this book to help you realize your dreams as a new century and a new millennium stand before us. If it has done so in even a small way, it has been successful.

APPENDIX:
THE ECONOMIC
──INDICATORS──

Economic statistics are like the gauges on the instrument panel of an airplane. They provide those in control with the information necessary to gauge the strength, speed, and safety of each of a multitude of functions that are all essential to the health and well-being of the ship—and of those aboard.

That's why we should take interest in several statistics which, while they apply to the economy as a whole, can help in individual financial planning.

A number of economists complain that the frequency and quality of some statistical analyses provided by the government have fallen in recent years, but, they note, the numbers being produced are still useful. And, because of computerization, the analyses and sometimes even the raw data themselves can be obtained, so that you can cross-reference them to suit your needs.

What statistics should we watch for? Why do they matter to people not directly involved in finance making the really big deals?

Here are a few, and why they're important:

- The Gross National Product. This is the big one. It's the total of the goods and services produced in the country, in short, an overall measure of whether and how quickly the economy is growing.

  The quarterly GNP numbers are absolutely vital to all of us, whether we know it or not. It's impossible to plan wisely without them. If the economy is growing too rapidly, it is in danger of "overheating," which is to say reaching a rate of growth that it can't possibly sustain. This results in corrective action, such as tightening of credit by the Federal Reserve Board. If the growth of GNP slows or, worse, the

334

GNP actually declines, times are rough. Two consecutive quarters of decline constitute a recession.

- The Consumer Price Index and the Producer Price Index. These monthly statistics measure the rate of inflation; the former at the retail level, the latter at the wholesale level. The PPI leads the CPI in that if retailers have to pay more for products and raw materials, the consumer is ultimately likely to have to pay more, too.

    These figures have been relatively unexciting in the last few years, but in the late 1970s and early 1980s, a time of double-digit inflation, they were crucial. Because inflation is literally a way of determining the value of money, those who owe money profit during a time of high inflation, while those who are owed money are repaid in dollars that aren't worth as much as the dollars they invested.

    If it looks as though inflation is on the upswing, it's a good idea to stay away from long-term, fixed-rate securities as investments. Those who have low fixed-rate mortgages make out like bandits during times of high inflation—a fact that caused many grey hairs to grow at savings and loan institutions in the early part of this decade.

- The employment figures. The most widely reported employment statistic is the monthly unemployment figure, which gives the percentage of American workers who are seeking jobs. But there are others. The percentage of the population that is employed is an important one. It's been hovering around 62 percent—the highest in the country's history.

    An important though little-reported employment figure is the total number of hours worked. It takes into account those who work part-time jobs and those who work more than one job.

    These statistics are important because they measure the demand for labor. The higher the demand, the higher the price. This can affect individuals in a variety of ways, from determining when to ask for a raise to planning when to build an addition to a home. They also are a leading indicator of inflation because when it costs more to hire workers, the prices of the goods and services they produce will rise.

- The government's monthly index of leading economic indicators. (See Chart 36.) This is a group of 11 statistics designed to predict the fate of the economy. When the figure is released, however, only nine components are included, because the other two aren't ready, so the figure must be revised each month.

Four important statistics. How important are they in your own financial

CHART 36

Components of the Index of Leading Economic Indicators

- Average workweek of production workers in manufacturing.
- Average weekly claims for state unemployment insurance.
- New orders for consumer goods and materials, adjusted for inflation.
- Vendor performance (companies receiving slower deliveries from suppliers).
- Contracts and orders for plant and equipment, adjusted for inflation.
- New building permits issued.
- Change in manufacturers' unfilled orders, durable goods.
- Change in sensitive materials prices.
- Index of stock prices.
- Money supply: M-2, adjusted for inflation.
- Index of consumer expectations.

planning? It depends on whether you'd rather be the pilot—or just a passenger.

They're the ones that receive enough news coverage that they're generally available to everyone. There are others, thousands of others, that are available to you.

Here is a brief rundown of some of the statistics that are available and the agencies that produce them:

BUREAU OF THE CENSUS. One of the government's big-three number crunchers, the Census Bureau produces a steady stream of statistics, released at specific times. Among the most important ones:

- Value of new construction put in place. This figure, calculated both nationally and by region, is released on the first business day of each month. The figures are not for the previous month, but for the month before that.

- New one-family homes sold and for sale. This statistic, which covers the previous month, is generally available on the second business day of the month.

- Manufacturing shipments, inventories, and orders. This statistic is of obvious importance to those involved in manufacturing, from raw materials suppliers to retailers of the finished products. Like the new construction report, it lags one month. It is available the second business day of the month.

- Wholesale trade. Released the second week of the month, it, too, lags a month in the figures it covers. For example, the numbers released on October 12 are for the month of August.

- Advanced retail sales. Released the second week of each month, these statistics cover the previous month.
- Manufacturing and trade: Inventories and sale. Lagging a month, this figure is usually released in the third week of each month.
- Advance report of U.S. merchandise trade. Important to market analysts, this analysis is, contrary to its title, released about seven weeks after the month it covers.
- Housing starts and building permits. An important measure of the vigor of the construction industry, this figure is released about three weeks after the end of the reported month.
- Advance report on durable goods shipments and orders. The indicator of the sales of "big ticket" items is released three weeks into the month, and reports on the previous month.

The Bureau of the Census also releases quarterly reports on housing vacancies; retail finance; plant and equipment expenditures; and manufacturing, mining, and wholesale trade.

BUREAU OF LABOR STATISTICS. Another of the government's big three, the BLS provides many of the reports that have an immediate effect on the financial markets.

- The employment situation. Customarily referred to as the unemployment rate, this is actually an elaborate, cross-referenced description of the labor force, broken down into regions, ethnic and age groups, and so on. It also lists the number and kinds of new jobs created in the previous month. It is issued on the first Friday of each month.
- The producer price index. Formerly called the wholesale price index, this analyzes the prices manufacturers and resellers are paying for their materials, and as such is a leading indicator of inflation. It is released the second week of each month and covers the previous month.
- Local area employment and unemployment. This is a deeper analysis of material first reported in the previous month's employment situation report, and is released the third week of each month.
- Consumer Price Index. While it may not be the best indicator of current inflation, it is certainly the most influential one. It is issued the

third week of each month and deals with changes in the prices of consumer goods the previous month.

- Real earnings. This report analyzes, in effect, the buying power of American consumers, based on fixed-value dollars. It is released in conjunction with the CPI.

The BLS also issues a number of quarterly reports, covering collective bargaining agreements and trends, U.S. import and export price indices, and the employment cost index.

BUREAU OF ECONOMIC ANALYSIS. The third of the government's analytical triumvirate, the BEA is responsible for the most basic measures of the health of the economy.

- Gross national product. This is issued quarterly, or is supposed to be. But there is a preliminary figure, called the "flash" GNP, which is followed by a revised figure, which itself can be—and usually is — revised yet again.

- The index of leading, lagging, and coincident economic indicators. This index is issued at the end of the month or the first business day of the new month, and has a one-month delay.

- Personal income and outlays. This is the basic measure of income and consumption, especially important to Keynesian theoreticians. It is issued the fourth week of each month and covers the previous month.

FEDERAL RESERVE BOARD. The Federal Reserve Board keeps track of those figures of greatest interest to monetarists—those who believe the economy can best be controlled by careful regulation of the supply and flow of money. It issues a number of reports, usually with very little lag time.

- Money stock. Usually called "the money supply," the money stock figure has been debated extensively by economists in recent years, because economists have come to disagree on what constitutes money. The report is issued weekly and deals with figures for the previous week.

- Selected interest rates. This report, also issued weekly, is less useful by itself than it is in conjunction with previous weeks' reports, which help the seers to divine trends in interest rates. These, in turn, can have a huge impact on securities markets and on industrial growth. The figures given are for the previous week.

- Consumer installment credit. This monthly report covers the total consumer debt in the country. It has a month's lag time and is issued about a week into each month.

- Production indices and capacity utilization rate. These reports, issued on the same day, provide an idea of how efficiently the economy is working. They are issued in the middle of the month and deal with the previous month.

U.S. DEPARTMENT OF AGRICULTURE. The U.S.D.A. conducts remarkably sophisticated analyses and projections of the supply and demand of a broad range of agricultural products both domestically and worldwide. These figures are the bread and butter of those in commodities-intensive industries.

DEPARTMENT OF THE TREASURY. A wealth of special-interest reports and statistical analyses are available.

These reports are available, generally in very generalized form, over the news media that broadcast or print economic news. Waiting for them to appear in these places can reduce the likelihood that you can immediately benefit from them, but this is less a worry than you might imagine.

There is an economic theory, called "rational expectation," that suggests markets will react, ahead of time, to events they believe will take place. The theory's validity is borne out by the panicked behavior following any surprising developments or reports.

(It differs from inside information in that it is based on the players' own analyses, rather than information leaked to them which they then use to their advantage. The line is a thin one. It has actually affected the way some reports have come to be issued. For instance, the "flash" GNP report was originally designed to be an internal working document. But its contents were leaked so consistently and selectively—and sometimes inaccurately—that the government decided to promote fairness by releasing it to everyone, along with the warning that the figures are preliminary and virtually certain to change.)

Although the urgency of instantly knowing the contents of these government reports is not great in most cases, they can help those who are very serious about their financial situation to become more aware of the complex interactions of the economy.

Those who wish to put the economy under a microscope with the government's help can easily do so. Late each year, the government issues a master list of the dates on which the following year's economic reports, fig-ures, analyses, and indices will be released.

On those dates, most of the reports are available through commercial data companies almost instantly, or through one of the government's own computer bulletin boards. The best way to get information on these is through the nearest regional office of the agencies involved.

INDEX